Dr Koowon Kim's exposition of 1 Samu  a gifted interpreter. He not only provides a clear and profound explanation of the meaning of the biblical book in its ancient context, he also shows its continuing relevance for today's church, particularly, but not exclusively, in an Asian context. His use of the medieval Chinese novel *Three Kingdoms* as a dialogue partner with the story of the biblical book was illuminating and interesting. I recommend this commentary for all readers.

Tremper Longman III, PhD
Distinguished Scholar and Professor Emeritus of Biblical Studies,
Westmont College, Santa Barbara, California, USA

A wonderfully clear, concise, theologically sensitive, and historically informed resource for pastors and students of Scripture. It is brimming with insightful and refreshing practical engagement with contemporary Asian contexts. A fine work! A joy to read!

Peter Enns, PhD
Old Testament Professor,
Eastern University, St Davids, Pennsylvania, USA

Koowon Kim has written an excellent commentary on 1 Samuel for readers in the Asian context. For instance, he incorporates relevant episodes from the medieval Chinese historical novel, *Romance of the Three Kingdoms*, to illustrate some biblical ways of viewing thought and human relations. *Three Kingdoms* is well-known among Chinese, Koreans, Vietnamese, and Japanese. The author is also an expert on Ugarit, so his explanations of Canaanite religious practices such as divination and necromancy are valuable. I hope this commentary will be used by many scholars in Asia and the rest of the world.

David T. Tsumura, PhD
Old Testament Professor,
Japan Bible Seminary, Tokyo, Japan

Asia Bible Commentary Series

1 SAMUEL

GLOBAL LIBRARY

Asia Bible Commentary Series

1 SAMUEL

Koowon Kim

General Editor
Federico G. Villanueva

Old Testament Consulting Editors
Yohanna Katanacho, Tim Meadowcroft, Joseph Shao

New Testament Consulting Editors
Steve Chang, Andrew Spurgeon, Brian Wintle

Published 2018 by Langham Global Library
an imprint of Langham Creative Projects
www.langhampublishing.org

Langham Publishing and its imprints are a ministry of Langham Partnership

Langham Partnership
PO Box 296, Carlisle, Cumbria, CA3 9WZ, UK
www.langham.org

Published in partnership with Asia Theological Association

ATA
QCC PO Box 1454 – 1154, Manila, Philippines
www.ataasia.com

ISBNs:
978-1-78368-517-2 Print
978-1-78368-518-9 ePub
978-1-78368-519-6 Mobi
978-1-78368-520-2 PDF

British Library Cataloguing in Publication Data
A catalogue record for this book is available from the British Library.

ISBN: 978-1-78368-517-2

Cover & Book Design: projectluz.com

To My Wife

CONTENTS

SERIES PREFACE

In recent years, we have witnessed one of the greatest shifts in the history of world Christianity. It used to be that the majority of Christians lived in the West, but Christians are now evenly distributed around the globe. This shift has implications for the task of interpreting the Bible from within our respective contexts, which is in line with the growing realization that every theology is contextual. Thus, the questions that we bring into our reading of the Bible will be shaped by our present realities as well as our historical and social locations. There is a need therefore to interpret the Bible for our own contexts.

The Asia Bible Commentary (ABC) series addresses this need. In line with the mission of the Asia Theological Association Publications, we have gathered evangelical Bible scholars working among Asians to write commentaries on each book of the Bible. The mission is to "produce resources that are biblical, pastoral, contextual, missional, and prophetic for pastors, Christian leaders, cross-cultural workers, and students in Asia." Although the Bible can be studied for different reasons, we believe that it is given primarily for the edification of the Body of Christ (2 Tim 3:16–17). The ABC series is designed to help pastors in their sermon preparation, cell group or lay leaders in their Bible study groups, and those training in seminaries or Bible schools.

Each commentary begins with an introduction that provides general information about the book's author and original context, summarizes the main message or theme of the book, and outlines its potential relevance to a particular Asian context. The introduction is followed by an exposition that combines exegesis and application. Here, we seek to speak to and empower Christians in Asia by using our own stories, parables, poems, and other cultural resources as we expound the Bible.

The Bible is actually Asian in that it comes from ancient West Asia, and there are many similarities between the world of the Bible and traditional Asian cultures. But there are also many differences that we need to explore in some depth. That is why the commentaries also include articles or topics in which we bring specific issues in Asian church, social, and religious contexts into dialogue with relevant issues in the Bible. We do not seek to resolve every tension that emerges but rather to allow the text to illumine the context and vice versa, acknowledging that we do not have all the answers to every mystery.

May the Holy Spirit, who inspired the writers of the Bible, bring light to the hearts and minds of all who use these materials, to the glory of God and to the building up of the churches!

Federico G. Villanueva

General Editor

AUTHOR'S PREFACE

When I was invited to write a commentary for the Asia Bible Commentary Series, I was more worried than happy. As a seminary professor based in Seoul, South Korea, who had a heavy teaching load in addition to administrative and ecclesiastical duties, I was not sure if I could ever finish this project, not to mention doing so in time. Further, the idea of contextualization in commentary writing posed an additional challenge to me. I was born and raised in the westernized city of Seoul in South Korea and acquired advanced degrees from American academic institutions. I found myself not quite up to the important task at hand. During the first couple of years since accepting the invitation, my worry appeared to prove true. I was not able to get much done and started losing confidence. Had it not been for the prayers and support of the Asia Theological Association, I could not have completed this book. They not only organized workshops as a way to support commentary writers like me technically and spiritually, but also arranged a visiting scholar program with Asbury Theological Seminary so that I might concentrate on the project away from my busy routine. I am especially grateful to Federico Villanueva, the general editor of the Asia Bible Commentary Series, for his prayer and encouragement. Also, I'd like to thank Reformed Graduate University for allowing me to have a sabbatical semester at Asbury Theological Seminary. The staff of Global Initiatives at Asbury Theological Seminary deserve my sincere gratitude for their hospitality and logistical support. I would like to thank Associate Provost Thomas Tumblin and his secretary Ashlyn Vasser. Most importantly, I'd like to express my deepest thanks to my wife, Sook Gyung Lee, who sacrificed herself by agreeing to live without her husband while taking care of three sons, Samuel (17), Elijah (15), and Isaiah (10), during my absence. I completed most of this book while I spent my sabbatical semester at Asbury Theological Seminary. I dedicate this book to her.

LIST OF ABBREVIATIONS

BOOKS OF THE BIBLE

Old Testament

Gen, Exod, Lev, Num, Deut, Josh, Judg, Ruth, 1–2 Sam, 1–2 Kgs, 1–2 Chr, Ezra, Neh, Esth, Job, Ps/Pss, Prov, Eccl, Song, Isa, Jer, Lam, Ezek, Dan, Hos, Joel, Amos, Obad, Jonah, Mic, Nah, Hab, Zeph, Hag, Zech, Mal

New Testament

Matt, Mark, Luke, John, Acts, Rom, 1–2 Cor, Gal, Eph, Phil, Col, 1–2 Thess, 1–2 Tim, Titus, Phlm, Heb, Jas, 1–2 Pet, 1–2–3 John, Jude, Rev

BIBLE TEXTS AND VERSIONS

Divisions of the canon

NT	New Testament
OT	Old Testament

Ancient texts and versions

LXX	Septuagint
MT	Masoretic Text

Modern versions

ESV	English Standard Version
NIB	New Interpreter's Bible
NIV	New International Version

Journals, reference works, and series

AB	The Anchor Bible
ABD	*Anchor Bible Dictionary*
BJWA	*Brown Journal of World Affairs*
BZWANT	Beiträge Zur Wissenschaft Vom Alten und Neuen Testament
CTM	*Currents in Theology and Mission*
ExpTim	*Expository Times*

HBM	Hebrew Bible Monograph
JBL	*Journal of Biblical Literature*
JCR	*Journal of Chinese Religion*
LBI	Library of Biblical Interpretation
NICOT	The New International Commentary on the Old Testament
TB	*Tyndale Bulletin*

INTRODUCTION

The book of Samuel covers a relatively short period of time in the history of ancient Israel – about eighty years of the early monarchy, but it has more chapters than the book of Kings, which covers nearly 380 years of Israel's monarchy. This disproportionate length points to the importance of the institution of monarchy, particularly the kingdom of David, in the redemptive history of Israel. Further, the book of Samuel provides a theological framework that informs the checkered history of Israel's monarchy for the entire period of its existence. It answers not only how monarchy began in ancient Israel but also why David was promised an eternal dynasty when Saul was rejected. In other words, its narrative is both historical and theological. The fact that the Davidic rule serves as a symbol for the Messianic rule adds extra significance to this book. Thus it is no wonder that the book of Samuel is widely read and loved both by Jews and Christians.

All modern translations divide the book of Samuel into two volumes, but the Jewish tradition did not construe the book as being bipartite. The Talmud never hints at such a division. The Masoretic notes are written on the assumption that 1 and 2 Samuel form one single book. Further, a single scroll was found in the fourth Cave of Qumran containing both 1 and 2 Samuel. The bipartite division of the book was introduced in the Greek manuscripts because scribes could not fit the Greek version into one physical scroll.[1] Thus 1 and 2 Samuel were originally intended as one book and should be read as such. But modern commentators tend to treat 1 and 2 Samuel separately for logistical reasons. The same practice will be adopted in the ABC series.

HISTORICAL SETTINGS: "THE PHILISTINE PROBLEM"

From a historical point of view, 1 Samuel answers the question about how monarchy originated in ancient Israel. So it would be apt to discuss one of the most important factors that fomented Israel's development into monarchy: the Philistines.

The Philistines emigrated from Greece several generations after Israel settled in Canaan. A complex set of natural and social factors in the Aegean world sent a wave of immigrants – the Egyptians called them "sea peoples" – eastward

---

1. The Hebrew original tends to be much shorter than its Greek translation because the Hebrew text consists of consonants only, whereas the Greek text spells out vowels.

both by sea and by land in the late-thirteenth century BC. The Philistines were one of those sea peoples, who arrived at the mouth of the Delta with the intention of settling in Egypt, only to be turned away by Ramesses III (1271–1155 BC).[2] After failing to settle in Egypt, the Philistines decided to make the southern coast of Canaan their permanent home. They conquered three Canaanite cities in the coastal region Gaza, Ashkelon, Ashdod – and made them into their own. They also built two cities further inland, Ekron and Gath. They ruled the southern coast of Canaan from these five city centers. Since they were immigrants from Greece, their political organization was different from that of indigenous peoples. Instead of having one king who wielded absolute power, they formed an alliance of five city centers. Decisions of national importance were made in the council of five city rulers (*seren*). In case of a war against an enemy, the five city rulers marshaled their respective armies in a place of assembly (e.g. Aphek) to form combined forces. In this sense, their political and military organization was close to that of Greece instead of the Oriental monarchy. The Philistine forces not only had iron chariots and sophisticated weapons but also monopolized the skill of smelting iron in the early Iron Age. The Israelites had to go down to the Philistines to sharpen their tools (see 13:19–21).

Earlier in the period of the Judges, the Philistines posed no threat to the Israelites, because they were busy with settling down, building cities, and consolidating their local rule. The Israelites, on the other hand, were occupied with dealing with indigenous enemies such as the Canaanites, Moabites, Ammonites, Midianites, Amalekites, and so on. Towards the end of the period, however, the Philistines became more threatening to Israel's existence. Unlike other peoples who attacked Israel mainly for the plunder (see 6:3–6), the Philistines made an effort to expand their territory into the land of Israel, establishing a permanent rule there. Part of the reason was population growth. As their population grew, they needed more agricultural land to support the population. They had the Mediterranean Sea to the west, the desert to the south, and high mountains to the north. The only direction they could expand was to the east, the Sharon plain of Israel. The last episode of heroic tales in the book of Judges reflects the beginning of this conflict between Israel and the Philistines.

---

2. The reliefs on the walls of Ramesses III's temple in Madinet Habu show that sea peoples arrived in oxcarts loaded with their wives and children. This implies that their intention was peaceful settlement in – not military conquest of – Egypt.

The story of Samson unfolds in border cities such as Zorah and Timnah in the Sharon plain. When the Philistines grew stronger, the area of conflict moved further inland, which often resulted in an all-out war between Israel and the Philistines. For instance, 1 Samuel 4 reports that the Philistines and the Israelites led by Eli's house fought each other at Aphek and Ebenezer. This battle ended in complete victory for the Philistines: as many as thirty thousand men of Israel were killed, including Eli's two sons; the ark of the Lord's covenant was taken; and Shiloh, the capital city of the northern tribes, was destroyed. After this victory, the Philistines succeeded in dominating the Israelite hill country. Although the Israelites had moments of victory over the Philistines under Samuel,[3] it is certain that by the time of Saul, the Philistines eventually regained the upper hand and practically ruled over the Israelites via a network of military outposts within Israel (see 10:5). Aharoni diagnoses the situation at the dawn of Israel's monarchy as follows: "The Philistine menace was the great challenge that forced Israel to face up to the question of its existence and continued development. This marks the end of the period of the Judges and the beginning of the United Israelite Monarchy."[4]

IDEOLOGY OF ISRAEL'S KINGSHIP

Kingship was divine in the ancient Near East, where kings were considered literally as gods. For instance, kings were divine from birth in Egypt, and in Mesopotamia they assumed divinity after death if not during their lifetime. Under the ideology of divine kingship, they enjoyed absolute power.[5] Their word became the law and their will defined what was good. This idea of divine kingship was most prominent in Egypt. In Mesopotamia, where kings became divine after death, there developed the tradition of written laws, along with the idea of rule of law. Mesopotamian kings even called themselves "the shepherd" of the land.[6] In Egypt, where pharaohs were divine from birth, however, there

---

3. See 1 Sam 7:14. As a result, the Israelites recovered the territory from "the towns from Ekron to Gath" from the Philistines.
4. Yohanan Aharoni, *The Land of the Bible: A Historical Geography* (Philadelphia: Westminster Press, 1979), 275.
5. The Babylonian priests may have had the authority to withdraw divine support from a king during the New Year festival, but it was only nominal. There was no case in which priests revoked the right to rule from a reigning king during the reenactment of the yearly coronation. See C. J. Gadd, *Ideas of Divine Rule in the Ancient Near East* (London: The British Academy, 1945), 49–50.
6. In royal ideology, ancient kings were expected to do justice to the people. Ibid., 38.

was no tradition of written law. A pharaoh ruled through his words and never took the title "the shepherd." The people were effectively his slaves.

It would be no stretch to say that Moses, not Rousseau, was the first to reject the idea of divine kingship. The ideology of Israel's kingship is epitomized in the law of Moses, which is lengthy but worth quoting in full:

> When you enter the land the LORD your God is giving you and have taken possession of it and settled in it, and you say, "Let us set a king over us like all the nations around us," be sure to appoint over you a king the LORD your God chooses. He must be from among your fellow Israelites. Do not place a foreigner over you, one who is not an Israelite. The king, moreover, must not acquire great numbers of horses for himself or make the people return to Egypt to get more of them, for the LORD has told you, "You are not to go back that way again." He must not take many wives, or his heart will be led astray. He must not accumulate large amounts of silver and gold. When he takes the throne of his kingdom, he is to write for himself on a scroll a copy of this law, taken from that of the Levitical priests. It is to be with him, and he is to read it all the days of his life so that he may learn to revere the LORD his God and follow carefully all the words of this law and these decrees and not consider himself better than his fellow Israelites and turn from the law to the right or to the left. Then he and his descendants will reign a long time over his kingdom in Israel. (Deut 17:14–20)

This law stipulated qualifications for a king of Israel, described his duty – both positive and negative – and articulated the nature of Israel's royal office. As for the qualifications of a king, there were two requirements. First, he had to be chosen by the Lord, not elected by popular will. This was very much the norm in the ancient Near East. But the second qualification differentiated the king of Israel from his ancient Near Eastern counterparts – he had to be chosen from among the Israelites. That is to say, he was the "first among brothers" and no different from his subjects in terms of his status before the Lord. His duty was also presented as a foil for an ancient Near Eastern king. He should not do what his counterpart did: he should not be in the business of "acquiring" things such as gold, horses, or women. Instead he should study the law all the days of his life. Finally, the king of Israel should be a God-fearer in the sense that he rules in accordance with all the laws of the Lord and treats the people as his brothers. What kind of a king was this, who obeyed the Lord his God and served his subjects as if they were his brothers? This idea of a king was hitherto unprecedented in human history.

One may call Israel's king a vicegerent, for he exercised delegated power on behalf of the true King of Israel. Further the people he ruled were not his own, but the Lord's. They were not his subjects to boss around but rather his brothers whom he was to serve. Since he ruled the people of the Lord on behalf of the Lord, obedient faith was an indispensable virtue for Israel's king. He might lack in many traits usually expected of a leader of the country but still serve as king of Israel as long as he remained obedient. But if he was disobedient deliberately and consistently, he could not stay in power, however competent he might be in other areas. However, obedient faith does not mean blind faith. Rather, true obedience involves human effort to understand the Lord's will. Thus Moses stipulated the study of God's law as the only thing the king must "do." In order to obey the Lord, the king must understand the Lord's will – although, in the context of 1 Samuel, he did so through the prophet Samuel. The reason that Saul was rejected as king and David was promised an eternal kingdom can be found in this unique ideology of Israel's monarchy. God looked for obedient faith in his king. That virtue was found in David, whereas Saul consistently rebelled against the Lord's commands as given through the prophet Samuel.

Where does all this go in the history of redemption? The reason God looked for an obedient king was not simply because he was supposed to act as God's deputy on earth, but also because through an obedient king, an obedient people could be formed. God's ultimate purpose was to have his own people in this world, a people who would earnestly seek God's will and live in total trust of the Lord. Samuel once said that God might abandon a king but would never abandon his people because it was God's desire to make the Israelites his own people (see 12:22). In order to have his own people, God was long-suffering in looking for an obedient king until he found one in Jesus Christ. Jesus' perfect obedience as demonstrated in his death and resurrection gave birth to a new people who were willing to live in complete obedience and trust in the Lord. 1 Samuel shows us how God's long search for an obedient king who would bring forth an obedient people began in the history of Israel.

MESSAGES

The narrative of 1 Samuel is as much theological as historical. Israel's history reflects both pastoral and theological themes. Following are some of the consistent themes in the book.

First, God counts on us for his kingdom project. He cooperates with us to advance his cause in the world. If we fail to live by faith, it may endanger God's plan for our family, our tribe, our nation. The story of Hannah illustrates this message. The narrator begins the story of Israel's monarchy with the story of an obscure woman suffering from childlessness. By so doing, the narrator metaphorically connects the fate of Hannah with that of her nation. Hannah's predicament recalls Israel's hopeless situation in the last days of the Judges. How Hannah responded to her problem would determine the fate of her nation. In total trust of the Lord, Hannah decided to arise from her place of despair and head to the temple to urge the one who had closed her womb to open it again. All she wanted was a son that might rid her of the shame of being barren. But her son turned out to be a kingmaker who would rid the nation of the condition of anomie. In other words, Hannah's victory in faith was intricately connected with the solution to Israel's problem. The institution of kingship in Israel would not have transpired if Hannah had not acted in faith. Hannah did not go to the temple with the intention of shaping Israel's history. However, when she responded with faith to her personal problem, the Lord used her faith to change the course of Israel's history. We learn from this that our everyday efforts to live out our faith matter in the kingdom of God. We do not need to be famous pastors or theologians or even politicians or scientists to make a difference in this fallen world that needs divine intervention. God uses our little acts of faith for his great purpose.

Second, obedience is one of the core virtues required of a king of Israel. Obedient faith in 1 Samuel, however, is not blind faith, but entails searching for truth with all our faculties as well as living that out in trust of the Lord. After anointing Saul as king, Samuel commanded him to attack the Philistine troops at Gibeah, Saul's hometown, so that his calling as king might be demonstrated in the people's eyes. But Samuel's actual words appear ambiguous in and of themselves: "Do whatever your hand finds to do, for God is with you" (10:7). This literally means that since God appointed Saul to be king of Israel, he must do what he was supposed to do as king of Israel. In other words, Samuel commanded Saul to attack the Philistines without actually saying it.[7] It was Saul who had to decide what he must do as king of Israel. This teaches us that obedience involves our rational efforts to understand the truth and specifically the Lord's will for us and to act that out in total trust in the Lord.

7. There is a saying in Tagalog, *Nasa Diyos ang awa, nasa tao ang gawa* ("Mercy comes from God, but humans have a part to play"). Federico Villanueva kindly brought this saying to my attention.

Third, the Lord is the God of second chances. He does not delight in destruction but always wants sinners to repent and be saved. Contrary to the common perception, Saul was not doomed from the beginning. He had genuine chances to establish his own dynasty by proving himself fit to rule Israel: "You have not kept the command the Lord your God gave you; if you had, he would have established your kingdom over Israel for all time" (13:13). Even after being rejected by God in chapter 13, Saul was given another chance to turn back to God when he was ordered to carry out the Lord's wrath against the Amalekites. God gave him the honor to act as the holy medium through which God fulfilled his promise for the Israelites. But Saul failed again. This teaches us that God is gracious to give sinners second chances all the time. The period of God's grace, however, leads some to repent and be saved while others harden their hearts, sealing their own doom. God never gives up on us, nor should we do so ourselves. It is never too late to turn back to God.

Fourth, there is no coincidence in the world that God created and rules. Everything is providential, although we cannot always make sense of it. In 1 Samuel, we do not see supernatural miracles, such as parting the Red Sea or stopping the sun, but God's interventions are disguised as coincidences. For instance, there are seeming coincidences that form a chain of events leading to Saul's encounter with Samuel: the missing of Kish's donkeys, Kish's decision to send Saul in search of them in the company of a servant, who had knowledge of a seer living in Zuph, and who happened to have a silver coin in his pocket that could be used as a gift. These were not coincidences but divine interventions (see 9:15–16).

Fifth, God's ultimate concern lies in the creation of his own people. Although 1 Samuel revolves around God's search for a king after his own heart, his search does not end there. He seeks to form a people after his own heart. A king after his own heart is a divine means to form a people after his own heart. God's constant desire is to have an obedient people who seek his will and live it out in trust of him. God's search for a king after his own heart culminates in Jesus Christ, whose obedience unto death created a new people of God, the Church. We are all part of this glorious body of God's people. It is encouraging to see that God's search for a king in 1 Samuel was, after all, shaped by his desire to gather all of us as his people in Christ.

TEXT OF 1 SAMUEL

The Masoretic Text (MT) of the book of Samuel is notorious for its numerous scribal errors and textual corruptions.[8] In order to deal with these textual problems, scholars use various ancient witnesses, the most important of which is the Septuagint (LXX), the Greek translation of the Hebrew Bible. The importance of the LXX in textual criticism has been proven beyond doubt by the discovery of the Qumran scrolls containing the text of Samuel (4QSam[a, b, c]), which reflect the text type of the LXX more closely than the MT. But emending problematic texts of the MT on the basis of the LXX or the Qumran witnesses must proceed with great caution, because the LXX and the Qumran witnesses may reflect a different "original" than the MT, let alone the LXX has its own share of textual critical problems. It appears that many different originals were available to different Jewish communities in the Persian period and the MT reflects only one of them (the Babylonian text-type).[9] But one cannot exaggerate the importance of the MT due to its status as *Textus Receptus* in Judaism and Christianity. Most English translations of the Bible use the MT as the original.[10] Further, the MT is more reliable than some scholars think, though it is not perfect. This commentary will, therefore, use the MT as the basic text for interpretation, with occasional adoptions of the LXX reading. For quotation purposes, the NIV is used.

READING 1 SAMUEL FROM ASIAN PERSPECTIVES

The biggest challenge in writing a commentary in the ABC series is to define what it means to read 1 Samuel from Asian perspectives. Besides the fact that Asian perspectives are many and varied and I, as a Korean biblical scholar, can represent only one of them, my upbringing in modern South Korea and my theological education in the USA may appear to delimit my capacity to interpret the Bible from an Asian perspective. But one should remember that the dependence on so-called Western scholars, at least in theological education, is not merely unavoidable, but is a necessary prerequisite to any indigenizing theology. Christianity, as well as the Bible, arrived from Europe and America to Asian countries as part of Western civilizations. For Asians, Christianity is a Western religion. Asian theologians, therefore, must begin by imbibing

---

8. Kyle P. MacCarter, *1 Samuel: A New Translation*, AB (Garden City, NY: Doubleday, 1980), 5.
9. Ellis R. Brotzman, *Old Testament Criticism: A Practical Introduction* (Baker Books: Grand Rapids, MI: 1994), 87–96.
10. Codex Leningrad or Codex Aleppo is medieval manuscripts that contain the MT.

theological traditions from the West. Western scholars are endowed with at least several hundred years of scientific studies of the Bible in addition to several thousand years of interpretive traditions. It would be unwise for Asian biblical scholars to study the Bible as if for the first time. Further, depending on Western scholarship does not "preclude the gaining of insights which are powerfully relevant to our respective Asian contexts."[11] For one thing, Western and Eastern peoples share life experience as human beings, although they have lived in different historical and cultural contexts. What is true of one is most likely to be so of the other. For another, Western and Eastern theologians belong to the same body of Christ. To ignore Christianity's Western heritage is "to cut ourselves off from the contributions of these brothers and sisters in the same body, and that is to impoverish ourselves to an unimaginable extent."[12]

Having said that, the task of contextualizing a biblical interpretation poses a doubly difficult challenge to Asian scholars. They must have a good grasp on both biblical scholarships of the West and Asian philosophical and cultural contexts.[13] For Asian biblical scholars who have been brought up in westernized Asian countries such as Japan, South Korea, Taiwan, or Singapore, it may take as many years of hard work to get reacquainted with their indigenous culture. Further, there has been no agreed upon method or procedure for contextualizing biblical interpretation. All this shows that there is no shortcut in the task of contextualization. It is a process that takes time. It cannot be done by any one genius, but rather should be a collective work by Asian scholars. Any endeavored work should serve as a stimulus and a stepping stone for a better work. My work presented in this commentary is no exception. A remark made by my friend and scholar at Trinity Theological College in Singapore is worth quoting here:

> As Christianity slowly takes root in Asia, contextualization is inevitable . . . But contextualization, especially for us younger theologians, sometimes takes place on an almost unconscious level, as subtle dissatisfaction with aspects of the theological heritage we have inherited begins to manifest itself and new ways of understanding and carrying out the theological tasks are tried out in response. This is necessarily a slow process, and its

11. Theng Huat Leow, *What Young Asian Theologians Are Thinking* (Singapore: Trinity Theological College, 2014), 9.
12. Ibid., 10.
13. Ibid.

fruits are not always evident. The fact that we write articles with heavy reliance on the Yale School, Max Scheler or Hans Urs von Balthasar does not mean we are not doing contextual theology. Contextualization is happening – we just need the senses to detect the almost imperceptible movement and the patience to wait for it to flower.[14]

Missiologists may call my commentary a "contextual interpretation of the Bible," biblical critics a "reader-response" or "post-colonial" reading of the Bible, and philosophers a "hermeneutical fusion of horizons." Whatever name one may give to it, one thing remains unchanged: I've tried to ground my interpretation in linguistic and historical meanings of the text. For this reason this commentary may not be so different from those commentaries written by Western scholars. After all, I've worked on the same Bible as everybody else. In the following three aspects, however, I tried to add Asian textures to it. First, I've tried to utilize Asian – especially Chinese, Korean, and Japanese – folk sayings or Confucius' teachings for illustrative purposes whenever possible. Second, I've tried to apply the text to current issues in Korean churches, with which I am most familiar. Finally, in expounding the story of David (1 Samuel 16–31), I've tried to incorporate relevant episodes from *Three Kingdoms*, a medieval Chinese novel, for comparison just as biblical scholars often do with ancient Near Eastern parallels. *Three Kingdoms* portrays a turbulent period at the end of the Han dynasty (206 BC–220 AD), when heroes and warlords competed for the future of China, often changing alliances. Its convoluted plot is full of "drama and suspense, valor and cowardice, loyalty and betrayal, power and subtlety, chivalry and statecraft the obligations of ruler and subject, conflicts in the basic ties of brotherhood and lineage."[15] It still influences the ways that Chinese, Koreans, Japanese, and Vietnamese think of politics, war, and human relations. Koreans like to say, "one is not worthy of conversation until he reads *Three Kingdoms* three times." The story of David recalls many episodes in *Three Kingdoms* in that both plots are in essence removing chaos in the country and establishing a kingdom or a dynasty that ushers in a period of peace. I hope that my work will serve as a catalyst for other similar efforts to contextualize the Bible for Asian Christians in a fruitful way.

---

14. Ibid., 11.
15. See John S. Service, foreword to *Three Kingdoms: A Historical Novel Attributed to Luo Guanzhong*, trans. Moss Roberts (Berkeley: University of California Press, 1994).

1 SAMUEL 1:1–20

THE STORY OF HANNAH:

THE BIRTH OF SAMUEL

Koreans like to say, "fighting!" to one another on a variety of occasions. They say it, for instance, when cheering for their favorite sports team. A Korean housewife may also say, "fighting," when seeing her husband off to work. Or it is not surprising to hear a radio show host say, "fighting," to his audience when concluding his show for the day. However, Koreans never say, "fighting," when picking a fight. This versatile use of the word represents what one may call the philosophy of life of modern Koreans. They look at life as warfare, a constant battle with oneself, people, and even one's fate. It may explain why Korean society has become overly competitive, but it also explains a fighting faith that Korean churches have demonstrated for the past decades. Korean Christians in the 1970s and 1980s refused to remain in the spiritual inertia and material poverty that they inherited from their ancestors and took initiative to change their lives for the better through aggressive prayer and strict discipline of life.

Hannah was a woman of fighting faith. Her life was a battle with herself, family members, and God himself. Not only did she emerge as a victor in her personal life of warfare, but her victory also changed the course of Israel's history. Because of this heritage, she may be compared to Jacob, the ancestor of Israel (see Gen 32:28), which may reveal why the narrator begins the history of Israel's monarchy with a private story about an obscure woman from an obscure family. Such a beginning is conducive to the message that our obedient life, however insignificant it may look, matters to God and his Kingdom. Had Hannah given into her personal misfortunes and not risen from a place of despair to go to the temple, Israel's history of redemption would have taken a different path from what we know now: history without Samuel! God uses our life of obedient faith – however insignificant it may look – to advance his Kingdom on earth. The Kingdom of God grows through every victory God achieves in our lives.

1:1–3 BACKGROUND: CHARACTERS

Verses 1–3 introduce major characters as a backdrop to the subsequent narrative. The genealogy of Elkanah comes at the beginning of the story (v. 1), creating the expectation that the story will be about Elkanah.[1] However, this expectation is soon thwarted. As the story unfolds, it becomes evident that Elkanah's barren wife, Hannah, is the focus of the story. The narrator prepares the reader for this surprise by the anonymity of Elkanah's forefathers. Jeroham, Elihu, Tohu, and Zuph never appear elsewhere in the Bible, which suggests that they were not men of distinction in those days. In this sense, Elkanah's genealogy fails to dignify Elkanah. In parts of ancient Asia influenced by Chinese culture, one's genealogy primarily determines his caste and moral worth in society. One's genealogy is worth quoting only if it includes one or two heroes of popular recognition. Thus by enumerating only obscure ancestors in the genealogy, the narrator appears to imply that Elkanah is not the hero of the story.

Immediately after Elkanah's genealogy, the narrator introduces Elkanah's two rival wives (v. 2).[2] Peninnah, as her name implies, had "branched out" many offspring, whereas Hannah, as her name implies, was in dire need of divine "grace" because she was barren. The observant reader may expect a reversal in fortunes later in the story because the narrator implies this through the chiastic structure he uses in relation to names. In such a structure, there is an enumeration of a series of items and then a repetition of them in reverse order. In the second half of verse 2, the names are repeated in reverse order, where "Hannah . . . Peninnah" becomes "Peninnah . . . Hannah." The chiastic structure is commonly used in Hebrew poetry, but when used in the narrative, it usually serves to foreshadow a reversal of fates or events later in the plot. Although Hannah was barren at the beginning of the story, her fate changed so that she became fruitful.

Although obscure in his social standing, Elkanah was certainly a man of faith. He visited the sanctuary in Shiloh every year together with his whole family (v. 3). In the three agricultural festivals stipulated in Exodus 23:14–19, only men were required to go up to the temple to Shiloh, and so the presence of Elkanah's whole family suggests that the purpose of the trip was not for one of those agricultural festivals. Rather, it might have been an inner-clan festival called "the annual sacrifice" (*zebah hayamim*; see 1 Sam 1:21; 2:19; 20:6). The

---

1. For instance, Matthew begins his gospel with Jesus's genealogy.
2. The practice of having multiple wives was common in ancient world. The Mosaic law assumes the practice as a given when it legislates inheritance rights of the firstborn right in Deuteronomy 21. But according to the Bible (Gen 2:18–24; 1 Cor 6:16), the practice of monogamy is the divine ideal. As in the case of divorce, one may say that polygamy was permitted in the Old Testament times because of the hardness of human heart (see Matt 19:8).

so-called "annual sacrifice" was not mandatory, but if someone observed it faithfully, it was seen as a sign of piety. Thus we can infer that Elkanah was a godly man. His godliness is put in perspective when we compare him with the corrupt priests of those days, which is what the narrator does: he introduces Eli's two sons, Hophni and Phinehas, right after mentioning Elkanah's annual sacrifice. As it turns out later, Hophni and Phinehas represent corrupt priests who were active at the last days of the judges (see 1 Sam 2:12). The fact that Eli's two sons have no role in Hannah's story underscores the narrator's intention to contrast the godly layperson Elkanah with the corrupt priests under Eli.

1:4–8 PENINNAH PERSECUTES HANNAH

Verses 4–5 set the plot in motion by introducing conflict in the narrative. When distributing meat after sacrifice, Elkanah gave Hannah "a double portion" in contrast to one portion for each of Peninnah's family. Peninnah was apparently outraged by this because, in her estimation, her eldest son deserved a double portion, as this was the lawful right of the firstborn. To Peninnah's further chagrin, Elkanah had been showing Hannah more affection. In fact, the text never mentions that Elkanah loved Peninnah. The Mosaic Law, however, seems to support Peninnah's side on the matter of the firstborn right.

> If a man has two wives, and he loves one but not the other, and both bear him sons but the first born is the son of the wife he does not love . . . he must not give the rights of the firstborn to the son of the wife he loves . . . He must acknowledge the son of his unloved wife as the firstborn by giving him a double share of all he has. (Deut 21:15–17)

Peninnah might have felt that her husband not only showed favoritism toward Hannah but also violated the divine law in turning a blind eye to her firstborn's right. It was one thing to be less loved but it was another to be denied this legal right. Thus Peninnah could not tolerate Hannah, which explains why Peninnah persecuted her so aggressively.

Verse 6 describes Peninnah's verbal abuse against Hannah as follows: "Her rival kept provoking her in order to irritate her." One of the hurtful words she said to Hannah was that "the LORD had closed her womb" (v. 6). It is worth noting in this regard that the narrator never utters the word "barren" in reference to Hannah. Instead he uses a euphemism, "The LORD had closed her womb," twice: first in the words of the narrator (v. 5) and second repeated by

Peninnah (v. 6).[3] It is one thing to say that Hannah was barren and another to say that the Lord had closed her womb. Not only is the latter more hurtful but it also snuffs out what little hope there was left for Hannah. Who could open a womb that the Lord had closed? To make things worse, Peninnah's attack was repetitive, not merely a one-time event. Every time they go to worship and offer sacrifice to God at Shiloh, Hannah was subjected not only to a sense of shame and worthlessness but also to her rival's verbal abuse. The fact that an annual sacrifice was an occasion for family members to have a festive time and strengthen their bonds made Peninnah's persecution even more unbearable. While everyone else ate and drank and laughed, Hannah shed tears and could not eat because of her pain.

Seeing Hannah weeping and fasting, Elkanah tried to console her (v. 8): "Hannah, why are you weeping? Why don't you eat? Why are you downhearted? Don't I mean more to you than ten sons?" (v. 8). Despite his good intention, Elkanah's words did not comfort Hannah for two reasons. First, he said the words in a rebuking tone. Elkanah's three questions all begin with, "Why," which represents a tone of rebuke or complaint in the Old Testament (see Gen 4:6; Exod 5:22). Second, Elkanah's fourth question reveals his self-centeredness in approaching Hannah's problem as well as his disinterestedness toward her bitterness of heart. If Elkanah had really wanted to console Hannah, he should have said, "Don't *you* mean more to me than ten sons?" Some scholars go further to argue that Elkanah was satisfied with the status quo by keeping one wife for fertility and another for pleasure. Be that as it may, it seems certain that Hannah was not comforted by her husband's well-meaning but insensitive words, for she left without answering her husband's questions (v. 9).

In sum, Hannah's pain reached a breaking point, for she was not only childless but also persecuted by Peninnah. Although her husband tried to comfort her, he offered no help. Nobody seemed to understand the depth of Hannah's pain. Further, she could not expect much from the priests at Shiloh, because they were corrupt. To top it off, it must have seemed to Hannah that even the Lord had abandoned her. Hannah was told that her barren womb was divine punishment. Put in Hannah's shoes, many people would give up and live the rest of their lives in chagrin and despair, if not killing themselves. But Hannah was different.

---

3. Hebrew conjunction *ki* may introduce a causal clause – "because . . ." (NIV), but it also introduces the content of what was said – "to the effect that . . ." I took *ki* in v. 6 in the latter sense.

1:9–11 HANNAH VOWS A VOW

Hannah had a fighting faith. She refused to stay in despair or chagrin and took the initiative to change things for the better. Her determination is shown in her act of "rising" in verse 9. The narrator begins verse 9 with the verb "she arose," which is couched in a verbal construction that denotes a definitive one-time act. Prior to this, the narrator uses verbal or nominal clauses that denote habitual acts or ongoing circumstances, suggesting that Hannah's barrenness, Peninnah's persecution, and Elkanah's failure to comfort Hannah all continue year after year until she finally decided to "arise" and break the cycle of despair and inertia.[4] Although the Hebrew text is ambiguous, the Septuagint makes it clear that she arose to stand before the Lord.[5] In other words, her strength came from her total trust in the Lord. She believed in a God who could close the womb and open it again, as she later confessed: "She who was barren has borne seven children; but she who has had many sons pines away" (2:5).

Godly people of Israel made a point of going into the temple to seek his face when faced with extreme difficulties in life or compounded by a riddle of life, such as sinners prospering. Unable to get an answer from any earthly beings, they decided to settle the matter directly with God, face to face. Job was one of those godly men who aspired to get an audience with God, even if it entailed his own death (see Job 19:25–26). Hannah likewise arose from a place of despair to go to the temple to seek the Lord's face. Hannah's arising, which symbolizes her fighting faith, is contrasted with Eli's inactive and perfunctory posture, for he is depicted as "sitting on his chair" (v. 9), which is associated with his priestly routine. Although Eli is portrayed in the narrative more positively than his evil sons, he has been affected by the general depravity of his era: he has become desensitized to the work of the Spirit. His spiritual insensitivity is underscored during his conversation with Hannah.

Once inside the temple, "In her deep anguish, Hannah prayed to the Lord, weeping bitterly" (v. 10). Obviously, she prayed for a son, but as verse 12 makes clear, Hannah continued to pray after she made her vow. The Hebrew phrase, *hitpallel 'al,* which can be translated, "prayed to the Lord" (v. 10), may also be rendered as "prayed for the Lord."[6] This rendering suggests that

---

4. Koowon Kim, *Incubation as a Type-Scene in the 'Aqhatu, Kirta, and Hannah Stories* (Leiden: Brill, 2011), 278–282.
5. The LXX renders the first part of v. 9 as, "And she rose after they ate in Shiloh and *stood before the Lord*" (italics added). It makes it clear that Hannah went to the temple.
6. This rendering is based on the use of the preposition *'al* instead of *'el* in conjunction with the verb *hitpallel.*

Hannah not only desired a son but also sought God himself. In a sense, Hannah was wrestling with the Lord, as Jacob did before her.

But for the plot of the story, the most important part of her prayer is her vow, which clearly expresses Hannah's initiative-taking faith. Her vow consists of two parts, which was typical of any vow in those days: "If you give X," "then I will give back Y." The "if" part of Hannah's vow is unusually long, consisting of four clauses. "[If you] give me a son" is preceded by three synonymous clauses: "If you will only look on your servant's misery and remember me, and not forget your servant" (v. 11). This lengthy preface to her actual request intimates that she was praying "in her deep anguish" (see v. 10). In the "then" part of the vow, Hannah promised to dedicate her son to the Lord as a permanent Nazirite. According to the Mosaic Law (see Num 6:1–8), the degree of purity required for Nazirites was the same as for the high priest. For instance, they must not touch the body of their own parents. By keeping themselves holy, Nazirites represented the holiness of God in a secular world. But since the Nazirite lifestyle could not be maintained with secular jobs, the period of Naziriteship was usually limited in time, ranging from six months to three years. A permanent Naziriteship, as implied by Hannah's vow, was an exceptional occasion. In fact, such a vow is evidenced only in the stories of Samson and Samuel. Further, Hannah's vow, "No razor shall touch his head," occurs in the same form as Samson's birth story (see Judg 13). These connections between the two birth stories foreshadow that the son Hannah asked for from the Lord will become an extraordinary deliverer like Samson.

Yet Hannah's story is different from the typical birth story of a hero, which emphasizes the baby's extraordinary future (e.g. the birth of Pak Hyukgese, the founder of Shilla).[7] In the story of Hannah, however, Hannah's piety is emphasized more than Samuel's heroic future. For instance, in Samson's birth story, the angel of the Lord predicted Samson's heroic future by imposing the Nazirite vow on baby Samson. The role of Samson's parents was very limited. In Samuel's birth story, by contrast, Hannah, rather than Eli the priest or an angel, imposed the Nazirite vow and thereby determined the heroic future of the baby. In other words, through her vow making, she provided Israel, albeit unconsciously, with a heroic kingmaker who would deliver Israel out of the moral and spiritual chaos in the last days of the judges. So even though the first chapter of 1 Samuel talks about the birth of Samuel, it deserves to be

---

7. Pak Hyukgese is known to have founded the kingdom of Shilla in the southeastern part of the Korean peninsula, which lasted as long as a thousand years (from 57 BC to AD 936). The legend has it that Pak Hyukgese was born out of an egg incubated by a divine horse.

called "the story of Hannah."[8] Ultimately, it is the story of a heroic woman who rises from her misfortunes in total trust of the Lord and shapes Israel's history in the form we now know.

1:12–18 ELI BLESSES HANNAH

Hannah's unusually intense and long prayer caught the attention of Eli, the priest, who was sitting on his chair by the doorpost of the temple. "As she kept on praying to the LORD" (v. 12), or, as the JPS (Jewish Publication Society) renders it, "as she prayed long," she might have entered into silent prayer. This inward prayer belies both Hannah's emotional turbulence caused by her external misfortunes and her desperate longing for divine intervention. During this prayer, Eli's eyes were fixed on Hannah's lips, which moved without making sound. He took her for a habitual drinker,[9] a misunderstanding that reflects the degree of moral and religious corruption during the last days of the judges, when it would not have been uncommon for a drunkard coming from a post-sacrifice feast to end up in the sanctuary. More importantly, Eli's mistake reflects his poor judgment in spiritual matters. Although Eli should have made his presence as high priest felt in the temple, Hannah dominates the dialogue scene. More verses are devoted to Hannah's words, and she also has the last word in the conversation. Furthermore, her words in verse 16 may be taken as an indirect criticism against the Elide family: "Do not take your servant for a wicked woman." For Eli's two sons (see 2:12) did evil before the Lord, and Eli himself honored his sons more than God. Hannah, whom Eli accuses of being habitually drunk, was, in fact, "pouring out" her heart, not wine, before the Lord and was "praying" out of her great anxiety and vexation rather than intoxication. Eli tried to save face by sending her away with a blessing, but even in this moment Eli had a moment of awkwardness, because he did not know the subject of Hannah's prayer. So he simply said, "May the God of Israel grant what you have asked of him" (v. 17). Hannah, on the other hand, accepted Eli's perfunctory blessing as if it had come from God himself, which is implied by her reaction: "Then . . . she ate something, and her face was no longer downcast" (v. 18). Before this encounter at the temple, she was

8. For this reason, the present writer has proposed to call the story of Hannah "the incubation type-scene" rather than "the annunciation type-scene." See Koowon Kim, *Incubation as a Type-scene in the Aqhatu, Kirta, and Hannah Stories*, 263–342.
9. The Hebrew *shikkorah*, "(she) was drunk" (v. 13), connotes alcohol addiction.

fasting and full of sorrow, but now she was certain that God had granted her petition. She found a new hope.

In a sense, her fervent prayer forced a blessing out of Eli. Although Eli was not a perfect priest, God still used him as a vessel through which to pass along his blessing to his people. Every generation has its own portion of problems with regard to their religious leaders, and our era is no exception. But God is able to use imperfect leaders for his good cause.[10]

1:19–20 THE BIRTH OF SAMUEL, KINGMAKER

The next morning, Elkanah's family headed back to their home at Ramah. God remembered Hannah's petition and gave her a son. Hannah named him Samuel, for she "asked the LORD for him" (v. 20). A few elements in the text underscore Hannah's fighting faith. In the traditional birth story of a hero, the sexual intercourse is never mentioned in relation to the birth of a child, for it not only makes the birth less extraordinary but also dilutes the sense of awe about a miraculous divine intervention. But in Hannah's story, the narrator mentions the intercourse of Elkanah and Hannah (v. 19). Furthermore, Hannah, not God, names her son "Samuel." These details underscore her assertive, gritty, and initiative-taking faith.

Based on Hannah's explanation of the name "Samuel," many scholars take this birth story as originally belonging to Saul, whose name means "one who is asked for."[11] Saul's name, they argue, is more fitting to the story than "Samuel," whose etymological meaning is "Sumu [a divine name] is a god." Be that as it may, the narrator certainly intends the birth story of Samuel to be read in relation to the birth story of the first king of Israel (i.e. Saul). The solution to Hannah's problem (i.e. Samuel, a king-maker) also serves as the solution to the nation's problem (i.e. the lack of a king). This shows how the private story of a barren woman is connected to the national history of Israel. Had Hannah not arisen from a cycle of despair to stand before the Lord in order to "force" a son from him, the history of Israel's monarchy would have been very different from what we know now. To put it another way, God took note of Hannah who, in total trust of him, refused to give into fate but always dared to make a difference in her apparently insignificant life. God used her faith to advance Israel's grand history of redemption.

---

10. However, this should not be used as an excuse for discouraging lay people from voicing their reasonable criticisms against religious leaders.
11. MacCarter, *1 Samuel*, 63–66.

We all want to be part of God's great plan of world redemption. For that, we do not need to be rich or famous. It all starts with our seemingly irrelevant and insignificant but godly decisions in life. It is crucial to practice godliness every day without growing weary. God is able and can make our life into an important puzzle piece for the picture of his great kingdom.

1 SAMUEL 1:21–2:11

SAMUEL'S DEDICATION

AND HANNAH'S SONG

As the Chinese say, "One heart in entering a backhouse, another heart in exiting it." This idiom suggests that after realizing a wish, people tend to change their mind about their previous commitments. This happens not only in the real world but also in a literary world. There are many stories wherein a person fails to keep his vows to his patron deity after his wish comes true. For instance, in the story of the Canaanite king Kirta (or Keret), Kirta does not fulfill his vow to his patron goddess even after successfully obtaining his wife with divine help. It's no surprise that the goddess becomes angry and makes Kirta seriously ill as a punishment. The prevalence of this motif in ancient literature underscores the truth of the popular Chinese saying: it is part of sinful human nature to be unfaithful.

Hannah, however, did not fall into the temptation to go against her vow. Right after weaning her hard-earned son, she dedicated him to the Lord, faithfully fulfilling her vow. This demonstrates the fact that she prayed in her deep anguish not only for a son but also for the Lord. Thus she did not use the Lord as a means to get what she wanted, for the Lord was her heart's desire. As Hannah's song articulates it, she came to a better understanding of God through her suffering. She was filled with new knowledge of God, which brought about significant growth and change within her.

1:21–23 HANNAH WEANS THE BABY

A couple of months after Hannah gave birth to Samuel, the time for the annual sacrifice came around again. As if to remind us of Hannah's vow, the narrator adds an extra purpose for this trip to Shiloh. Elkanah goes up to the sanctuary not only to offer the annual sacrifice but also "to fulfil his vow."[1] Now that God had fulfilled his part of the transaction, Hannah was expected to do her part. The annual sacrifice provided such an opportunity. But we are told in verse 22 that Hannah did not go with the family to Shiloh, announcing the need of a weaning period for the baby.

---

1. What "his vow" refers to is not clear in the text, but it is certainly not Hannah's vow.

21

At first glance, Hannah's decision is understandable. Since the baby came to her after a long period of waiting in anguish, it would have been very hard for Hannah to give him up right away. Further, the priests at Shiloh had a reputation for abusing temple workers in the precinct, and Hannah must have been reluctant to deliver her two- or three-month-old baby into their hands. In terms of the plot, her delay in dedicating the baby to the temple creates tension in the story, raising a suspicion about her willingness to honor her vow to God. This actually has more to do with the fact that there was no fixed period for weaning a baby in ancient Israel. Scholars speculate that three years was the average, but the timing varied from mother to mother[2] and was ultimately up to the mother to decide. So if Hannah wanted to hold the baby back for a longer period of time, she could have done so.

But her delay creates tension in the narrative, which is subtly implied by the narrator's intentional juxtaposition of the phrase, "to fulfill his vow," at the end of verse 21 and the phrase, "[But] Hannah did not go up," at the beginning of verse 22. Although we are not sure of the nature of "his [Elkanah's] vow," the narrator's mention of it certainly recalls Hannah's vow to give her son to God. Elkanah's words in verse 23 are suggestive in this regard: "Do what seems best to you . . . only may the Lord make good his word." The phrase, "do what seems best," is contrasted with, "may the Lord make good his word." The former is reminiscent of the refrain that punctuates the last chapters of Judges: "people did what was right in their own eyes" (Judg 21:25). When we do what is right in our own eyes (or what "seems best"), we usually establish our own agenda rather than honoring "God's words." These subtle nuances in phrasing create tension in the story, which is reminiscent of ancient tragedies about unfaithful oath-makers.

This tension is soon resolved by another act of initiative-taking faith. As discussed before, it was up to Hannah to decide when to wean her baby. It did not take long for Hannah to make the decision to bring her baby to the temple, which is demonstrated by the narrator's short note: "he was very young" (v. 24).[3] Although we are not sure how many months or years Hannah breastfed Samuel, she did not hold him back out of an unwillingness to dedicate him to the Lord, for when the right time arrived, she took initiative in weaning the baby and presented him to the Lord. The narrator's fourfold use of the Hebrew *gamal*, "to wean," is noteworthy in this regard. The first use is

---

2. Philip J. King and Lawrence E. Stager, *Life in Biblical Israel* (Louisville, KY: Westminster/John Knox Press, 2001), 41.
3. My translation; NIV: "young as he was."

spoken by Hannah in a passive form: "after the boy is weaned" (v. 22). The second use is spoken by Elkanah in an active form, as if to remind Hannah that it is her decision to wean her baby: "Stay here until *you have weaned him*." The third and fourth uses are part of the narration, which confirms that Hannah took initiative to wean the baby and to dedicate him to the Lord: she "nursed her son until she had weaned him" and "*After she weaned him*, she took the boy with her" (v. 24).[4] Once again, she proved herself to be a woman of an initiative-taking faith, though this does not mean that she was free from struggling. A life committed to God is not free from struggling, for Hannah must have fought against her desire to keep the baby with her, however short that struggle might have been.

1:24–28 DEDICATION OF SAMUEL TO THE TEMPLE

This section concerns the dedication of the infant Samuel to the temple in Shiloh. The dedication ceremony consisted of a bull sacrifice (v. 25), the presentation of Samuel to Eli (v. 25), and Hannah's public pronouncement that she was hereby dedicating her son to the Lord (v. 28). Samuel's service to the Lord was permanent, for Samuel stayed in the temple "for his whole life" (v. 28). Although the biblical tradition is ambiguous about Samuel's priestly genealogy,[5] Samuel soon replaced Eli as the leading priest in the country.

This section also includes a few indications about Hannah's prominence in the narrative. First, Elkanah's absence is noticeable. The context makes it unambiguously clear that Elkanah was present along with Hannah at this dedication ceremony, but the narrator does not mention anything about him. Instead Hannah is the main actor and the subject of most of the verbs. Further, she is the only one who talks in this scene. Even Eli's answer to Hannah's confession is silenced.[6] Furthermore, if we accept the Septuagint's reading of verse 28, it was "she" (Hannah) that worshiped the Lord, not "he" – which could refer either to Samuel or his father. All these show that Hannah took initiative in dedicating her long-awaited child to the Lord.

---

4. My translation; emphasis added. The NIV translation, "After he was weaned," is a sufficient English idiom but does not reflect the Hebrew original faithfully.
5. Compare 1 Sam 1:1 and 1 Chr 6:26–28.
6. Eli could have said something after v. 26 or v. 27. The narrator does not record it.

HANNAH'S UNYIELDING FAITH AND ITS IMPLICATION TO US

For any mother, giving up a long-awaited child would be a heartbreaking experience. Hannah undoubtedly experienced that heartbreak, but honoring her vow was a powerful expression of her unyielding faith. Hannah fulfilled her vow and willingly offered her son to God with praise and thanksgiving. For Hannah, dedicating Samuel to the temple meant more than physically giving him up, for it implied her relinquishment of all the joys of motherhood – the blissful moments of laughter and tears she could have shared with her precious child. Hannah also let go of the source of her security, for if Elkanah died before Hannah could give birth to another child, her future would be at risk. Despite this, Hannah resolutely bound herself to her vow and dedicated Samuel to the temple.

How could Hannah exert such remarkable faith? Her experience with God – which began with the long suffering of infertility and climaxed in the miraculous birth of her child – made her realize that God, not Samuel, was the true treasure she had been seeking in her life. Over the course of her journey, Hannah came to know God intimately and discovered the Immanuel God who is bigger than life, who was attentive to her outcry and provided her peace in the storm of her suffering. God saved Hannah by bringing her out of darkness and into the light and demonstrated his creative power through the birth of Samuel. Confident that God would remain her protector and provider, Hannah could willingly give away her child, entrusting both her life and the life of her child into God's hands. Thus she could do what seemed humanly impossible.

As with Hannah, God performs wonderful miracles in our lives and answers our prayers beyond our imagination. Out of desperation, many "Hannahs" kneel in prayer, petitioning God to change their unfavorable circumstances, grant their desires, and end suffering in their lives. We can all look to God with our petitions and trust in his goodness.

Jung Jun Kim

2:1–10 HANNAH'S SONG OF PRAISE

The story of Hannah aptly ends with her prayer, praising God.[7] Although some scholars doubt that Hannah's song is original to the story, her prayer not only recalls her personal tribulation but also completes her story by showing how her suffering changed her perspective about God. Further, it is not uncommon to have poems as part of narratives.[8] Ancient Chinese historiography also uses poems at crucial junctures in the story as a way of presenting life lessons of eternal significance.[9] By presenting Hannah's prayer in Hebrew poetry, the narrator lays out the theology that informs the whole book. Moreover, the narrator's reference to "his king" (v. 10) outlines the subsequent plot of the story.

In order to appreciate Hannah's prayer, one should remember that this prayer was not sung on the occasion of Samuel's birth but when she dedicated her baby to the temple. The song not only traces Hannah's joyous reaction to the event which removed shame from her but also the change in her perspective about God because of her experiences. In other words, Hannah's elation was not merely owing to the gift that God gave her but to the giver himself: "My heart rejoices in the LORD" (v. 1). Hannah's experience of God's salvation led her to confess her faith in the one and only God: "there is no one holy like the LORD; there is no one besides you; there is no rock like our God" (v. 2). Hannah's confidence stemmed from her personal encounter with God in the temple. Before the encounter she was bitter and hopeless, but afterwards she became confident that God had vindicated her, that her barrenness was a blessing in disguise for the sake of the greater glory of God in her personal life as well as in the broader history of redemption. In verse 3, Hannah addresses her (and God's) enemies whose wickedness culminates in their arrogant derision of God's wisdom: "How can God know? Is there knowledge in the Most High?" (see Ps 73:11). She refutes those deriding God with the following words: "the LORD is a God of knowledge" (v. 3). She affirms that God knows how to rule the universe, although man is not always privy to God's wisdom. Hence mortals should not speak proudly or let arrogance come from their mouths

---

7. Scholars have noted that Hannah's song provides basic themes for the Magnificat of Mary in Luke 1:46–56. See Grail O'Day, "Singing a Woman's Song: A Hermeneutics of Liberation," *CTM* 12 (1985): 203–210.

8. The narrator of 1 and 2 Samuel often uses poems to deliver theological lessons. For example, Samuel's speech to Saul about the importance of obedience is presented in Hebrew poetry (see 15:22–23).

9. Luo Guanzhong, author of *Three Kingdoms*, uses poetry extensively in his narrative. For example, poems ascribed to Cao Cao, king of Wei, became so popular that they were later published in a separate volume.

too hastily. Rather the Lord judges the human according to his deeds (v. 3). At this point, Hannah might have been remembering Peninnah's judgmental remarks: "the LORD had closed your womb"![10] Although Peninnah "thundered" against Hannah (see 1:7), the Lord will "thunder from Heaven" against those who are proud and arrogant like Peninnah (see 2:10).

The central part of the prayer (vv. 4–8) is devoted to the proclamation of the core theology of 1 Samuel: the sovereignty of Yahweh. Verses 4–5 give examples of how Yahweh reverses human fortunes. For instance, the strong become weak while the weak become strong (v. 4). The rich become hirelings and the poor become rich (v. 5a). The most relevant example to Hannah, however, comes at the second half of verse 5: "She who was barren has borne seven children, but she who has had many sons pines away." The focus is not on the barren or fertile woman whose fortunes are somehow reversed, but on Yahweh, who reverses human fortunes according to his free and good will. Hannah trusted that Yahweh, who had closed her womb, had the power to open it again. Verses 6–8 continue the same theme of God's sovereign rule and yet shift focus regarding its extent. For that purpose, the poetess uses a merism, a rhetorical device in which two words on both ends of a scale are used to represent everything in the scale. In verse 6, "the LORD brings death and makes alive; he brings down to the grave and raises up," for instance, Hannah proclaims that the Lord controls all the affairs concerning life and death. The merisms in verses 7–8 suggest that the Lord controls everything about wealth and honor:

The LORD sends poverty and wealth;
    he humbles and he exalts.
He raises the poor from the dust and lifts the needy from
    the ash heap;
he seats them with princes and has them inherit a throne
    of honor.

Thus the merisms in verses 6–8 encompass all three major areas of human affairs: health, money, and fame, underscoring the exhaustive extent of God's sovereign rule over the world. As Abraham Kuyper once said, "There is not a square inch in the whole domain of human existence whereof Christ, who is Sovereign over all, does not say: 'Mine!'"[11] And what is the basis of Yahweh's

---

10. See the comment on 1:6 in chapter 1 above.
11. James D. Bratt, ed., *Abraham Kuyper: A Centennial Anthology* (Grand Rapids, MI: Eerdmans, 1998), 488.

claim to such universal sovereignty? The latter half of verse 8 provides the justification of such a claim: he is the creator of the universe! He is the one who established the foundations of this earth and set the world on them at the beginning of time. The Creator rules!

Hannah's prayer reaches its climax in verses 9–10. God's sovereign rule is not simply powerful and absolute but also merciful and just. Not only is he able to defeat anyone who rebels against him by sending thunder from heaven but he also reveals himself to be just by differentiating between the faithful and the wicked in his judgment: "He will guard the feet of his faithful servants, but the wicked will be silenced in the place of darkness" (v. 9a). In a world ruled by the merciful God, a man prevails not by might (v. 9b) but by grace (see Zech 4:6). The Lord judges "the ends of the earth" (v. 10a), or the whole world, with his anointed as vicegerent. He will anoint a man after his own heart as king of Israel so that he may administer divine goodness and justice to his people (v. 10b). Hannah is almost prophetic in anticipating not only the eventual arrival of a monarchy in Israel but also her son's crucial role as kingmaker. On this prophetic note Hannah ends her prayer.

DESIRING GOD

Once we receive a long-awaited "gift" from God, we tend to invest less in our relationship with God and seek God less until a new prayer request visits us. Our ingrained self-centeredness tends to lead us to serve God only when God serves our needs. Thus we fail to follow in Hannah's faith journey in seeking God and praying for the Lord. God has been sidelined in our hearts by the "functional" gods we dearly serve, such as material blessing, security, recognition, and so on. What is our true motivation for seeking God? Do we love God for who God is, or for what God can do for us? One concrete way to have our hearts in check is to take time to review the contents of our need-focused prayers and compare them with Hannah's God-centered prayer.

The growth in popularity of the prosperity gospel in Asia reveals that we Asian Christians are in danger of praying self-centered and need-focused prayers. Considering the historical context of poverty, war, and colonization in many Asian countries – especially Korea – we have a strong desire to receive "blessings" from God: a secure, healthy, and wealthy life. However, if the pursuit of such earthly blessings gets in the way of us getting to know our Lord intimately, we need to repent of our idolatry. The true blessing that Hannah had the privilege of enjoying, and which God wants us to have, is to taste and see that the Lord is good (Ps 34:8)! What "Samuels" do we need to give up and dedicate to the Lord today?

Jung Jun Kim

2:11 SAMUEL SERVES THE LORD UNDER ELI

The Hannah story concludes with the characters returning to their rightful places. Elkanah returned home to Ramah, which confirms that Elkanah was present with Hannah in the dedication ceremony at Shiloh, although his presence was ignored by the narrator until here. Meanwhile, "the boy served the LORD under Eli the priest" (v. 11, my translation). The narrator calls Samuel "the boy," which does not simply refer to his age but also to his status as the apprentice of Eli. More interesting to note is the fact that Samuel "served the LORD," not Eli. Humanly speaking one may say that Samuel was serving Eli, but Samuel was under the tutelage of the Lord. This explains how Samuel was able to nurture his integrity among corrupt priests in the sanctuary. We learn from this that God cares for his people no matter where they may find themselves.

1 SAMUEL 2:12–36

THE SIN OF ELI'S FAMILY

For the past ten years or so, several megachurch pastors in South Korea have been criticized for financial or sexual misbehavior. Many people have expressed concern that these are not isolated cases but the tip of an iceberg, so to speak. This crisis was set in motion by the gradual nominalization of Christianity in South Korea. As Christians grew in number and influence, pastors got too comfortable in their vested offices and gave into temptations. It is always sad to watch saints who begin good end badly. Eli was one of those saints. This section contrasts the evil acts of Eli's two sons with Samuel's growth in stature and favor with the Lord and the people. Eli's two sons, though they were priests, proved themselves to be scoundrels by doing what was right in their own eyes under the pretext of temple service. Father Eli was not without fault, for he did not take any punitive actions against his recalcitrant sons except for a half-hearted rebuke. Eli's perfunctory mentorship is contrasted with Hannah's passionate care for young Samuel, symbolized by "a little robe" which she made for him. At the end of chapter 2, the oracle of judgment is pronounced by an anonymous man of God. According to the prophecy, the Elide line of priests will be removed from temple service due to their sins against God and replaced by an alternative line of priests.

2:12–17 ELI'S WICKED SONS

Eli's two sons are first introduced as "priests of the Lord" in 1:3, where their priestly office at Shiloh is juxtaposed with layman Elkanah's pilgrimage to Shiloh. The narrator subtly contrasts the priests' perfunctory manner with the layman's piety. But chapter 2 reveals Eli's sons' true identity: they are described as "scoundrels" (*bene beliya'al*; 12a), an epithet that is reserved only for the worst sinners in the Hebrew Bible, such as murderers, rapists, and mockers of the Lord. Eli may have used this word to describe Hannah when he calls her "a wicked woman" (*bat beliya'al*: 1:16) without realizing that his own sons were actually the wicked ones. The Korean saying, "the foot of an oil lamp is dark!" teaches that we tend to overlook what is right under our nose. Further, the narrative says that Eli's two sons "had no regard for the Lord" (v. 12b) even though they functioned as priests. The Hebrew original suggests that they did not even know the Lord. Even though they had been groomed to become priests of the Lord, they had no authentic experience of who God was and what he did for them. Based on this characterization as scoundrels who did not know the Lord, one may easily judge that they did not belong in the sanctuary.

Verses 13–16 illustrate why Eli's sons deserved to be called scoundrels who did not know the Lord. As a backdrop, the narrator begins by describing the customary procedure about how to separate the priests' portion from the sacrificial meat. First, the fat portion had to be burnt for the Lord; second, the meat had to be boiled in water; after this, the priests could send their servant to get their portion. Only the portion that was picked up from the cooking pots by the servant's fork with one poke could go up on the priests' table. But Eli's sons violated this customary procedure – a custom that was not based on the Mosaic law – by demanding raw rather than boiled meat as a priestly portion, even before the fat was burnt for the Lord. To enforce their will, they were prepared to use violence (see v. 16).

To put the sin of the Elide priests in perspective, we should remember that the way in which the Elide sons conduct the procedure not only violates the Levitical law (see Lev 7:32), but also reflects the moral and spiritual chaos in the last days of the Judges, especially with respect to the priests. First, the use of a three-pronged fork is unprecedented.[1] It appears to have been the device used to take the most meat out of the cooking pots. The three-pronged fork speaks to the priests' greed. Second, the enumeration of various cooking pots is also suggestive. According to Alter, the unusual catalogue of implements "serves a satiric purpose: Eli's sons are represented in a kind of frenzy of gluttony poking their three-pronged forks into every imaginable pot and pan."[2] Thus, the custom concerning the priestly portion may have been designed to put a cap on what the priests could take from the offering, but the custom was itself based on the "fallen" condition of priests, not to mention that it went against the Levitical law. But what made the sin of Eli's sons most flagrant was that they did not even burn the fat as an offering for the Lord. This amounted to the sacrilege of robbing the Lord.

The narrator identifies the exact nature of the Elide priests' sin, which was not only robbery from the Lord but also contempt for the Lord (v. 17). Their sin was more a matter of blasphemy than ethics. The expression "treating the

---

1. Mary J. Evans, *1 & 2 Samuel* (Grand Rapids, MI: Baker Books, 2000), 23. The fork was a latecomer to the table. People used a knife point to pick up food before the invention of a fork. The earliest forks were two-pronged.
2. Robert Alter, *The David Story: A Translation with Commentary of 1 and 2 Samuel* (New York: W. W. Norton & Co., 1999), 12.

Lord's offering with contempt" (v. 17) is a euphemism for treating the Lord with contempt. The ancient Jews feared to pronounce the name of the Lord, let alone curse or despise the Lord. By saying that the sons despised the Lord's offering, the narrator suggests that they had a blaspheming contempt for the Lord. This explains why their sin is characterized as unforgivable even "by sacrifice or offering" (see 3:14). Denying the Lord in contempt is as unforgivable as it is to deny Jesus willfully and consistently without repenting (see Matt 12:31; 1 John 5:11).

It is important to remember that the Lord gave the land of Canaan as a gift to the Israelites hundreds of years prior to this narrative. After receiving the land, the Israelites were given the mission to work the Canaanite land and turn it into a land filled with the knowledge of the Lord. But after all those years, they obviously failed in that mission and instead became like the Canaanites. The priestly corruption in this narrative reflects the depth of Israel's Canaanization. Eli's sons had become like pagan priests; personal piety was no longer necessary to be a religious functionary. They worked for money and fame. As the Koreans say, "if a monk was interested only in his rice bowl, the country would fall." This saying originates from the historical experience that the fall of the state always comes in tandem with religious corruption. The corruption of the Elide priests shows that the history of Israel had passed the point of no return. There was no way to establish the old order. Something drastically new had to happen in order to fix the problem of Canaanization.

2:18–21 HANNAH AND SAMUEL

The narrator gives a glimmer of hope by punctuating the description of the sinful priests with a mention of Samuel's service and growth under the tutelage of the Lord. "But Samuel was ministering before the Lord – a boy wearing a linen ephod" (v. 18). In verse 11, we see Samuel serving the Lord as Eli's apprentice. The use of the phrase "under Eli" in this verse reminds us of Eli's role as Samuel's master priest. But in verse 18, after describing the sin of Eli's two sons, the narrator replaces "under Eli" (*et-pene Eli*) with "before the Lord" (*et-pene YHWH*). In the Hebrew original, the narrator uses the same preposition *et-pene* in both phrases. The change from "under Eli" to "under the Lord" underscores that God, not the Elide priests nurture Samuel in matters of priesthood.[3] Moreover, the note about Samuel wearing a linen ephod points to his faithful service as a priest, for the Levitical law stipulates that a linen garment is the proper attire for a priest on duty (see Lev 16:32). The fact that the narrator mentions this detail suggests that, in contrast with Eli's two "young men" (*na'ar.* v. 17) who flagrantly abused the Law in matters of temple service, Hannah's "boy" (*na'ar.* v. 18) faithfully obeyed it.[4]

This contrast extends beyond the "boys" to their parents. Elkanah and Hannah continued their annual sacrifices as before: note that the phrase "each year" (*miyamim yamimah*) in verse 19 is the same in Hebrew with "year after year" (*miyamim yamimah*) in 1:3. They did not neglect worshipping and sacrificing to the Lord even after their problems had been solved – for Elkanah, intra-familial dispute, and for Hannah, childlessness. The faithfulness shown by Samuel's parents is exemplary even now, let alone in the darkest age of Israelite history. Furthermore, every year Hannah brought a small garment (*me'il*) to Samuel at Shiloh. The small garment illustrated Hannah's passionate and unceasing care for her son. It was no small thing to make a new garment every year. First, Hannah had to anticipate Samuel's growth in size and cut his clothes accordingly. In other words, she had to know Samuel's needs accurately. Second, making a garment in the ancient world took a long time, since it entailed the whole process, from growing or acquiring materials for cloth to weaving, dyeing, cutting, and knitting them into a garment. It is no exaggeration to say, therefore, that although Hannah was physically separated from Samuel, she constantly thought and prayed about him as she made his garment. Thus she was able to influence him even though they were not living under the same roof. On the contrary, Eli was not able to influence his sons even though he lived near with them and was supposedly in regular contact with them as their senior priest.

The little garment that Hannah made for Samuel each year later became the garment that symbolized his authority as a prophet. He always wore the prophetic mantle when he went about the land of Israel discharging his duty (see 15:27–28). People recognized Samuel by this outer garment (see 28:14). Thus Hannah's love and prayers influenced little Samuel to grow to become the prophet Samuel. This teaches us that parents' faithful love matters in the character development of their children. One does not need to be present with

---

3. Further, the phrase "before the Lord" may denote the sanctuary in the temple. Hannah arose to pray before the Lord: "As she continued praying before the LORD" (ESV, 1:12). It was also in the same place that Eli's sons had sexual relations with temple workers (see 2:22).
4. Hebrew *na'ar* "boy" may refer to any man, minor or adult, under authority.

children all the time to influence them. Hannah saw Samuel only a couple of days a year. Every family is different, but the truth remains that the children of faithful and prayerful parents are not likely to fail.

2:22–26 ELI REBUKES HIS SONS

Eli's inability to influence his sons is implied by the word "very old" in verse 22, which not only points to his physical age but also to his spiritual dullness. Another hint about his spiritual dullness – or his failure to get access to knowledge – is the fact that Eli found out about his sons' evil acts through rumors spreading among his people (v. 24). Although he was their biological and spiritual father, Eli was the last person to learn about their sins. Apparently Eli lost his authority over his sons, for they would not listen to him when he confronted them about their wrongdoings (v. 25). This underscores Eli's failure both as parent and as priest. Further, it highlights not only Eli's personal failure but also the failure of the whole family as a priestly line. Thus God rejected the Elide priests from serving him, which is implied by the narrator's note: "For it was the LORD's will to put them [Eli's sons] to death" (v. 25). The death of Eli's two sons is used as a prophetic sign confirming the divine rejection of the Elides as priests of the Lord (see v. 34).

Verse 22 also reveals another crime: Eli's sons had sexual relations with the women "who served at the entrance to the tent of meeting." Eli seemed to interpret this crime as being against the Lord rather than against the women, judging from his remark in verse 23: "If one person sins against another, God may mediate for the offender; but if anyone sins against the LORD, who will intercede for them?" The Hebrew word[5] that refers to the violated women and the location of the unfortunate crime confirms Eli's judgment that his sons sinned against the Lord himself. The narrator calls the women who were violated by Eli's sons *tsobe'ot* (literally, "female workers"). Interestingly the sound for this phrase recalls the title of the Lord of Almighty (*YHWH tseba'ot*). The narrator seems to be arguing that Eli's sons violated both the women as well as the Lord. In other words, the sin of Eli's sons was more blasphemous than moral in nature. Further, the Hebrew text allows us to understand that the crime happened at the sanctuary, where people worshipped and prayed,

---

5. The Hebrew author resorts to an indirect way of saying "rape," so the reader must judge by context whether a particular sexual intercourse was forced in any sense. The Hebrew *škb*, which is used in reference to the sexual sin of Eli's two sons (v. 22), may refer to a rape, as the same verb is used in Deut 22:23 and in 2 Sam 11:4.

which suggests that the crime was a sacrilege committed against the temple of the Lord. In this sense, their sexual sin was the same in nature as robbing the Lord of his offering, and neither sin was forgivable by sacrifice or offering.

The narrator concludes this section with a note that refers to the physical and spiritual growth of Samuel. In contrary to Eli's blasphemous sons, Samuel "continued to grow both in stature and in favor with the LORD and also with man" (v. 26). Soon Samuel would establish himself as a new political and religious leader, essentially replacing the Elide priests.

2:27–36 PROPHECY OF DOOM AGAINST THE ELIDE PRIESTS

An anonymous "man of God" came to Eli and sealed the fate of his household by declaring the Lord's rejection of Eli's descendants as priests. The so-called "messenger formula" – "This is what the LORD says" (v. 27) – identifies the anonymous man as a prophet. The narrator, however, calls him "a man of God" (v. 27). This is interesting because the word "prophet" (*nabi*) is usually reserved for those prophets who were active during Israel's monarchy. Prior to the monarchy, they were called "a seer" (*ro'eh*). The difference in terms reflects different functions. Seers, such as diviners in the neighboring countries, worked miracles and wonders, possibly in exchange for rewards.[6] Monarchic prophets, on the other hand, proclaimed divine messages, mostly of doom to covenant breakers. The title "man of God" may have been either a seer or a prophet or both, but what's peculiar about the man of God in this passage is that his message recalls the messages of monarchic prophets in general and of Samuel against King Saul in particular (see chs. 13 and 15).

The man of God's prophecy of doom consisted of three parts, arranged according to temporal order. First, the Lord reminded Eli about how he had dealt favorably with his family in the past. God had chosen Eli's ancestor out of all the tribes of Israel to be his priestly family while they were still slaves to the house of Pharaoh, and he had given Eli's family all the privileges of serving God, such as "to go up" to his altar, "to burn incense," "to wear an ephod" in his presence, and to eat "all the food offerings presented by the Israelites" (v. 28). But Eli and his sons had not lived a life worthy of the grace bestowed upon them. Instead of serving the Lord with all their hearts, they had scorned God's sacrifice and offering (v. 29; see v. 17). Further, we are told that Eli had "honored" (*kbd*) his sons more than God by "fattening" (*kbd*) himself and his

---

6. For instance, a seer could be consulted about the whereabouts of runaway donkeys for a quarter of a shekel of silver (see 9:8).

sons on the choicest part of the offerings made by God's people. The Hebrew root *kbd* means both "to be honorable" and "to be heavy." The narrator employs wordplay to accuse the Elide priests of robbing God of his honor by putting weight on themselves. Noteworthy in this regard is that Eli is described later as being heavy (see 4:18). In sum, the Elide priests broke the covenant with the Lord, and so they could not receive God's grace.

Therefore the Lord cancelled the covenant he had made with Eli, which would have continued forever if Eli had fulfilled his part (v. 30; see 13:14). According to the very principle of the covenant, "Those who honor me I will honor, but those who despised me will be disdained" (v. 30; see 15:23). Thus God renounced his special relationship with Eli and his family (v. 30).

The man of God continued to enumerate the misfortunes that would haunt the Elide priests in the future. First, Eli's descendants would die young, a sign of divine disfavor (v. 31). Second, although they would witness the good that the Lord would do to Israel, they would not be part of it (v. 32).[7] The third misfortune outlined in verse 33 is ambiguous in its Hebrew meaning. Either God would leave the Elide priests alive to witness in pain the destruction of their family – "all your descendants will die in the prime of life." Or, those who were left alive to serve at the Lord's altar would have failing eyes and melancholic souls – "I will spare [you] only to destroy your sight and *grieve your soul*" (italic mine), which would ultimately make them unfit for the job both physically and mentally. Having said these things, the man of God gave a short-term sign that would demonstrate the veracity of his prophecy: Eli's sons would "both die on the same day" (v. 34; see 28:19). This sign was fulfilled in the battle against the Philistines at Aphek (see 4:11; 31:2).

The man of God's prophecy against the Elide priests reaches its climax when he declared a new choice by the Lord of "a faithful priest, who will do according to what is in my [God's] heart and mind" (v. 35; see 13:14; 15:28). This priestly house will replace Eli's priestly house, and he will serve the Lord's anointed always. Speaking from a later vantage point, the faithful priest in question may have been Zadok, whom Solomon first installed as the high priest serving in his administration. The establishment of a new priestly line provides a backdrop for the further humiliation of the Elide priests.

> Then everyone left in your family line will come and bow
> down before him for a piece of silver and a loaf of bread and

---

7. This interpretation is based on my translation of v. 32: "And oh enemy of the temple, you will see the good that will be done to Israel, but no one in your family will ever reach old age."

plead, "Appoint me to some priestly office so I can have food to eat." (v. 36)

Whereas verse 33 focuses on the physical and emotional unfitness of the Elide priests left alive to carry out the priestly duty, verse 36 focuses on the shameful motivation in their filling of any priestly office. Just as Hophni and Phinehas were more interested in getting themselves rich than serving the Lord, their descendants will only want to work in the temple so they can have food to eat.

The prophecy of judgment uttered by the man of God also prepares the reader for the future plot of the story in the book of Samuel. The sins of Eli and his sons and the subsequent cancellation of God's covenant with their family line anticipate Saul's failure to obey the Lord and his subsequent rejection as king. In fact, many elements in the prophecy against Eli are also found in Samuel's prophecy of doom against Saul. First, Samuel said that if Saul had kept the command of the Lord, the Lord would have established Saul's kingdom over Israel forever (13:14; see v. 30). Second, Samuel said that Saul's rejection as king was a natural and logical outcome of his rejection of God: "Because you have rejected the word of the LORD, he has rejected you as king" (15:23; see v. 30). Third, the Lord appointed a man after his own heart as a new king of Israel (13:14; 15:28; see v. 35). Fourth, the short-term sign that proved the verity of the prophecy was that Saul and his sons would die soon (28:19; see 34).

It is always sad to watch someone who began well end badly. In a sense Eli was a decent leader who struggled to serve the Lord in one of the darkest periods in Israel's history. He was Samuel's mentor and taught him how to answer to the Lord's callings. Further, he was humble enough to accept the Lord's judgment with aplomb. But at the same time, he was not entirely free from the influence of the general corruption of his time. He did not uphold the Mosaic law faithfully in carrying out his priestly duty. He was willing to compromise to satisfy the needs of the corrupt system of his day. In some parts of Asia, where Christianity has rapidly grown in size and influence, Christian leaders may face challenges similar to those that brought down Eli. Eli's failure should be "the other mountain's stone that can polish jade" for us.

1 SAMUEL 3:1–21
THE LORD CALLS SAMUEL

All spiritual leaders have their moments of enlightenment. Siddhartha had his moment under the Bodhi tree, a kind of old fig tree, in Bodh Gaya and became a Buddah, "an enlightened man." *Mudangs,* Korean spiritists, have to go through an initiation rite called *Naerimgut,* the first possession by a spirit, before he or she can officially function as such. Biblical prophets also had moments of enlightenment, which are referred to as a "calling." The prophetic calling is distinguished, however, from enlightenment experiences of Asian spiritual leaders in that God, rather than spiritual seekers, take the initiative in the process of initiation. Notable in this sense is the fact that biblical prophets often demur before accepting a divine calling.

This episode relates Samuel's call narrative, depicting how Samuel grew to replace Eli as a spiritual leader of the whole nation.[1] The narrator assumes that the social and religious chaos in those days was owing to poor spiritual leadership. In particular, the Elide priests could not function as the medium of divine revelation because of their total corruption. Leaderless people did what was right in their own eyes, which resulted in lawlessness. Samuel succeeded, however, where Eli and his sons failed. On a fateful night, God spoke to Samuel rather than the Elide priests, and thereafter, he continued to speak to Samuel until Samuel was established as a prophet of the Lord across the country.

3:1–3 SAMUEL SLEEPS AT THE TEMPLE

The narrator introduces Samuel as the boy ministering "before the LORD under Eli" (v. 1a). The word "boy" refers both to his young age and to his status as Eli's apprentice. The latter sense is especially noteworthy at this point in the narrative, because later Samuel is no longer called Eli's "boy" but "a prophet of the LORD" (v. 20). Samuel will eventually become a religious leader, independent of the Elide priests, and he will be recognized as such across the country. The theme of this chapter is Samuel's transformation from Eli's boy into a prophet of the Lord.

---

1. Chapter 3 is the first literary unit which is wholly dedicated to Samuel. This is prepared by the brief notes about young Samuel's ministry at the temple in Shiloh in 2:11 and 2:18 and by those that mention his physical and spiritual growth in 2:21 and 2:26.

During Eli's tenure as spiritual leader of the nation, Israel fell into a spiritual stupor; they were in the dark in terms of divine-human communication: "The word of the LORD was rare; there were not many visions" (v. 1b). The Hebrew *yaqar*, "rare," was merchant's language used to describe their most expensive merchandise. By applying this word to the word of the Lord, the narrator subtly criticizes the spirit of Eli's period, when the word of the Lord was treated like an item on a merchant's table instead of something to be obeyed. It is also worth mentioning that the Hebrew phrase *eyn hazon niprats*, "there were no frequent visions," can be literally translated as "no vision was able to break through" to the Israelites. This suggests that God never stopped sending his words and visions to his people but some obstacles blocked the way. As it turned out, the corrupt leadership constituted the obstacles that prevented the words and visions of God from making it to the nation. Only when Samuel became the new leader of Israel could change come about. The situation in modern churches is not much different from that of Israel under Eli. The church organization has become like a business. They sell sermons to the congregants as merchandise, and church leaders themselves often block the way of evangelism instead of serving as a medium of divine blessing. Those who are in church leadership should remember the importance of their office. The fate of the whole congregation depends on their spiritual health.

Verses 2–3 provide the background for the subsequent narrative. First, Eli's spiritual dullness is implied by the narrator's note about his poor eyesight: his "eyes were becoming so weak that he could barely see" (v. 2). Poor eyesight may have been a sign of Eli's seniority, but the narrator uses it as a metaphor for Eli's gradual alienation from divine revelation.[2] Second, Israel's crisis in spiritual darkness is compared to the lamp of God that has almost, but not yet, gone extinct (v. 3).[3] In other words, Eli's corrupt leadership has driven the nation near to death, but there is still hope. The lamp of the Lord has not yet gone extinct but is still burning. Soon, Samuel will turn that failing fire into a flaming torch. Third, as another piece of background information, the narrator contrast Eli's sleeping quarters with Samuel's. Eli sleeps in his own place while Samuel is lying down "in the house of the LORD, where the ark of God was" (v. 3). The mention of the ark of God is noteworthy and may suggest Samuel's purpose for sleeping in the temple. The ark was believed to be part of God's throne, and when God spoke to the Israelites, his voice came from between

---

2. See 2:33. Losing one's eyesight was one of the curses against the Elide priests.
3. Hebrew *terem* may be translated as both "not yet" and "almost."

the two cherubs on top of the ark. Further, in the ancient Near East, priests often spent the night at the temple in order to obtain revelations from the gods. All this may suggest that Samuel slept or was instructed to sleep in the temple for the purpose of obtaining divine revelation. If that was the purpose of temple sleep, however, Eli should have slept in the temple and asked the Lord to speak to him because he lived in the season of spiritual drought (v. 1). But he had his apprentice Samuel sleep in the temple in his place. Further, he did not expect God to speak to Samuel, judging from the fact that he had not taught Samuel how to answer the Lord. Although he continued the practice of temple sleep through his apprentice, he did not believe in it.[4]

3:4–9 GOD CALLS SAMUEL

Then an unexpected incident occurred: "The LORD called Samuel" (v. 4). Since Samuel was an inexperienced acolyte, he did not realize that the call was coming from the Lord. So he ran to Eli in his quarters and woke him up, saying, "Here I am; you called me" (v. 5). But Eli said, "I did not call," and sent him back to lie down in the temple again. The Lord called Samuel again, and again Samuel ran to Eli and woke him up. This time Eli paused a little by calling Samuel, "my son," but he sent him back the same as before. The exchange suggests that Eli loved obedient Samuel as his own son. Then God called Samuel a third time, and when Samuel ran to Eli and woke him up again, Eli realized that the Lord had been calling the boy and gave Samuel a quick lecture about how to respond to divine revelation: "Go and lie down (*lek shekab*), and if he calls you, say, 'Speak, LORD, for your servant is listening'" (v. 9). Notice Eli's first two words, "Go and lie down." These are slightly different from his previous words, "Go back and lie down" (*shub shekab*; v. 5, 6). The Hebrew *shuv*, "go back," is often used adverbially as "again" in conjunction with another verb. Thus "Go back and lie down" means the same as "Lie down again" or "go back to sleep." But when Eli sent Samuel back a third time, he chose a different word, "Go (*lek*)," by which he meant that Samuel should lie down not to sleep again, but to hear God's voice. This is corroborated by some medieval Jewish manuscripts in which the phrase, "if he calls you"

---

4. Verses 1–3 are couched in iterative verbal forms, namely, participles and imperfects. This suggests that the current state of affairs continued for a long time. This ongoing state will change through a definitive event that follows. This pattern recalls a similar pattern in the Hannah story, where Hannah's definite act of "arising" to go to the temple is set within iterative actions surrounding the annual sacrifice of Elkanah's family.

(v. 9), is replaced by "when he calls you."[5] Eli knew that it was not a matter of "if" but "when." Then he taught Samuel five secret words to induce divine revelation: "Speak, LORD, for your servant is listening." The Hebrew *shomea,* "listening," is reminiscent of Samuel's own name. This word defined Samuel's identity and mission as a prophet throughout his career.

Why did God call Samuel as many as three times? Since Samuel did not respond to him the first two times, why did he not simply go away from Samuel? We learn from this that the Lord would not give up on the people of Israel. Though the word of the Lord was rare and there was not much vision, God would not give up his efforts to communicate with his people. He was always looking for a proper channel of revelation. In a sense, the real hero of chapter 3 is God himself, who relentlessly called out to Samuel in order to talk to his people through him. God's calling of Samuel three times is more literary than literal, for God would have called Samuel as many times as necessary until Samuel was ready to respond to him properly. God is the same even now. He is looking for people like Samuel in our time. God continues to speak, but we need to grow a spiritual antenna within us to receive the Lord's signal for ourselves, our family, and our people.

A comment on verse 7 is in order: "Now Samuel did not yet know the LORD: The word of the LORD had not yet been revealed to him." The narrator appears to have inserted this comment in order to explain Samuel's initial failures to respond to God. On a deep level, however, it may refer to the sad reality that Samuel had no experiential knowledge of God until then. As a temple acolyte, he was exposed to the so-called "theological training" of the time. Further, Samuel was a man of integrity unlike Eli's two sons. Even still, he was not ready for an intense spiritual experience with God. This underscores the limit of our institutionalization of theology, ministry, and mission. For instance, we cannot say that three years of MDiv education alone can make one ready for field ministry.

3:10–14 SAMUEL RECEIVES A DIVINE MESSAGE

Verse 10 concerns divine revelation, which is both visual and aural: "The LORD came and stood there, calling as at other times, 'Samuel! Samuel!'" The expression, "[the LORD] came and stood there," is an idiom that is often depicted in theophany scenes of ancient Near Eastern literature. It denotes a

---

5. *'im* is replaced by *ki*. See the textual apparatus of 3:9 in BHS.

divine act of entering a room and towering over the head of a prostrate person. It also conveys the overwhelming feeling that the person might experience at the appearance of the looming divine. The visual aspect of divine revelation is corroborated by the word "vision" (v. 15), which the narrator uses to refer back to the theophany that Samuel experiences. This visual aspect is immediately followed by an aural aspect. God called Samuel's name twice, as he did before: "Samuel, Samuel!" This conveys a sense of urgency, as when God called Abraham's name twice to stop him from killing Isaac (Gen 22:11), or when God called, "Moses, Moses!" out of the burning bush (Exod 3:4). Samuel's life would never be the same after his encounter with the Lord who summoned him so urgently.

The subsequent revelation of the Lord shocked and disturbed Samuel. In fact, God began by warning Samuel: "See, I am about to do something in Israel that will make the ears of everyone who hears about it tingle" (v. 11). The message itself concerned Eli and his family. Part of the reason the message was so shocking was that Eli and his sons were honorable senior priests to Samuel. When he heard God accusing Eli and his sons of sin that could never be atoned for by sacrifice or offering and pronouncing irrevocable judgment against them, Samuel must have been speechless, fearful, and confused. In order to understand what might have gone through Samuel's mind, we may think of an analogous situation, where a young intern pastor finds out about his senior pastor's secret sins for the first time. Further, some of what God said to Samuel did not make any sense, because Samuel had not heard the prophecy of doom that the anonymous man of God had delivered to Eli. Samuel might have wondered what God meant by "the sin he knew about" (v. 13) or "everything I spoke against his family" (v. 12).

Although Eli's sin was not specified in God's words to Samuel, a couple of textual details shed some light on the matter. First, the phrase, "from beginning (*halal*) to end (*kalah*)" (v. 12), is worth further discussion. While the phrase emphasizes the thoroughness of divine judgment against Eli's family, it consists of terms that are reminiscent of Eli's dim eyesight (*kalah et-eyn*; see 2:33; *halal kahah*; see v. 2). Further, the Hebrew *kahah* connects Eli's dim eyesight (v. 2) to his poor oversight of his sons (v. 13). This shows that the sin of the Elide priests and God's judgment are ultimately a function of Eli's spiritual blindness. A large cause for the disaster on Eli's family is the result of Eli's failure in leadership. He fails to restrain his sons. Second, the clause, "his sons blasphemed God," shows that the sin of the Elide priests is more spiritual than moral: Hophni and Phinehas committed a sin against the Lord, not merely humans, when they stole from sacrifices and violated women working at the sanctuary. This places their sins in the same category as an unforgivable sin, such as "blasphemy against the Holy Spirit" (Matt 12:31–32). This explains why God says in verse 14, "The guilt of Eli's house will never be atoned for by sacrifice or offering." When Eli rebukes his sons by saying, "if any sins against the LORD, who will intercede for them?" (2:25), he must have understood this. He may have known all along what was coming.

It appears that God's words, "he [Eli] failed to restrain them," in verse 14 contradict the fact that Eli appeared to rebuke them (see 2:23–25), although they did not listen to him. The solution to this problem lies in the sophisticated way in which the narrator puts the Hebrew *dabar* to use in chapter 3. The Hebrew *dabar* may denote both "word" and "action." For instance, the divine *word* that Samuel requested in verse 10 ("*Speak*, your servant is listening") is the same as the divine *action* that God promised to carry out in verse 11 ("See, I am about to *do something*"). By skillfully moving from one meaning to another, the narrator shows that the word, whether human or divine, must be accompanied by action. Eli's words of rebuke or restraint in 2:23–25 apparently did not bring about change in his sons' actions. One may speculate that Eli did not follow up on his own words with any punitive actions, although bad public opinion forced Eli to talk to his sons about their sins. From God's perspective, that is neither rebuking nor restraining. All ministers of God's words may take this as a warning for themselves, taking care that their words, whether at or away from the pulpit, should be accompanied by genuine efforts to live them out.

3:15–18 SAMUEL INFORMS ELI

After his nocturnal encounter with the Lord, Samuel could not go back to sleep: "Samuel lay until morning" (v. 15). This clause is a variation on the motif of "rising early in the morning," which typically closes the scene of theophany and begins a new scene of action. This motif usually assumes that the one who has been visited goes back to sleep after experiencing theophany. By using its variation, the author intimates that Samuel did not sleep a wink after hearing the divine judgment against Eli's family. This is understandable, since the shock of the divine word must have made Samuel unable to asleep. The fact that Samuel is depicted as an obedient servant of Eli would have made the divine judgment even harder. No wonder Samuel was afraid to tell the vision to Eli (v. 15). But for the people of Israel, the news that threw Samuel into great confusion was good news. The people had been suffering from a lack of God's revelation because of the corrupt priests who had failed to function as a medium of divine revelation. The people had lived without divine guidance during a time when it was greatly needed. The news about the demise of Eli's house would have brought hope back to the people. Further, God spoke directly to Samuel, which had never happened under Eli's leadership. Samuel would serve as a medium of divine revelation. This change in mood is expressed through the metaphor of opening the door: "he opened the doors of the house of the LORD" (v. 15). Although this literally refers to Samuel's duty as a junior priest, we can also discern a figure of speech, as a new breath of air would have come into the sanctuary along with a shaft of sunlight as he opened the door. Just as we can read a metaphorical meaning into the lamp of Yahweh becoming nearly extinguished, we can do the same with Samuel's opening the door of the house of Yahweh: an influx of wind and light would bring revival into that place of worship.

The words of the Lord were not new to Eli – or the reader – because he had been privy to the anonymous man of God's prophecy against Eli's house. But the shift of leadership in this episode is new, and this is made clear in the reversal of Eli and Samuel's roles in verses 16–18. Previously Samuel asked Eli for divine words, but here Eli asked Samuel about God's revelation, and Samuel relayed divine words to Eli. Thus Samuel served as a medium of divine revelation. Finally, it is noteworthy that Eli accepted God's judgment through Samuel with dignity. Although he had many issues and his descendants fell from grace, he himself was an honorable priest of the Lord who served Israel for forty years (see 4:18).

3:19–21 SAMUEL BECOMES A PROPHET

This section shows the process through which Samuel established himself as a full-fledged prophet independent of the Elide priests. Finally, all the Israelites from Dan to Beersheba recognized Samuel as their spiritual leader (v. 20). The people no longer had to suffer from the dearth of divine revelation because Yahweh began to appear at Shiloh and speak through Samuel (v. 21). We must remember, however, that Samuel did not wake up to find himself so famous. This is implied in verse 19: "The LORD was with Samuel *as he grew up*, and he let none of Samuel's words fall to the ground" (italics added). Through a long process, which took as many as twenty years of the ministry of words and love, Samuel came to be recognized as a prophet whose authority reached every corner of the country.[6] After all, the theophany that Samuel experienced about Eli's judgment was not broadcast nationwide, and so it is extremely unlikely that the whole nation knew about it. Instead, the judgment must have stayed among the Elide priests at Shiloh, because the content of the revelation pertained only to Eli and his house, and it was detrimental to their priestly authority. Thus we may gather that Samuel's installment as a prophet with nationwide authority was not the result of an overnight miracle but rather a result of his unceasing hard work as a minister of words and love.

For decades, it has been a fad among Korean pastors to pursue advanced degrees such as a PhD or DMin, especially from Western schools. But Korean Christians, including pastors, are now learning that spiritual authority does not come with an academic credential, much less overnight. As we have discussed, the institutional theological education at the Elide seminary did not help Samuel come to know the Lord intimately. Spiritual authority is also something to be earned in the field of ministry through serving the people of God with words and deeds. Samuel was no exception to these principles, nor are we.

---

6. See my comment on 7:2 about these twenty years of Samuel's ministry.

1 SAMUEL 4:1–22

THE DEMISE OF ELI'S FAMILY

AND THE LOSS OF THE ARK

The ancient Chinese in the Chou period (1040–771 BC) believed in heaven as a supreme and moral deity. The so-called Mandate of Heaven dictated that good conduct would ensure good fortune and evil conduct would bring about misfortune. But this mandate was always confronted by the fact that Heaven did not always reward the good people and punish the bad ones, especially when the Chou slipped into a long period of civil war. Thus there came into being the problem of theodicy in ancient China, similar to the problem of Christian theodicy: why were the covenantal people destroyed whereas the idolaters prospered?[1] The defeat of the Israelites by the Philistines poses this question of theodicy. The capture of the ark of the covenant exacerbates this question. Why did the Lord allow the Philistines to take the ark for a war trophy? A close reading of chapter 4 will shed light on this intractable question.

Chapter 4 serves as a pivot point in the narrative, closing the story of Hannah's family ascending and Eli's family descending, and beginning the story of the ark of the covenant (chs. 4–6), in which human protagonists recede into the background and the Lord emerges as the hero of Israel.[2] Some scholars argue that the story of the ark is not original to the Samuel narrative, based on the absence of Samuel in chapters 4–6.[3] But there are several textual details in these chapters that connect them with the previous story of Samuel's birth and growth. For instance, the narrative identifies the defeat of Eli's army by the Philistines (ch. 4) as a fulfillment of the prophetic oracle by an unnamed man of God (2:34). Also, chapters 1–3 and chapters 4–6 contribute to the subject

---

1. For further studies of this subject, see Ning Chen, "The Problem of Theodicy in Ancient China," *JCR* 22 (1994): 51–74.
2. Chapters 4–6 are distinguished from chapters 1–3 in many respects. Whereas the story in the latter chapters focuses on two individuals' families – Hannah's family ascending and Eli's family descending – the story unfolding in chapters 4–6 has two nations – Israel and the Philistines – as main characters. Samuel, whose birth and growth have dominated chapters 1–3, drops entirely out of the latter story. Further, chapters 4–6 disclose the external problem of Israel that forces her to establish a monarchy, whereas the internal problem of moral and religious anarchy is exemplified in the sins of the Elide priests in chapters 1–3.
3. See MacCarter, *1 Samuel*, 23–26.

of a larger literary unit by providing internal and external reasons – moral corruption and the Philistine threat – for establishing the monarchy in Israel.

Chapter 4 is divided into two sections. The first section (vv. 1–11) narrates Israel's defeat by the Philistines, during which Eli and his two sons were killed and the ark of Yahweh was captured. The second section (vv. 12–22) concerns the reactions of the community of Shiloh, the priest Eli, and his daughter-in-law to this disastrous news. The whole community sent up a cry, Eli fell from his chair to his death, and Eli's daughter-in-law died in childbirth. The name of the newborn, Ichabod, encapsulates the despair of the whole nation of Israel: "The Glory has departed from Israel" (v. 22). But God started his work of restoration just as the Israelites felt they were finished.

4:1–2 ISRAEL DEFEATED BY THE PHILISTINES

The introduction of the Philistines is a bit abrupt. We do not even know how their fight with the Israelites began. We are just told in verse 1 that the Philistines drew up a battle line at Aphek, the northern border town of the Philistines at the source of the Yarkon, while the Israelites camped at Ebenezer about three kilometers east of Aphek. It is interesting to note that these two place names function as a literary connector to future events of great significance. Aphek foreshadows the battle of Mount Gilboa, where Saul and his sons were killed because the Philistines mustered their combined forces at Aphek before moving up to Mount Gilboa (see 29:1). This connection helps us to see the fates of Eli and Saul as reminiscent of each other. Ebenezer, on the other hand, anticipates another battle against the Philistines, wherein the Israelites achieved a decisive victory under the leadership of Samuel. In this sense, the tragic defeat in chapter 4 is compensated by Samuel's victory, which is commemorated by setting up a stone named "Ebenezer."

The battle described in this section may be understood in terms of the general rivalry between the Israelites and the Philistines, who encroached into the hill country of Canaan, then populated by the Israelites. Usually, the Philistines invaded Israelite border towns for the plunder, but the Israelites typically responded with a counterattack, as illustrated in the story of Samson (Judg 13–16). Since this was a time of continuous action and reaction between the two opposing sides, border skirmishes were common. This battle at two border towns, Aphek and Ebenezer, was one such skirmish. However, some scholars find a specific background to this battle at the beginning of verse 1:

"And Samuel's word came to all Israel."[4] They argue that Samuel's ministry of words awakened the people of Israel from moral and spiritual stupor and unified the once-divided Israelite tribes. With Israel united as a serious threat, the Philistines launched a preemptive strike. Regardless of what is behind this battle, it goes poorly for the Israelites, and about four thousand men fall on the battlefield (v. 2). As for the number four thousand, the Hebrew *'elep*, "thousand," may also mean a military unit of an indeterminable number of soldiers. So "four thousand" suggests a hyperbolic number, or it refers to forty units of soldiers. In either case, the narrator emphasizes that a large number of soldiers were killed in the first bout of battle.

4:3–5 THE ARK OF THE LORD'S COVENANT CARRIED TO THE ISRAELITE CAMP

Upon seeing defeated soldiers return to the camp, the elders of Israel asked a question that has percolated throughout the history of Israel: "Why did the LORD bring defeat on us today before the Philistines," who are idol worshippers? (v. 3). Although this question might lead to theological enlightenment for Israel, her elders decided to put the question to rest by bringing the ark of the Lord's covenant to the battle lines. They might have expected that such an uncomfortable question would no longer arise if they could make the ark work a miracle for them. Thus they resorted to a magical solution instead of tackling the question squarely.

Who are these elders of Israel? And why did they decide to bring the ark of the covenant to the battlefield? The "elders of Israel" refers to the national council of elders, consisting of representatives dispatched from each local council of elders. Prior to the monarchy, Israel was a loose confederation of twelve tribal groups. Each tribal group was governed by its local council of elders. In dealing with problems of national significance, however, a national council of elders was convened. For instance, the elders of Israel proposed that the near-extinct Benjamites should have a new beginning (Judg 21:16–19). The elders of Israel also visited Samuel in Ramah to request a king. After Israel's sore defeat by the Philistines, the elders decided to bring the ark of the covenant to the battlefield.

---

4. K. Bodner, *1 Samuel: A Narrative Commentary*, HBM (Sheffield: Sheffield Phoenix Press, 2009), 44.

The elders' decision was motivated partly by the fame of the Lord as a God of war and also by the belief that the ark of God would secure a victory at war. The role of the ark in the battle was most prominent in the days of Israel's wandering in the desert. Numbers 10:35–36 preserves an interesting prayer in this regard:

> Whenever the ark set out (for war), Moses said, "Rise up, Lord! May your enemies be scattered; may your foes flee before you." Whenever it came to rest [from war], he said, "Return, Lord, to the countless thousands of Israel."

Further, Numbers 14:44 mentions an incident wherein the failure to bring the ark of the covenant to the battlefield led to the defeat of the Israelites. One may also think of the role of the ark in the battle of Jericho. All these contributed to the elders' decision to bring the ark to the battlefield in order to compensate for their initial failure. The high expectations that the Israelites had for the ark is intimated in the full epithet given to the ark in verse 4: "The ark of the covenant of the Lord Almighty, who is enthroned between the cherubim." The people of Israel seemed to support the elders' decision, which is made clear from their reaction to the arrival of the ark in the camp: "All Israel raised such a great shout that the ground shook" (v. 5). One may even argue that the elders' decision reflected the popular will of the people.

4:6–11 THE PHILISTINES CAPTURE THE ARK OF THE LORD'S COVENANT

Verse 6 rephrases what is said in verse 5 from the vantage point of the Philistines: they heard Israel's uproar (*hamam*), wondered what it was about, and learned that the ark of the Lord had come to Israel's camp. Israel's uproar of elation was loud enough for the Philistines to be alarmed by it, but in the midst of Israel's uproar, we do not hear her confession of faith in the Lord. Ironically, the pious confession of Yahwistic faith came from the mouth of the Philistines. For the Philistines were "afraid" – a proper attitude to the holy God – when they learned that the ark came to Israel's camp (v. 7). Further, the Philistines acknowledged the mighty power of the Lord as shown in the events of Exodus (v. 8). Noteworthy in this regard is the narrator's use of *hamam* to refer to Israel's elated uproar. The Hebrew *hamam* is often used to refer to the confusion that the Lord threw into the midst of Israel's enemies (see 14:15). But the narrator applies the term here to the Israelites. These narrative details serve as an ominous foreshadowing of Israel's defeat. One may assume that the ark of the Lord would do nothing for the Israelites, who did not have faith in the Lord himself. An additional omen for Israel's defeat may be discerned in the apparent misunderstanding of the Philistines about Israel's religion. The Philistines assumed wrongly that the Israelites were polytheists, serving multiple gods: "Who will deliver us from these mighty gods?" (v. 8).[5] This distortion of facts may be expected since the Philistines might have been informed through a rumor. But at a deeper level, one can discern the narrator's intention to criticize the Israelites for serving other gods besides the Lord. Influenced by Canaanite religions, many Israelites served Baals and Ashtoreth in the last years of the Judges. Samuel's later exhortation to remove Baals and Ashtoreth confirms the prevalence of syncretistic religion among the Israelites (see 7:3). Thus it is no surprise that the Philistines "mistook" the Israelites as polytheistic.

The Philistines feared the news of the ark's arrival, but fear was not their only response. Verse 9 records a dramatically different reaction to the news: "Be strong, Philistines! Be men, or you will be subject to the Hebrews, as they have been to you. Be men and fight" (v. 9). This word might have come from a different person, perhaps a Philistine general who was trying to boost the flagging confidence of his soldiers, for his motivational speech resembles other war speech in Greek literature. This is not surprising considering the Greek origin of the Philistines. The motivation for the Philistines to fight against such great odds was freedom: "fight lest you should become slaves to Hebrews." To die as a free man in the battlefield was better than to live perpetually as a slave. This war speech works, and the Philistines defeated the Israelites again, killing about thirty thousand soldiers. This number of casualties is almost ten times that of the previous battle. Among the dead were Eli's two sons, Hophni and Phinehas – thereby fulfilling the prophecy of the man of God (see 2:34). Worst of all, the ark of covenant was captured! The fact that the Israelites had fought alongside the ark of the covenant made this defeat even more devastating and perplexing. The capture of the ark by the Philistines posed a theological conundrum for the Israelites – and also for the audience. Does this story suggest that Yahweh was defeated by the Philistine gods?

What went wrong? Three points may help to answer this question. First, the Israelites tried to use the ark of the Lord's covenant for their own agenda. By doing so, they tried to turn the Lord into a magic wand. Count how many

---

5. They also mistook the plagues as having struck the Egyptians in the wilderness as they crossed the Red Sea in pursuit of the Israelites.

"us" or "our" are used in the speech made by the Israelites in verse 3: "Let *us* bring the ark of the Lord's covenant from Shiloh, so that he may go with *us* and save *us* from the hand of *our* enemies" (italic added). In the original Hebrew, "we" is used five times in that speech, which intimates that the elders were minding "our" agenda rather than God's. However, God does not allow himself to be manipulated or deceived by humans. Second, the presence of Hophni and Phinehas made the whole business of enlisting the help of the ark dubious. As discussed in chapter 3, Eli's two sons were "scoundrels" who did not know the Lord (see 2:12). The Mosaic law dictated that the Israelite camp should keep itself holy in order to secure divine help in the battle (Deut 23:14–15). But the presence of Hophni and Phinehas made the Israelite camp unclean, thus obstructing God from protecting the Israelites. The presence of the ark did not automatically secure God's aid. Our faith in God effects our salvation. Third, the soldiers' elation about the arrival of the ark implies that the elders' decision to fetch the ark was made on the basis of the popular will rather than the will of the Lord. They should have sought advice from Samuel in Shiloh. If they had done so, Samuel would have told them that the defeat by the Philistines was part of divine judgment on the Elide family. The total silence of Samuel in this chapter after so much attention in chapter 3 suggests this point. God's will was for Israel to be defeated in the Aphek-Ebenezer battle. Sometimes God wants us to be losers. Winning is not always God's plan for Christians. Just as the elders of Israel did not accept this truth, many Christians do not accept it today. But we should all remember that Jesus died on the cross like a sinner. God is able, and he can make good out of our failures if we trust him.

4:12–16 A MESSENGER ARRIVES AT SHILOH

The location of the narrative shifts from Aphek to Shiloh, where Eli anxiously awaited a messenger from the battlefield because of his concern for the ark of the Lord's covenant. He sat on his chair in the watchtower rather than his chair in the temple in order to hear the news before anyone else. But when a Benjamite messenger arrived from the battlefield with his clothes torn and with dust on his head – traditional signs of mourning – he somehow bypassed Eli, who was the last person in Shiloh to hear the news. The citizens of Shiloh heard the news first and "sent up a cry" (v. 13). Although Eli sat waiting in the watch tower, he could not see the messenger passing because he had become totally blind, and the messenger might not have noticed Eli because he did not expect him to be at the gate; Eli should have been sitting "on his chair by the doorpost of the Lord's house" (1:9). Interestingly, Eli's delay in hearing the news about the battle fits the pattern, since Eli had been denied access to knowledge repeatedly. For instance, Eli did not know anything about Hannah's problem of childlessness or her vow concerning her son when he pronounced a blessing on her (1:17). He learned about it only later at the dedication ceremony. Also, Eli was the last person who became aware of his two sons' evil acts (2:23). In a similar vein, God's words and visions were rare under Eli's leadership, and he had to ask Samuel what God had told him. Thus Eli was repeatedly alienated from the truth. Further, Eli's spiritual dullness coincided with his gradually worsening eyesight. Eli's observing eyes mistook praying Hannah as a drunkard (1:12–14). Samuel's experience of theophany at the temple occurred after Eli's eyes had become so weak that he could barely see (3:2). On the day when Eli's fate was finally sealed, Eli had gone completely blind (4:15). The degradation of Eli's eyesight dovetails with his increasing spiritual dullness.

Two textual details indicate that Israel's loss in battle was due to divine punishment against Eli's house. First, the phrase "that same day" in verse 12 recalls the phrase "at that time" in 3:12. These two phrases are identical in their Hebrew original (*bayyôm*). The day when God said he would "carry out against Eli everything I spoke against his family – from beginning to end" (3:12) was the very day when thirty thousand Israelite soldiers, including Hophni and Phinehas, were killed in the battle against the Philistines. This helps us understand Israel's defeat as a fulfillment of the judgment oracle pronounced against Eli's house. Second, the question that Eli posed to the messenger may be taken as Eli's request for God's words. "What happened, my son?" in verse 16 may be rendered literally as, "What was the word [*dabar*], my son?" Considering that *dabar* may denote both a word and a deed, we can hear a double meaning in Eli's question to the messenger. Whatever God did to the Israelites in the Aphek-Ebenezer battle was the actualization of his own words.

4:17–18 ELI DIES

In answering Eli, the messenger mentioned Israel's defeat by the Philistines, the death of Eli's two sons, and the loss of the ark of the covenant. As soon as the messenger mentioned the ark of the covenant, Eli fell from his chair and broke his neck. Although some scholars speculate about the location of Eli's chair in order to discern the medical reason for his death,[6] the text holds his obesity accountable: "for . . . he was heavy [*kabed*] (v. 18)." Thus far, this information about Eli's obesity has been held back from the readers. As with Eli's eyesight, his weight also serves as a metaphor for his sin. The metaphoric meaning of "weight" is based on the double meaning of the Hebrew word *kbd,* which may denote "weight" or "glory." The narrator, for instance, plays on the double meaning of *kbd* when the man of God says, "Why do you *honor* [*kbd*] your sons more than me by fattening yourselves [*kbd*] on the choice parts of every offering made by my people of Israel?" (2:29). The narrator implies that Eli's "weighty" body is due to the sin of stealing the "honor" from the Lord.[7] This shows that Eli's death is both divine punishment and poetic justice.

The narrator, however, concludes the story of Eli's death with a short note about Eli's forty-year reign as Israel's judge (v. 18). This note is given in the context of a negative evaluation of Eli's house, but it is not necessarily intended as a criticism against Eli. Instead, it appears to command the reader's respect for Eli's long service for his country. Just as Samson's deviant acts could not nullify what he did for his country, neither could Eli's sin.[8] We should be careful not to throw the baby out with the bathwater when we criticize our spiritual leaders.

4:19–22 THE BIRTH OF ICHABOD

The focus of the narrative shifts again from Eli to Phinehas's pregnant wife. When she heard the news about her husband's death, she went into labor and gave birth to a son (v. 20). Although welcoming a newborn baby is a joyful occasion, Phinehas's wife was in a different mood. When the midwives said, "Don't despair; you have given birth to a son!" she responded out of her deepest despair by naming him "Ichabod." She then explained the name as meaning, "The Glory has departed from Israel" (v. 22). It is interesting to note that Eli did not leave us any commentary about the incident of the ark being captured – and thus we are clueless about how the religious leader of the time

6. It is very likely that Eli sat in the watchtower, which was part of the gate structure. He fell from the tower and died, which is implied in the phrase *yak derek metsapeh* "[Eli was sitting on his chair] on the way of a watchman" in v. 13 (my translation).
7. During the Spanish colonization of the Philippines, the priests were the fattest among the people (Villanueva: personal communication). Needless to say, Eli's partaking of the fat taken by his sons contributed to his obesity.
8. The fact that Eli's sin was similar to an unforgivable sin does not change it. We should remember that God is the ultimate judge in matters of salvation.

interpreted that theological conundrum. However, Phinehas's wife named his grandson "Ichabod," which can be taken as the authoritative theological interpretation for this national tragedy. This episode constitutes a fitting closure to the literary unit of chapters 1–4, which trace the rise of the Hannah-Samuel family and the demise of Eli's house. Just as the unit begins with a woman (Hannah) outdoing Eli in communicating with God, it ends with another woman (Phinehas's wife) outdoing Eli in making sense of the national tragedy.

One question remains: why did God allow the ark to be taken by the Philistines? They took it to their temple to prove that their god was mightier than the Lord! So why did God allow it? He could have killed the Philistines the moment they touched the ark, as he did when Uzzah tried to stabilize the ark. This suggests that God purposefully allowed them to capture it. The Hebrew *niqlad*, "(the ark of God) has been captured" (v. 22), may refer to a voluntary and purposeful expedition.[9] In this case, the ark was not taken captive to Philistine territory but rather sent on an expedition to achieve the Lord's purposes. Although that purpose remains to be seen, the fact that the Lord had a plan even in what appeared to be Israel's total failure encourages us not to despair about any misfortune. The so-called "teleological theodicy" in Chinese philosophy provides a similar way out of the problem of theodicy. It argues that Heaven's plan is to make evil people successful so that they can be happy with what they have done and continue to do evil until they meet Heaven's final punishment.[10] God is able to surprise us under any circumstances. God can make a way where there seems to be no way!

---

9. For a similar meaning, see Esther 2:23. Instead of being forced to go to the harem, Esther volunteered to go in order to achieve a purpose, possibly as instructed by her uncle Mordecai.
10. Ning Chen, "The Problem of Theodicy in Ancient China," 55.

1 SAMUEL 5:1–7:1

THE ARK IN PHILISTINE TERRITORY

The Philistines must have celebrated a complete triumph as they installed the captured ark of the Lord in the temple of Dagon at Ashdod without knowing that it was the beginning of a nightmare that would haunt the whole country for the next seven months. What an irony of fate! The ark of the Lord showed forth his power and majesty right in the heartland of the Philistines, the archenemy of Israel, not only by subjugating the chief god of the Philistines, Dagon, but by sending plagues among the people and making a triumphant return to the land of Israel. Although the Philistine lords, being rational thinkers, doubted the connection between the outbreak of the plague and the holy ark, their rational doubt soon turned into blind superstition, while the God of Israel was vindicated when the Philistines sent the ark back to Israel with gifts.

In this section the ark of the Lord is depicted as the king of Israel, who goes on an expedition to the Philistine land in the spring to show forth his power by subjugating the Philistines under his feet, and then returns to Israel with plunder in the autumn. In other words, the ark of the Lord was not taken as captive but left Israel in order to establish God's sovereignty in the Philistines' land, proving the Lord as king of every nation. The ancient Near Eastern notion of a tribal god, whose power was limited to his jurisdiction, does not apply to God of Israel, the creator of the universe.

5:1–5 YAHWEH BEHEADS DAGON

The Philistines brought the ark of the Lord from Ebenezer to Ashdod, the religious and political center of Philistia, and installed it at the temple of their chief god, Dagon, right next to his image.[1] Ancient Near Eastern custom commonly installed the image of a defeated deity at the temple of a triumphant deity. Installing the ark of the Lord at the temple of Dagon reminded the Philistines of Dagon's superiority over Yahweh. Dagon was a Semite deity, known to be the father of Baal and associated with grain fertility. The Philistines may have

---

1. The scene of the Philistines capturing and installing the ark of the Lord at the temple of Dagon in Ashdod is contemporaneous with the scene of the wife of Phinehas giving birth to a son and calling him "Ichabod." This is implied by the pluperfect form of the verb "had captured" in v. 1. One may say that the glory of the Lord departed from Israel to Philistia, but the glory in Philistia turns out to be destructive.

1 SAMUEL

adopted him as their chief god because Dagon was Baal's father. As recent immigrants to Canaan, they needed an ideological and religious anchor that would secure them in the land of many competitors. Adopting Dagon, Baal's father, as their chief god provided them with an ideological superiority over the Canaanites, who served Baal as their chief god.

To the Philistines' misfortune, the joy of triumph did not last long. The next morning, the Philistines found Dagon face down on the ground before the ark of the Lord (v. 3). Although the author does not tell us what went through the minds of the Philistines, the prostration of Dagon before the ark of the Lord, as if worshipping Yahweh, must have been a theological enigma. Dagon's falling before the Lord belied the Philistines' political and military dominance over the Israelites. When something unexplainable happens, we often take it as a coincidence. So the Philistines took it as a coincidence and put Dagon back in his place without saying a word. But their silence speaks volumes about their theological and emotional shock.

The next morning, they found Dagon's torso on the ground before the ark of the Lord and Dagon's head along with his two hands lying on the threshold. Given the considerable length of the main sanctuary,[2] the position of Dagon's severed head and two hands cannot be explained by physics. If the head and two hands were cut off from Dagon's body when they fell to the ground, the impact from the free fall would not have been enough to send those limbs to the threshold of the porch, which was around thirty meters away from the place where the image of Dagon had once stood. Furthermore, the severed body parts suggest Dagon's defeat by the Lord. In the ancient Near East, soldiers used to cut off the head and the hands of enemy soldiers as a way of "finishing" them. So the fact that Dagon's head and hands were lying on the threshold, separated from the body, points to a hypothetical scenario such as the following. In the previous night, Dagon tried to escape from his own house in fear of the Lord. The Lord killed Dagon as he stepped over the threshold. After cutting off Dagon's head and two hands, he pulled the torso back to his original place. That is why Dagon's head and both hands were found lying on the threshold of the porch, but his body was near its original place. All this was an undeniable sign of Yahweh's victory over Dagon.

---

2. By comparison, the length of Solomon's temple was about twenty-seven meters long. For the comparison in size and structure of Solomon's temple with Syrian temples, see Ammon Ben-Tor, ed., *The Archaeology of Ancient Israel* (New Haven: Yale University Press, 1992), 310–315.

Interestingly, the author does not report the Philistines reaction. We do not know what went through their minds when they found Dagon brutally murdered in his own house. Instead, the author connects this incident to the origin of the custom of Dagon's priests and his worshippers not to tread on the threshold of Dagon's temple in Ashdod. Historically speaking, the custom may have originated with the belief that spirits live in the threshold. But by appropriating the custom in a new literary context, the narrator imbues the custom with a new meaning. That is, the custom is re-used in criticizing the blind faith of the Philistines in Dagon. Despite all the telltale signs to the contrary, they believed that Dagon was a powerful god, worthy of their worship. They idolized even the threshold where Dagon's head and two hands lay cut off from its torso. The logical conclusion is that Yahweh, not Dagon, is the true god, worthy of worship. This story mirrors the psychology of unbelievers who swing back and forth between rationalists and cult beliefs. At one point they deny, even mock, the existence of God, but at another time, they visit a fortune teller to find out their fate.

5:6–12 THE LORD'S HAND

After subjugating Dagon, Yahweh attacked the idol-worshippers in Ashdod and its vicinity. Dagon's helpless hands cut off from its torso can be contrasted with the Lord's powerful hands, which rested heavily on the people of Ashdod. Although "the hand of the Lord" might have been a well-attested idiom for a plague, the context makes it clear that the outbreak of tumors was caused by the Lord himself: "he brought devastation on them and afflicted them with tumors" (v. 6). What sort of plague struck the Philistines? This question is still debated among scholars.[3] Some argue that it was hemorrhoids, since its original Hebrew is related to the Aramaic cognate meaning "strain at the stool." But this is problematic because hemorrhoids are not a fatal disease. Others assert that it was the bubonic plague carried by rodents. The bubonic plague was highly contagious, and if not quickly contained and properly treated, 70 percent of the infected could die within four days. The mention of golden rats as a guilt offering seems to support the latter opinion.

The people of Ashdod quickly realized that the Lord God of Israel was behind the outbreak of a deadly plague (v. 7), and so they gathered together all the rulers of the Philistines. Unlike other peoples in Canaan, the Philistines

---

3. See J. Wilkinson, "The Philistine Epidemic of 1 Samuel 5 and 6," *ExpTim* 88 (1977): 137–141.

did not have a king who ruled over the entire territory. Instead, Philistia was ruled by a council of five city rulers, reminiscent of the *polis* system of ancient Greece. Since returning the ark to Israel would have meant denying the military victory over Israel, that sort of decision could not be made by the Lord of the city of Ashdod alone, which explains why the people of Ashdod summoned all five lords of the Philistines.

The decision from the council was that the ark should "be brought around to Gath" (v. 8). One may wonder, Why to Gath and not to Israel? If the plague had come from the hand of the God of Israel, sending his ark from one Philistine city to another would not stop the plague but rather strike the people of Gath with the same plague! The council's decision, therefore, reveals that the five lords did not believe in any causal relationship between the plague and the presence of the ark. Although the suffering people in Ashdod were already convinced of it, the rest of the Philistines remained suspicious – until they experienced the heavy hand of the Lord. By sending the ark around to Gath, they were testing out what they suspected to be a superstitious belief.

The Septuagint reinforces this point. According to the Greek translation of verse 8, the people of Gath – rather than the council – took the initiative in deciding that the ark of the God of Israel should be brought to Gath.

> And they sent and gathered together to them the satraps of the Allophiles and said, "What should we do with the ark of the God of Israel?" And the Geththites said, "Let the ark of God come over to us," and the ark of God came over to Geththa.[4]

But why did the people of Gath allow the ark of the God of Israel to come to their town? Elsewhere in the Bible, Gath was known for its giants and warriors. The Anakim once lived in Gath (Josh 11:22) and Goliath was from that city. The people of Gath were rational and daring enough not to believe in the superstitious connection between the recent outbreak of the plague and the presence of the ark of the Lord. The decision to bring the ark to Gath rather than returning it to Israel shows the hardness of their hearts. But this decision also provided the Lord with the opportunity to show his glory among the Philistines once more. The Philistines eventually had to confess that Yahweh's reign had reached their own territory.

The unbelief of the Philistines put them in a more difficult situation. When they brought the ark to Gath, the hand of the Lord caused a great panic in

---

4. New English Translation of the Septuagint. "Geththites" is a wooden translation of Greek *Geththaioi*, which may be rendered alternatively as "the people of Gath."

the people (v. 9). The word *mehumah,* "panic," is often used in the context of the battles in which the Lord fought alone on behalf of the Israelites (see 1 Sam 14:20; Deut 7:23). Further, the Lord's attack on the people of Gath was indiscriminate: "He afflicted the people of the city, both young and old, with an outbreak of tumors" (v. 9). So the people of Gath sent the ark of God to Ekron without even asking for permission from the council! They were too baffled to follow the normal procedure of decision-making. Their previous confidence was gone without a trace as they hastily sent the ark around to Ekron.

The ark arrived at Ekron and the deadly plague broke out among its people. The Ekronites then summoned all the Lords of the Philistines to propose something that no one had dared thus far: "Send the ark of the god of Israel away; let it go back to its own place" (v. 11). The people of Ekron believed in the deadly power of the ark, and they cared more about their own survival than the country's political causes. Noteworthy in relation to this change is that chapter 5 ends with the note, "the outcry of the city went up to heaven" (v. 12). This reminds us of the outcry of the Hebrews under Egyptian slavery. Whenever the outcry of the people reaches Heaven, God acts. The note that the cry of the Philistines reached heaven signals the beginning of a new phase in the story of the ark of God.

6:1–9 DIVINERS' ADVICE

Chapter 6 begins with the chronological note that "the ark of the LORD was in the Philistine territory for seven months" (6:1). For seven months, the ark struck the Philistines with a plague, killing many of them. Seven months may not be a long period to those living in peace, but to the suffering Philistines, it must have felt like forever. Further, considering that the number seven connotes completeness, one may argue that God *completely* established his sovereignty over the Philistines during those months. Now God was ready to return home.

After deciding to send the ark of the God of Israel to its original place, the Philistines had to decide *how* to send it back. To answer this question, the Philistines called for the help of priests and diviners to learn the proper procedure for returning the ark to the Israelites. Since ancient Near Eastern peoples identified a god's statue with the person of a god, it stands to reason that the Philistines thought that the God of Israel must be appeased before his ark could be sent to Israel. Thus they called for the help of their religious leaders – particularly "diviners" – because they were known to be privy to divine knowledge through various natural and artificial means.[5] The diviners advised the Philistines not to send the ark of the Lord back without a gift, and they suggested a guilt offering (v. 3). Ironically, these words from pagan priest diviners declare two theological truths, which may be applicable to the ark narrative as a whole. First, the idea of returning the ark with a gift underscores the truth that the Lord is worthy of honor. He should not be dealt with lightly. Proper glory should be ascribed to him. This recalls the battle at Aphek in which the elders of Israel dealt lightly with the ark of the Lord and brought it to the battlefield at the hands of corrupt priests to realize a popular, not divine, will. Second, the idea of a guilt offering underscores the truth that repentance is necessary in gaining divine grace. By preparing a guilt offering, the Philistines effectively admitted their sin in not honoring the God of Israel. The Israelites, on the other hand, continued to sin by doing what was good in their own eyes. Third, for the guilt offering, the priest diviners proposed "five golden tumors and five golden mice" (v. 4). The number "five" here represented the five major cities of the Philistines: Ashdod, Gaza, Ashkelon, Gath, and Ekron (see v. 17). The purpose in sending the gifts was to give "glory to the God of Israel" (v. 5). The priest diviners became almost like prophets of the Lord when they urged their own people not to harden their hearts, as Pharaoh once had. During those painful seven months, it seems that the Philistines had grown in the knowledge of God. Seven months before, they had not even known how many gods the people of Israel worshiped, but now they were calling the God of Israel by his personal name, "Yahweh" (see v. 4: NIV "the LORD"). The ark's presence in the Philistines' territory caused the people to grow in the knowledge of Yahweh, which shows that one cannot remain the same after encountering the true God! This awakening among the Philistines forms a sharp contrast with Israel's spiritual darkness in the last days of Judges.

The Philistines, however, were a people outside the Lord's covenant. Their religious leaders did not worship the Lord even when they saw the Lord's power manifested against Dagon. Still in doubt, they continued their experiments to determine whether the recent national disasters had come from the God of Israel or happened by accident. First, they tried to use the guilt offering as an apotropaic object. The priest diviners advised the Philistines to "make models of your tumors and of the rats that are destroying the country" (v. 5). By sending away those images along with the ark, they tried to cause the expulsion of

---

5. Here the narrator seems to use priests and diviners synonymously. In the ancient Near East, priests divined by using the internal organs of sacrificial animals.

the plague. This practice is an exercise in magic, not faith. Second, they tried to use the behaviors of nursing cows as a sign to see if the plague had come from the Lord. They instructed the Philistines to prepare a new cart and two milk cows that had never been yoked (v. 7). After loading the ark on the cart, along with a box containing the golden tumors and rats, they sent the cart off to the wilderness with no one to drive it (v. 8).

> If it goes up to its own territory, toward Beth Shemesh, then the Lord has brought this great disaster on us. But if it does not, then we will know that it was not his hand that struck us but that it happened to us by chance. (v. 9)

As a test, this scenario was predisposed to have a "chance" verdict, since the cows had no experience of walking under a yoke and could not even walk straight under the yoke. Further, they were nursing cows. How could one expect nursing cows to walk away from lowing calves? There was little or no chance that the cows would go across the wilderness straight to Israelite territory, but the priest diviners would only believe if that should happen. Even though they had experienced the Lord's judgment, they still did not believe in him. Even in their acts of repentance and surrender, the priest diviners hatched a scheme to reverse the verdict at the last minute. They represent the sort of people who deny the truth consistently and intentionally. Moreover, the way in which the ark of the Lord returned home (v. 9) supports the image of the Lord coming and going at his own pleasure.

6:10–12 THE COWS HEAD TO BETH-SHEMESH

In spite of impossible odds, the cows went straight to Beth-Shemesh. The report in verse 12 has two interesting details about how the cows traveled in the direction of Beth-Shemesh. First, the cows were lowing as they went, which shows that the cows were going against their motherly instincts. How was this possible? Although some give credit to the cows, the God of Israel should get all the credit. Second, the cows went "along one highway" (ESV: v. 12). It is one thing to arrive at the destination, but another to arrive there while keeping to one road. The narrator adds, "they turned neither to the right nor to the left" (v. 12). This idiom is often used in referring to Israel's faithful observance of the Law (see Deut 5:32 and 28:14). This also underscores the Lord's sovereignty: he could make animals obey his words!

6:13–18 THE ARK ARRIVES AT BETH-SHEMESH

When the ark of the Lord finally returned to Israel, it was the wheat harvest season (v. 13). The connection between harvesting wheat and the ark's arrival is related to the fact that ancient Assyrian kings went out on military campaigns in the spring and came back home in the fall. The narrator describes the return of the ark in terms that recall the triumphant return of a king from abroad. This confirms that the ark of the Lord was never captured as a trophy by the Philistines. Rather, the ark of the Lord went on a military campaign to show forth God's honor and power among the Philistines. Now the Lord returned back after seven months of defeating the enemy.

The ark arrived at the field of Joshua beside a large rock.[6] The Levites took down the ark of the Lord and the box containing the golden tumors and rats and set them upon the great rock at the field of Joshua. There they "chopped up the wood of the cart and sacrificed the cows as a burnt offering to the Lord" (v. 14). The mention of the Levites may be abrupt here, but Beth-Shemesh was a Levite city (Josh 21:16). Further, the positive role of the Levites in Israel's reception of the ark reinforces the idea that the ark of the Lord had to be handled in a proper manner. A severe consequence soon follows the mishandling of the ark in verses 19–21.

The city rulers of the Philistines watched the whole process of Israel's receiving the ark of the Lord at the field of Joshua, which reveals how much the ark of the Lord had affected the lives of the Philistines over the previous seven months. After seeing with their own eyes that the ark of the God of Israel had been properly accepted by the people of Beth-Shemesh so that it would not come back to haunt them again, they left for Ekron (v. 16).

---

6. The story of the ark recalls the story of Exodus in several respects. First, the ark stops at the field of Joshua. Just as the Exodus was brought to its completion through the work of Joshua, the arrival of the ark at the field of Joshua completes the ark's exit out of Philistia. Second, like the Exodus, this story bears witness to the sovereignty of Yahweh, the divine king of Israel.

HOW MANY MODELS OF RATS?

Verse 18 raises an interesting question about the number of the golden images. How many golden rats were sent as a guilt offering? Verse 4 seems to answer, "five." But according to the explanation in verse 18, the number of golden rats seems to be larger than five, because its number should match the number of "Philistine towns belonging to five rulers, both fortified towns along with their country villages." This partly explains why the Septuagint omits "five" as the number of golden rats in verse 4.

The scene of the arrival of the ark at Beth-Shemesh ends with an etiological note: "the large rock on which the Levites set the ark of the LORD is a witness to this day in the field of Joshua of Beth-Shemesh" (v. 18). A standing stone in a field could function as an idol in the ancient Near East, but the biblical author attributes a new meaning to the great stone in the field of Joshua, transforming it from an object of pagan worship to serve as a witness to Yahweh's great salvation. The stone should encourage people to *pass on* what God has done for them. All this shows the essence of the biblical religion. God so much wants to communicate with us that he talks in terms that are familiar to us. This entails transforming things of the world into his holy mediums by imbuing new meaning into them. A standing stone is one such example. As Christians, we were once followers of the world, but God has transformed us into his vessels.

6:19–7:1 THE ARK KILLS MEN OF BETH-SHEMESH

The successful reception of the ark of the Lord by the Levites is followed by a deadly incident, wherein "seventy men" of Beth-Shemesh were killed "for looking *upon* the ark of the LORD" (v. 19, italics added). Although the NIV translation, based on the Septuagint, gives the impression that a limited number of people were affected by this incident, the Masoretic text tells us the opposite. According to the Hebrew text, 50,070 men of Beth-Shemesh were killed. Although the number is too large to be real, it conveys the impression that a large number of people were killed in that incident.[7] Whereas the

---

7. Archaeologists estimate that the population of Judah in the eighth century was around 100,000 and that of Jerusalem was no more than 15,000. Israel Finkelstein and Neil A.

Philistines grew in their knowledge and fear of the Lord over the past seven months, this scene shows that the people of Israel remained in spiritual darkness. They learned nothing from their disastrous defeat at the battle of Aphek. The people of Israel still handled the ark of the Lord flippantly by leaving the ark in the field of Joshua without any protection. They stationed no priestly guards to keep it from prying eyes, thereby making the holy ark of the Lord a spectacle. Yahweh's anger went out to kill those who "looked upon the ark of the LORD" as if it were a circus.[8] Though the men of Beth-Shemesh belonged to the chosen people of God, they were not safe in the holy presence of the ark of the Lord. "Who is able to stand before the LORD, this holy God?" they asked (v. 20).

Shocked by the dangerous presence of the holy God, the people of Beth-Shemesh gave up the ark of the Lord to the people of Kiriath-Jearim. The latter came to Beth-Shemesh and "took up the ark of the LORD and brought it to the house of Abinadab on the hill. And they consecrated his son Eleazar to guard the ark of the LORD" (7:1). Some details need explanation. First, why did the people of Beth-Shemesh call the people of Kiriath-Jearim to receive the ark of the Lord? The answer to this question is related to the fact that the people of Kiriath-Jearim were Gibeonites, who had deceived Joshua into making a peace treaty and then been allowed to live among the Israelites as laborers. In other words, they were the 'second-class' citizens who may have found it hard to refuse the request of the Israelites. Furthermore, the people of Kiriath-Jearim might have wanted to return a favor to their hosts when they were asked to receive the ark.

Second, the people of Kiriath-Jearim carried the ark to "the house of Abinadab on the hill" and "consecrated his son Eleazar" to guard the holy ark (7:1). A house on a hill connotes a holy place, which infers that the Canaanites prepared a special place to enshrine the ark of the Lord and consecrated a special person to guard it. This stands in stark contrast with the way the men of Beth-shemesh left the ark of the Lord unattended in the open field of Joshua. The people of Kiriath-Jearim presumably did not know the law about the ark of the Lord, yet they did their best in fear of the Lord and in love for

---

Silberman, *The Bible Unearthed: Archeology's New Vision of Ancient Israel and the Origin of Its Sacred Texts* (New York, NY: Touchstone, 2001), 3, 208.

8. This interpretation assumes that "looking" rather than "touching" was the cause of the death. This better explains the large number of the dead. But whether it was "touching" or "looking," the point remains the same: the ark of the Lord should be dealt with in a proper, deferential manner.

their hosts. This teaches that the Lord dwells among those who are loving and sacrificing, whether they are Israelites or pagans. It is no surprise that the ark of the Lord found rest at Kiriath-Jearim until King David brought it to Jerusalem. Many Asians used to live under colonial rule. They know what it means to be discriminated against and persecuted. But when the colonizers leave, a new type of discrimination and persecution takes place. There are minority groups in India and China who are discriminated against and even persecuted by fellow citizens just because they are different. For instance, the Naga people are often spoken of disparagingly by fellow citizens in the streets of Mumbai. Christians should remember that God cares for those who are persecuted and loves those who fight against oppression.

1 SAMUEL 7:2–17

THE MIZPAH REVIVAL

Samuel reached the zenith of his career as a judge of Israel when he assembled the people of Israel at Mizpah, led them back to the Lord, and established "peace from strength" with enemies all around. In a sense, he proved himself as the answer to both internal and external problems that plagued the nation in the days of Judges. Under Samuel's leadership, the people began to seek the Lord with all their heart instead of doing what was right in their own eyes, and foreign oppressors such as the Philistines were not able to infiltrate beyond the border of Israel. No wonder the Lord compared Samuel's leadership to Moses, the greatest leader of Israel (Jeremiah 15:1). Yet all these things happened in a place called "Mizpah," which means "a place of longing." Responding to Samuel's preaching, the Israelites gathered themselves in Mizpah and lamented after the Lord (see 7:2). Later, the Jews made a point of gathering there to pray for the nation in times of trouble, because they understood that the Lord was their hope in a time of no hope (see 1 Macc 3:46). Mizpah may symbolize a place where we all go to be reminded that our longings should be for God himself. As Kierkegaard once said, "For in the longing itself the eternal is, just as God is in the sorrow which is sorrow unto God."[1]

7:2–4 SAMUEL'S CALL FOR REPENTANCE

From the day when the ark of the Lord lodged at Kiriath-Jearim, twenty years passed. Although the text does not tell us what went on during those years, we can infer from verses 2–4 that during this time the hearts of the people of Israel were prepared for spiritual revival. In other words, the twenty-year period was one of spiritual growth for the Israelites. They changed from a people doing what was right in their own eyes to a people "turning back to the LORD" (v. 2). The Hebrew phrase *yinnahu*, "[they] turned back" (v. 2), may be rendered literally as "[they] lamented." For twenty years, the people of Israel "lamented" because the Philistines resumed hostilities against them despite their firsthand experience with the power of the Lord. The reason for the resumption of Philistine oppression seems to be related to Israel's

---

1. Søren Kierkegaard, "Discourse on Luke 22:15," *Christian Discourses*, trans. Walter Lowrie (New York: Oxford University Press, 1961), 267.

apostasy, judging from Samuel's challenge to "put away the foreign gods and the Ashtaroth from among you" (v. 3). Once again, God gave the idolatrous people of Israel over to their inveterate enemy the Philistines. Although we find the people of Israel lamenting under Philistine oppression, their mourning was not simply because of their miserable life under foreign oppression; rather, their sorrow was "onto the LORD," and so they sought "after the LORD" (*aharey YHWH*) in lamentation (v. 2). This is reminiscent of Hannah, whose lament was at first occasioned by Peninnah's oppression, but later became a means for seeking the Lord's face and lamenting after the Lord.

The twenty years while the ark remained at Kiriath-Jearim was indeed a time of spiritual growth for the Israelites. The ministry of the prophet Samuel helped to prepare Israel for this time of revival. Samuel's ministry began after the death of Eli and his sons and the destruction of Shiloh.[2] Here it is worth remembering that Samuel did not wake up to find himself a prophet of the Lord who was recognized across the country (see my comments on 3:19–22). Rather, it took many years of faithful ministry for Samuel to become an authoritative prophet of the Lord. During those decades, Samuel served the people humbly in their towns and villages through preaching and good deeds. Gradually, the people of Israel were transformed into a people lamenting after the Lord in a time of despair. Verse 3 summarizes the message that Samuel preached to the Israelites:

> If you are returning to the LORD with all your heart, then rid yourselves of the foreign gods and the Ashtoreths and commit yourselves to the LORD and serve him only, and he will deliver you out of the hand of the Philistines.

The if-clause here in verse 3 explains the meaning of the expression, "[they] lamented after the LORD," in verse 2. Israel's lament was not a passive one caused by the Philistine oppression, but an active one that led to their whole-hearted return to the Lord. Since the "heart" represents one's whole person in Hebrew, Israel's whole-hearted return to the Lord entails a change of behavior. Samuel urged the Israelites to put away "the foreign gods and the Ashtoreths" which they enshrined in their houses. Throwing away gold or silver idols was not an easy thing to do, because they were part of a family's saving. Throwing them into the fire was equal to burning a wad of cash. Israelites may have wanted to keep these valuables in their house by saying that they would

---

2. Shiloh was destroyed right after the defeat at the battle of Aphek. See Aharoni, *The Land of the Bible*, 275.

not worship them anymore. Such an attitude can be compared to modern people who want to serve the Lord and money at the same time. But the Lord demands our full commitment to him. Returning to the Lord with all our heart entails completely severing our tie with idols so that we can focus on God alone. The Lord demands our undivided love!

For the Israelites who were surrounded by people who believed in many gods, a syncretistic religion was a real temptation. The people of Israel were constantly tempted to serve other gods in addition to the Lord. In ancient Near Eastern myths, every god or goddess is believed to have a special function in the universe and is worshipped by those who need his or her expertise. For instance, Baal and Ashtoreth were favored because of their connection to rain and fertility. In the eyes of the pagans, the God of Israel was a war god who earned his reputation when he defeated the Egyptians in Exodus for the Israelites. But for anything other than the matter of a war, the God of Israel could not be trusted. Further, ancient people took it for granted to serve as many gods as possible since their life abounded with various challenges. It would be unwise to throw all the eggs into one basket, so to speak. In polytheism, people do not need to forsake one god for another god, and so the Israelites may have believed that they could worship the Lord along with other pagan gods. But Samuel did not endorse such a syncretistic religion and demanded a whole-hearted and exclusive commitment to the Lord with the divine promise of deliverance from the Philistines. Samuel's insistence on the exclusive worship of God was certainly unpopular, as it went against the flow of the time. It must have made Samuel's job of turning the Israelites away from a syncretistic religion even harder. But as Samuel served the people faithfully in their towns and cities for these twenty years, they eventually responded to Samuel's call to put away foreign idols and serve the Lord alone (v. 4). Their obedience confirms Samuel's authority as a prophet of the Lord.

In South Korea each year, different denominations organize their own so-called Mizpah revival meetings by renting a stadium and filling it with tens of thousands of people. But these meetings do not result in any significant change in Korean churches. Yet the success of the original Mizpah meeting was Samuel's faithful ministry to the people living in towns and villages. The great revival of the nation will not come through an event, but through each local pastor's faithful ministry to his or her congregants, however small and insignificant that may look.

7:5–6 AN ASSEMBLY AT MIZPAH

Samuel gathered all Israel at Mizpah, thirteen kilometers north of Jerusalem (modern Tell en-Nasbeh). This gathering came as a culmination of Samuel's ministry as a prophet of the Lord. Only a prophet of Samuel's caliber could have gathered "all Israel" at one place. The immediate purpose of the meeting was twofold. The first purpose was to exercise Samuel's priestly duty, namely, to "pray to the LORD for" the people of Israel (v. 5). The second purpose was to rule the people as judge (v. 6). These verses seem to imply that penitent people of Israel still needed Samuel's priestly intercession before they could enjoy the divine rule through Samuel's judgeship. Samuel's intercessory prayer recalls Eli's rebuke to his sons: "If one person sins against another, God may mediate for the offender; but if anyone sins against the LORD, who will intercede for them?" (2:25). Samuel took on the role of the intercessor for Israel who had sinned against the Lord. It is important to remember, however, that Samuel's intercessory prayer was accompanied by the people's confession of sin, without which Samuel's prayer would have been ineffectual. The people drew water and poured it out before the Lord and fasted on that day to show their penitent heart: "We have sinned against the LORD" (v. 6). The ritual act of pouring water on the ground is not attested to elsewhere in ancient Israel.[3] But we can infer from the general symbolism of water and its use in the context of penitence that they poured water on the ground in order to make themselves ritually pure and thereby ready to experience the Lord's rule. The final act of the Mizpah "revival meeting" was Samuel's judgment of the people of Israel (v. 6). Samuel's role as judge represented the Lord's rule over Israel, for it brought salvation to the people.

7:7–12 A VICTORY OVER THE PHILISTINES

A crisis of faith develops with the Philistine invasion, for "When the Philistines heard that Israel had assembled at Mizpah, the rulers of the Philistines came up to attack them" (v. 7). Why did the Philistines attack the people of Israel at Mizpah when they were holding a religious meeting? There is a good possibility that the Philistines mistook the gathering at Mizpah as marshaling for war. After all, the Israelites used to gather at Mizpah before launching military attacks (see 20:1–3; 21:1–8). If so, then the Philistine attack was a

---

3. This should be distinguished from a drink offering of wine which accompanies animal offerings (see Num 15:1–10).

preemptive one. Samuel may have been fully aware of the danger when he gathered all Israel at Mizpah. The people of Israel, in turn, took the risk and obeyed Samuel's summons. This reinforces the image of the Israelites earnestly seeking God's face under Samuel's leadership. They were, indeed, returning to the Lord with all their heart! They trusted that the Lord would deliver them out of the Philistines' hands just as Samuel promised in verse 3. Their trust is confirmed through their reaction to the news of the Philistine attack. Although they were afraid initially, they asked Samuel to pray for them. Here we may discern a significant change in the people of Israel. Faced with similar crisis twenty years earlier, the frightened people of Israel took the matter into their own hands by bringing the holy ark into the battlefield without asking the Lord's will through the prophet Samuel. Now, turning to Samuel at the moment of crisis, they said, "Do not stop crying out to the LORD on Israel's behalf, and the LORD answered him" (v. 8; see 12:23).

Just as the people of Israel responded to Samuel's call for repentance at Mizpah, Samuel responded to their request for intercession affirmatively. First, he offered a nursing lamb as a whole burnt offering to the Lord (v. 9a).[4] Then he cried out to the Lord for Israel's salvation (v. 9b). It is interesting to note that the narrator reports the Lord's answer immediately and succinctly: "The LORD answered him" (v. 9c). By doing so, the narrator underscores the intimacy between Samuel and the Lord. In this sense, Samuel was a perfect medium for God's rule in the land of Israel. Verse 10 fleshes out what the Lord's answer looked like in the battlefield. As the Philistines drew near to attack Israel, the Lord "thundered with loud thunder against the Philistines and threw them into such a panic that they were routed before the Israelites" (v. 10). Such words as "thunder" and "panic" often occur in the context of a divine war in which God himself engages in battle while the Israelites stand still and watch (Exod 24:14; 23:27; Josh 10:10; 1 Sam 2:10). Thus verse 10 describes the Lord as a fighter striking enemy soldiers in the field. The Israelite army, on the other, served only as an armor-bearer for the Lord. They finished up the Philistines who had been fatally wounded by the Lord. After a decisive blow had been dealt to the Philistines, "the men of Israel rushed out of Mizpah and pursued the Philistines, slaughtering them along the way to a point below Beth Kar"

---

4. It is not clear why he chose a nursing lamb as an offering. It may be intended as a literary link both to the Hannah story and the story of the ark. Hannah had to wean baby Samuel in order to bring him to the Lord. In some sense, Hannah offered "a nursing lamb" to the Lord. The cows in the story of the ark also abandoned their nursing calves to carry the ark of the Lord.

(v. 11).[5] In order to remember the victory, Samuel set up a memorial stone called "Ebenezer," which means, "Thus far the LORD has helped us" (v. 12). This recalls the earlier battle fought against the Philistines at Ebenezer when the Israelites lost to the Philistines even after bringing the ark of the Lord to the battlefield (see 4:1–11). The victory that the stone "Ebenezer" commemorated reversed or nullified the shameful defeat inflicted by the Philistines some twenty years earlier. It is important to remember that this victory began with the people of Israel repenting and praying at Mizpah. The Lord ruled over Israel through Samuel with grace, giving the Israelites chance after chance to repent and serve as agents seeking to bring about God's *shalom* in the land.

7:13–17 GOD'S PERFECT RULE THROUGH SAMUEL

After this decisive victory over the Philistines, the land of Israel enjoyed a time of peace. The narrator suggests that this time of peace was due to Samuel's leadership by identifying the period of peace as coterminous with Samuel's tenure as judge. We are told in verse 13 that the Philistines did not invade the land of Israel as long as Samuel lived. There was also peace between Israel and the "Amorites," which is another term for the Canaanites. Further, the cities that the Philistines had taken from Israel were restored to Israel, from Ekron to Gath (v. 14).[6] But these claims may be an example of hyperbole, a literary exaggeration, for many episodes in the subsequent narrative show the Philistines still occupying Israelite territory and engaging in military actions against the Israelites (see chs. 13–14; 17–18), not to mention Nahash the Ammonite king's invasion of Jabesh-Gilead (see ch. 11). Nevertheless, this hyperbole emphasizes the perfect rule of God over Israel through Judge Samuel. This provides a backdrop for understanding the episode of the elders of Israel requesting a king in chapter 8, for they requested a king when there was no need for one.

The narrator concludes with a summary of Samuel's ministry as Israel's judge in verses 15–17. The expression "[Samuel] judged Israel" is used three times over the span of three verses. The first occurrence needs to be read in connection with the previous section on Israel's victory over the Philistines and

---

5. The exact location of Beth Kar is unknown.
6. Ekron and Gath are two of the five major cities of the Philistines. These are located near the border with Israel, so the cities restored to Israel must have been the border cities of Israel. Not only did Israel restore the once-lost border towns, but they also delivered Philistine border towns. "Their territory" in verse 14 may be rendered as "their border."

their peace with the Canaanites. Thus Samuel's judging of Israel in verse 15 has a military connotation, which would have solved Israel's external problem during the last days of the Judges, namely, foreign oppression. The second occurrence of Samuel's judging in verse 16 identifies Samuel's judiciary role: he "went on a circuit year by year to Bethel, Gilgal, and Mizpah.[7] And he judged Israel in all these places." This second aspect of Samuel's judging goes beyond the role of a judge in a modern-day courthouse. Samuel attended to all aspects of the people's lives. Prior to the establishment of a monarchy in Israel, prophets served the people in a similar way to today's missionaries in rural areas of the world. They were expected to give some answer, by prayer or miracle, to all issues of life – from illness, to legal or personal conflict among neighbors, to a runaway donkey. Samuel's visitation ministry taught the Israelites how to live as members of a covenantal community, solving the problem of moral corruption that plagued Israel in the period of the Judges (see Judg 19–21). The third occurrence of Samuel's judging is related to his priestly function (see v. 17). After completing the year's visitation of Bethel, Gilgal, and Mizpah, Samuel returned to Ramah, where his house was and where he had built an altar. From this detail, we can infer that Ramah replaced Shiloh as the cultic center of the Israelite religion. Samuel's priestly rule instructed the Israelites about how to cultivate their relationship with the Lord, which thereby solved the problem of spiritual corruptions during the last days of Judges (see Judg 17–18). This aspect of Samuel's leadership reinforces the impression that the people of Israel did not need a human king, for God's rule was well established through Samuel's judgeship.

---

7. These towns are located at the Benjamite territory in close proximity to one another.

1 SAMUEL 8:1–22

THE PEOPLE OF ISRAEL

DEMAND A KING

Although Israel enjoyed a period of peace under Samuel, the people came to Samuel in Ramah and demanded a king because they desired to be like "all the other nations" (v. 5). This desire was more economic than political and can be compared with developmental authoritarianism in many parts of Asia.[1] The people wanted a king who would build the nation for them. They were not satisfied by the way their men and women had to work long hours for a meager income in the harsh mountain environment. They wanted to build great cities such as Assur and Babylon. Looking at the developed kingdoms all around, they reasoned that a monarchy would lead them to a new period of safety and prosperity. But Samuel felt betrayed by their demand for a king, which would practically force Samuel to retire. When Samuel turned to God in prayer, God comforted his prophet by construing the people's request for a king as a sin of rejecting God as king. Yet he instructed Samuel to give them a king while warning them about the dangers of monarchy. Thus chapter 8 captures one of the most important pivot points in Israel's history.

8:1–3 SAMUEL'S SONS BECOME JUDGES OF BEERSHEBA

Chapter 8 begins by noting that Samuel "grew old" (v. 1). The seniority may be a symbol of wisdom and blessing (see Prov 16:31; 20:29), but here it seems to refer to Samuel's physical and mental weakness. Because Samuel was old and weak, he bequeathed his office as judge to his two sons, Joel and Abijah. Unlike the priestly office, the office of judge was not meant to be hereditary and could only be transferred to whomever God endowed with his Spirit. God alone could choose a judge to serve Israel, but Samuel violated this by appointing his two sons as judges at Beersheba. Since the text gives us no hint that God's Spirit was upon them, verse 1 suggests that Samuel, despite his otherwise perfect track record, makes this error because of his advanced age. Joel

---

1. For the relationship between authoritarian regimes and economic development, see Lawrence Sáes and Julia Callagher, "Authoritarianism and Development in the Third World," *Brown Journal of World Affairs* 15 (2009): 87–101.

and Abijah failed to realize the Lord's good and just rule over Israel. Despite their godly names – "The LORD is God" and "The LORD is my father" – Joel and Abijah accepted bribes and perverted justice (v. 3). Instead of walking in their father's footsteps, they turned aside after unlawful gains. Thus the elders of Israel used the sins of Samuel's sons as an excuse to demand a king.

It may seem strange that Samuel's sons became judges at Beersheba, the southernmost city of Israel. This might be compared to the president of the USA moving its administrative capital to a Key in Florida or to the president of South Korea moving the Blue House to Jeju Island. Why didn't Samuel's sons rule Israel from a more central location, such as Ramah in the Benjamite territory? Josephus may have been aware of this question when he recounted that Joel became a judge at Bethel and Abijah at Beersheba (*Antiquities* 6.32). Josephus implies that Samuel's two sons divided the nation into two and ruled their respective halves from Bethel and from Beersheba. But the text says that Samuel's two sons "served at Beersheba" (v. 2). Thus a more plausible explanation is that Samuel did not retire but continued to judge from Ramah. He appointed his two sons as judges of Beersheba to see how they would do before passing on his full authority, establishing a kind of co-regency with a probationary purpose. In this case, the jurisdiction of Joel and Abijah was limited to Beersheba, which debunks the elders' complaint about Samuel's two sons and reveals the real motive for their request for a king. As we mentioned earlier, the people of Israel had no urgent need for a king under Samuel's judgeship. The Philistines had been subdued, and there was peace between Israel and the Canaanites. Further, Samuel's prophetic and priestly ministry restored the people's heart to the Lord. Despite all these, the elders of Israel insisted on having a king like all the other nations and took advantage of Samuel's mistake of passing on his office to his sons. They justified their demand for a king based on the sins of Joel and Abijah. But the fact that the unjust rule was restricted to the area of Beersheba, not to mention that Samuel still ruled from Ramah, seems to suggest that the damage done by Joel and Abijah was contained within Beersheba. One may argue that the elders' request for a king had no ground and that their complaints about Samuel's sons were simply an excuse to cover up their real motive for demanding a king.

DID SAMUEL FAIL IN CHILD EDUCATION?

Asians place much emphasis on child education. For instance, middle-income Korean families spend around 30 percent of their income to send their children to private academic institutions for after-school classes. Asian Christians are no exception to this and want their children to grow up to be responsible and beneficial members of society. However, not all Christian parents are fortunate enough to afford high education expenses. Many work until late hours and cannot attend to their children in person. But they trust that God will guide their children to become great Christian members of society if they remain faithful and obedient. To these parents, this passage is a stumbling block, for even Samuel spoiled his children! It makes it seem as if parents' faith is one thing and children's faith is another. But did Samuel really fail in raising his children in faith?

Clearly, Samuel did not fail in educating his two sons to become faithful leaders of the Israelite community. To make sense of this claim, we need to compare Samuel's family with Eli's family. The narrator provides many textual details that make this comparison viable. First, their names indicate different upbringings. Samuel enclosed his own confession of faith in his sons' names: Joel means "the LORD is God" and Abijah means "the LORD is my father." Eli, on the contrary, gave secular Egyptian names to his sons: Hophni means "a tadpole" and Phinehas means "a southerner." Because Egyptian culture was considered "high culture" in Eli's days, we may assume that Eli gave his sons fashionable names, but he did not enclose his faith in their names. Second, after Hophni and Phinehas were ordained as priests in Shiloh because the office was hereditary, they committed heinous sins against the Lord. In contrast, even though Samuel may have been wrong in bequeathing non-hereditary office to his two sons, he was prudent enough not to give them full authority over Israel. Instead, he entrusted them only with Beersheba to give them an opportunity to prove their worthiness to follow in his footsteps. The fact that Samuel appointed his two sons as judges shows that they must have been faithful and obedient men of God. If they had been scoundrels like Eli's two sons, one may assume, Samuel would not have appointed them as judges. Moreover, the fact that he entrusted his sons only with Beersheba suggests that he continued to exercise supervision over them. Though the moral sin of taking bribes is grave considering their status, it must be juxtaposed to and compared with Eli's two sons' sin against the Lord. After all, the moral sin of Samuel's sons does not nullify Samuel's efforts as a father. It would be unfair to blame Samuel for his adult children's mistake. Similarly, if we are faithful and obedient in our walk with the Lord, we can trust the Lord with our children's education.

8:4–5 ISRAEL DEMANDS A KING

All the elders of Israel visited Samuel at Ramah and demanded a king. Though this has no justification, the elders made up excuses to justify their request. First, they pointed out Samuel's seniority: "Behold, you are old" (v. 5), which implies that Samuel had no physical or mental strength to lead the people. Second, they complained about Samuel's sons, though the damage done by their sin was not so extensive as they lead us to believe. Further, it is possible that Samuel still ruled the country from Ramah. Furthermore, the Lord himself ruled Israel under the judges. God does not grow old, nor does he die. He is able to rule perfectly through imperfect or elderly judges. Like an earthen pot, he puts sinners to good use for his own glory (see 2 Cor 4:7). Samuel's seniority cannot be a hindrance to God in ruling. This raises a question about the real reason for their request for a king, which may be discerned in the expression "as all the other nations" (v. 5).

Monarchy was the oldest polity in the ancient Near East, which began with the invention of written language. Several advanced civilizations composed the so-called kinglists – e.g. Sumerian Kinglist – that traced their kings back to the time before the flood. The history appears to prove the efficacy and longevity of rule by a king in creating civilization. Kings could mobilize human and material resources at will for massive building projects. They built cities and filled them with people and culture. In the elders' estimation, the rule by king was the common denominator of all advanced countries in the ancient Near East. Israel, however, was considered a backwater in the region because the people lived at a subsistence level scattered in the mountainous areas without a central government. The elders reasoned that adopting kingship would be the first step towards a better life and a stronger country. By adopting a monarchy, they hoped to become as strong and prosperous a country as the other nations.

In addition, a centralized kingdom would bring a strong army. Since a king's order was mandatory, he could muster a big army quickly in times of national crisis. In times of peace, kings maintained a standing army. A judge's call for war was, by contrast, often ignored, even in times of national crisis. The tribes of Dan, Asher, and Gilead, for instance, did not respond to Deborah's call for help when Jabin, the king of Canaan, invaded the country (Judg 5:17). Jephthah also failed to enlist the aid of other tribes when he tried to save the Gileadites from the hand of the Ammonites. The twelve tribes of Israel remained independent with no central leadership to force them to stand together for the same cause. To make things worse, the tribes often fought with one another. The elders of Israel reasoned that this would change if they installed a king on the throne. All the tribes would listen to their king, and all Israel would be united under the king's standard. Thus the country would be better prepared to deal with international conflicts.

Most Asians in developing countries would not blame the elders of Israel for their desire to modernize Israel by instituting a monarchy. They might also agree with the elders that it was their divine calling to install a king for the good of the nation. After all, kingship was the time-tested polity that many civilized peoples adopted. Anyone who dared to oppose it could be called names such as "one who went against the flow of time" or "one who lacked vision." Was it really wrong for the people of Israel to ask for a king to build their nation like all the other nations? In our modern context, is it a sin to desire to make our nation as safe and prosperous as "all the other nations"? Of course, the desire to have a greater nation or a better life is not bad in itself. However, the elders wanted a king in order to become like all the other nations. In the ancient Near East, a king was a god – they were either divine from birth or assumed divinity after death. This ideology of kingship made their demand for a king idolatrous, for seeking a human king for a better life and a more advanced society would have been equivalent to forsaking the Lord for "money and fame." Moreover, God chose Israel out of all the other nations to be his holy people. God ruled Israel as king and gave the people God's law. By living according to God's laws under God's rule, the Israelites were different! Thus having a king like all the other nations was an abandonment of their identity as a covenantal community.

We all are like the elders of Israel. We want to serve a visible king who promises wealth and power instead of trusting the invisible God. Further, we expect our leaders to be perfect and even divine. In politics, this tendency has led to the emergence of authoritarian regimes in some Asian countries, where some people are willing to sacrifice their own freedom for the cause of nation building, but others suffer from persecution. In the church, our desire for superhero leaders may force our pastors and missionaries to hide their personal weakness and show only what looks good on the outside. When we live a life of pretension, we begin to fall from grace. Israelite judges were faulty human beings who needed God's grace and trusted in God's good and just rule. We need to trust God to rule through imperfect leaders, adjusting our expectations and nurturing a community where they are encouraged to share their shortcomings.

8:6–9 GOD COMFORTS SAMUEL

Samuel was displeased with the elders' demand for a king, which essentially forced him to resign from his office as judge! This becomes clear in the way they qualified their request for a king: "Give us a king to lead us" (v. 6). The Hebrew phrase *leshapenu*, "to lead us," is literally rendered as "to judge us." This implies that Samuel would be replaced by a king. Samuel would no longer lead the people, but a king would. We all can relate to Samuel's feelings about this ungrateful betrayal. For after Samuel served the people for over twenty years by praying for them, offering sacrifices, visiting towns to provide legal and pastoral service, Israel overcame their moral and spiritual anomie and lived in safety from foreign oppression. Then all the elders of Israel came to his hometown and demanded a king! Imagine Samuel's sense of rejection and of humiliation! But rather than cursing the people, Samuel knelt with his broken heart and *prayed to the LORD*" (v. 6, italics added). Koreans would say, "prayer runs in his blood." His mother Hannah had been a woman of prayer, for she conceived him and raised him up in prayer. No wonder Samuel himself was a man of prayer who ran to the Lord in times of trouble. Although the narrator omits the content of Samuel's prayer, we may infer from God's reply (see v. 7) that he asked God for the answer that he should give to the elders of Israel.

Before answering Samuel's question, the Lord provided pastoral counseling. He began by articulating the sin that the elders committed in requesting a king: "It is not you they have rejected, but they have rejected me as their king" (v. 7). In other words, the Lord defined the nature of their sin as more theological than political. In essence, they rejected God as their king. In effect, the Lord went on to say, "Calm down! Don't take it too personally. Let's go over some history of redemption and learn from it." The point of the Lord's lecture on the history of redemption was that the people of Israel had a track record for rejecting God, who delivered them out of foreign oppression: "As they have done from the day I brought them up out of Egypt until this day, forsaking me and serving other gods, so they are doing to you" (v. 8). From Samuel's plea to put away foreign gods in Mizpah, we may infer that the Israelites continued to betray God until rather recently. So God was saying to Samuel: "so they are doing to you. Now you begin to understand how painful it is to be betrayed." There is a Korean saying: "Fellow sufferers sympathize with each other." God attempts to comfort his fellow sufferer Samuel by showing sympathy.

But it is one thing to feel sympathy and another to concede to those who are causing you to suffer. Yet the Lord commanded Samuel to "listen to" the elders (v. 9). Although he also said "listen to" the elders at the beginning of his speech (v. 7), his intention there was more ambiguous than it is here. For after making it clear that the elders' request for a king was a sin of idolatry, God allowed the people of Israel to have a king. Why did God allow his people to walk the wrong path? Why didn't God impose his good and right way upon the people? Apparently, the most effective way to bring about an awareness of sin is to let sinners suffer the consequences of their sin so that they can be ready to obey God. Further, God does not force us to live for his kingdom, but rather waits for us to choose what is good over evil. Yet we are in God's hands even when we are walking through the darkest valley, away from God. Although some may complain, "Why does God allow us to sin?," a human without free will is no longer a human. Our free will is a precious gift from God, which we ought to use to live in and for God's kingdom.

8:10–22 THE WAYS OF THE KING

As a warning to the people of Israel who requested a king, the prophet Samuel announced, "what the king . . . will claim as his rights" (*mishpat hammelek*: v. 9). The Hebrew for this phrase may be rendered literally as "the law concerning the king." Some scholars take it as a satire, since the title does not match its content.[2] What is subsumed under "the law concerning the king" reflects only negatives relating to the new institution, as if Samuel were saying, "you will only lose under the rule of a human king." Samuel appears to deliberately avoid mentioning the positives of a monarchy. Further, the title "the law concerning the king" reminds us of the Mosaic Law relating to the institution of a monarchy in Israel (Deut 17:14–20). This law lays down the qualifications for kings of Israel, his duty, and the nature of Israel's royal office. As for the qualifications for a king of Israel, there are two requirements. First, he must be chosen by the Lord – not elected by popular will (v. 15). Second, he must be an Israelite, not a foreigner (v. 15). The law stipulates his royal duty in terms of what he should and should not do: he should not be in the business of "acquiring" (*laqah*) worldly things such as gold and wives, but should study the law all the days of his life (vv. 16–19). Finally, the nature of Israel's royal office is revealed in the statement that the king should be a God-fearer, ruling in accordance with all the laws of the Lord, and he should not regard himself as being above his fellow Israelites (see vv. 19–20). In other words, king and people are brothers in Israel! What kind of a king is this? A king who obeys the

---

2. M. Garsiel, *The First Book of Samuel: A Literary Study of Comparative Structure, Analogies and Parallels* (Winona Lake, IN: Eisenbrauns, 1983), 68.

Lord his God and serves his people as if they were his brothers? This idea of a king is unheard of in human history. A king was a god in the ancient Near East whose word was the law and whose will defined the good. He regarded himself as being qualitatively different from his people, and his right was defined in terms of "acquiring" worldly things from his people. Samuel's discussion of "the law concerning the king" reflects the pagan ideology of kingship.

The key word in Samuel's warning is the word "to take" (*laqaḥ*). Various rights of a king boil down to the business of "taking" things from his people. First, he will "take" their sons and daughters to work for him. Some of their sons will be part of the king's standing army (v. 11) and some of their daughters will perform house chores for the king (v. 13). Others will farm the land for the king and others will make weapons and tools for his army (v. 12). Second, he will "take" things from his people. He will take the land from the people (v. 14), along with their servants and livestock (v. 16). Further, he will take a tithe of their income (v. 15). This tax of commodities will be used to reward his loyal servants and finance his palatial bureaucracy (vv. 14–15). Finally, Samuel concludes his warning by articulating what it means to live in a kingdom: "You yourselves will become his slaves" (v. 18). To top it off, Samuel warns that the Lord will not save the Israelites even when they cry out "for relief from the king you have chosen" (v. 18). One can discern a principle of retribution in these words: since Israel rejected God as king by requesting a human king, God will also reject them as his people and not answer their pleas for help. The phrase "the king you have chosen" (v. 18) is contrasted with the king whom God chooses (see Deut 17:15). Samuel tried to tell the people that the king they asked for would do more harm than good and was not the king whom God intended for them. Samuel may have been hoping that the people would take back their demand.

But even after hearing all the negatives of a monarchy, the people of Israel did not retract their demand for a king. They said, "No! We want a king over us. Then we will be like all the other nations" (v. 19). It is as if they had already calculated the pros and cons of a monarchy and still wanted a king. This is made clear when they remind Samuel of one of the good things about kingship: a king will "lead us and fight our battles" (v. 20). Although, generally speaking, a king was recognized as a warlord, it is not because of any imminent military threat that the elders of Israel demanded a king; Israel was enjoying a period of peace in those days under Samuel. Just as the elders' complaint about Samuel's sons was an excuse for hiding their real motive, the king's role as a warlord here was also an excuse for hiding their real motive.

The people of Israel seemed to prefer a prosperous life with limited freedom to a life of freedom with limited resources. All of us can relate to this. We may stay in a job even though it is not fulfilling, or when we are mistreated or yelled at, because regular income gives us a sense of security. We, too, may be willing to sacrifice our freedom to generate steady income. In this way, we are accomplices in the sin of the Israelites, who chose material well-being over freedom in God by preferring a human king to invisible God.

Finally, it is interesting to note that Samuel responded to God's command to install a king by dismissing the people of Israel (v. 22). The meaning of this act is not clear. Is Samuel refusing to obey the Lord's command? Or was he trying to buy time to search for a candidate for the role of king of Israel? The fact that he could have cast lots for that purpose (see ch. 11) makes the latter proposition less likely. Further the fact that the next chapter is about God sending a candidate to Samuel, rather than Samuel searching for a king, suggests that Samuel was refusing to obey the Lord's command to appoint the people a king.

1 SAMUEL 9:1–25

SAUL IN SEARCH OF KINGSHIP

Aristotle defines a tragic hero as "a literary character who makes a judgment error that inevitably leads to his/her own destruction."[1] Some of the common traits of a tragic hero include suffering from fate more than he/she deserves, falling from great heights because of his/her own error, and accepting death with honor. Most importantly, according to Aristotle, a tragic hero "must be noble in nature, but imperfect so that the audience can see themselves in him."[2] Saul fits this definition of a tragic hero perfectly. Chapter 9 introduces him for the first time, where we see Saul in his noble but imperfect character. Koreans express a prejudice against men of great height in the saying, "tall people always turn out to be insipid." But rather than being insipid, the tall and handsome Saul turns out to be intelligent and even passionate, though he doesn't take initiative. In other words, the prophet Samuel had good reason to anoint him as king of Israel besides the divine command.

9:1–4 SAUL IN SEARCH OF DONKEYS

Chapter 9 begins with a genealogy of an individual whose tranquil private life appears to be miles away from the story of national importance recounted in chapter 8, where the institution of monarchy was hotly discussed between the prophet Samuel and the people of Israel. The introduction of the genealogy of a certain man named Kish, therefore, is a perplexing sequel to the previous story about God's instruction to Samuel to appoint a king over Israel. This sense of confusion increases when we consider that Kish belonged to the tribe of Benjamin, about whom the people of Israel in the last days of Judges may have said, "Can anything good come out of the tribe of Benjamin?" The Benjamites committed a heinous crime against their own brothers and were almost annihilated in the subsequent war of retaliation (see Judg 19–21). Most likely, the tribe of Benjamin commanded little or no respect from other tribes. A Benjamite was the last person one would expect to become king of Israel. In this regard, neither Kish nor his son Saul was a promising candidate as king,

---

1. https://www.bisd303.org/cms/lib3/WA01001636/Centricity/Domain/593/10th%20english%20Fall/C%20-%20The%20Tragic%20Play/Antigone.Medea/Definition%20of%20Tragic%20Hero.pdf (accessed on 11 October 2016).
2. Ibid.

although they were men of wealth (v. 1).[3] Furthermore, Kish's forefathers were otherwise unknown in the Bible, a sign of mediocrity. Although details might seem to suggest that the author of 1 Samuel is changing the subject, the literary strategy of beginning the story of public significance with a seemingly unpromising individual is not uncommon. In 1 Samuel, this strategy is employed to deliver the message that a great step forward in the history of redemption begins with a humble and faithful individual. We have seen a similar strategy in the story of Hannah. Kish's humble genealogy and the repeated mention of his problematic Benjamite clan in verse 1 emphasize that God's great work of redemption has a humble and even mysterious beginning (see Mark 4:30–32).

Verse 2 introduces Kish's son, Saul, whose name means "one whom they demanded." The name "Saul" becomes prophetic when we consider that the people of Israel demanded their king in chapter 8. Further Saul had an ideal appearance for king: he was "as handsome a young man as could be found anywhere in Israel" (v. 2a) and he "was a head taller than anyone else" (v. 2b). In ancient China, four traits were considered essential to public leadership: *shen* (appearance), *yan* (speech), *shu* (writing), and *pan* (judgment), among which appearance was preeminent. In ancient Israel, good appearance was an important trait expected of a leader (see 1 Kgs 1:6). Saul was born with a physicality that made him a perfect candidate for the king of Israel, and he was also a heroic warrior (see Gen 39:6; 1 Sam 16:12; Esth 2:7). Thus he was just right in the people's eyes. But, as it turns out, Saul's good looks become a byword for human misjudgment, and his tall stature becomes a symbol for human arrogance against God. In fact, the Hebrew *gabah* used to describe Saul's stature in verse 2 is used earlier to refer to arrogant speeches against the Lord in Hannah's prayer (see 2:3).

The story is set in motion by some runaway donkeys that belong to Kish (v. 3). Kish sent his son Saul on a mission to retrieve the missing donkeys. Since it was not always safe to travel in the countryside, Kish had one of his servants accompany Saul. Beyond this, Kish has no role in the narrative – in fact, he disappears from the scene completely. But his actions in verse 3 become crucial in making Saul king of Israel, and since Kish did not expect this, we can discern here the invisible hand of God. God works through common people, whether they are aware or not, to achieve his good purpose. Later,

---

3. The Hebrew phrase *gibbor hail*, "a man of standing," originally refers to the ideal Israelite, who was "a man of wealth, power, and integrity" (see Ruth 2:1). The NIV, "a man of standing," does include the nuance of his being wealthy, but it may be used more specifically for a valiant soldier (Judg 11:1), a man of wealth (see Isa 60:5), and a man of morality (1 Kgs 11:28).

the anonymous servant turns out to be doing much more than escorting his master's son, for he plays an important role in leading Saul to the prophet Samuel. Some of us might wonder why a wealthy man such as Kish put his son in harm's way to retrieve a few runaway donkeys, as Samuel later implies (see v. 20). But donkeys were expensive assets, and they were also like pets in that owners developed emotional bonds with them, since donkeys carried their owners and luggage and slept under the same roof.[4] So it is no surprise that Kish sent his son and one of his servants to retrieve his missing donkeys. Interestingly, Saul's journey in search of the donkeys turned into a journey in search of kingship.

Saul obeyed his father's instruction, and verse 4 places him on the mission in the hill country of Ephraim. This shows Saul to be a man of filial piety in contrast to the disobedient sons of Eli and Samuel. Saul and his servant traveled for about three days before they arrived at Zuph (v. 20). They passed through the hill country of Ephraim, the land of Shalishah, and the land of Shaalim, but they did not find the donkeys. It is not certain where Shalishah and Shaalim are located now, but one may argue that these place names, rendered as "three-forked road" and "fox alley," respectively, are imbued with folkloristic and mysterious airs. It appears that Saul passed through these mysterious places to arrive in a different world. By the time Saul left those places behind, he was embarking on a totally different journey.

9:5–10 SAUL VISITS SAMUEL AT RAMAH

After passing through Shalishah and Shaalim, Saul and his father's servant came to the land Zuph in the Benjamite territory. Zuph is first introduced as Samuel's eponymous father (see 1:1), but here it refers to the area where Samuel's hometown was located. Then Saul said to his servant, "Come, let's go back, or my father will stop thinking about the donkeys and start worrying about us" (v. 5). This is Saul's first recorded utterance. In the biblical narrative, the first recorded utterance of a character always deserves special attention, because it often reveals an important character trait. Saul's first utterance, "Let's go back," suggests that Saul lacks confidence in taking initiative. This impression is reinforced by Saul's subsequent utterance, "Good . . . Come, let us go" (v. 10). Although Saul, as the master, was supposed to give decisive orders, his servant took the initiative and set an agenda. Saul's first utterance

---

4. Houses in ancient Israel accommodated animals in the first floor while humans slept in the upper room.

also infers that Saul was a man of filial piety who did not want to worry his father (see v. 10). Filial duty, according to Koreans, means not worrying the parents. Although not perfect, Saul appears to have many positive character traits that would make him appealing to the people.

In response to Saul's suggestion to return home, the servant proposed that they go to "a man of God," or seer, in the city of Zuph. "Going to a seer" was an idiomatic expression for inquiring of the Lord (v. 9). A prophet used to be called a seer before the Israelite monarchy. This change signifies the change in function. Unlike a prophet, who proclaimed judgment against a king or the people, a seer helped individuals solve their problems through counseling, prayers, or miracles – much like the role of a diviner in neighboring countries. The man of God or seer lived among the people and solved their problems by using their extraordinary skills. In a sense, the seer's role was similar to that of Christian missionaries serving in remote areas of the world.

By inquiring of the Lord through the seer, Saul and his servant wanted to know "what way to take" (v. 8; see v. 6). They expected the seer to tell them where their donkeys might be found. But it is also possible to discern a metaphorical tone in their words "what way to take." Although the story in chapter 9 begins with a private matter (i.e. Kish and his missing donkeys), it ends in an event of public significance. The narrator makes an artful transition from one to the other by investing some of his phrases with double meaning. The expression "which way to take" is a perfect example. Although Saul was seeking which way he should take to find his runaway donkeys, the man of God guided him toward the course that the nation should take to restore *shalom* to Israel. Israel wandered from the Lord, doing what was just in their own eyes. The people of Israel (including Saul) did not know where they should go. The man of God told Saul what he should do in order to restore *shalom* in Israel.

As implied by Saul's words, "what can we give the man?" seers normally received compensation for their service. We should not be too judgmental about this, for living in a village in ancient Israel was hard, and life threw many curve balls to the people. In moments of crisis, people turned to the seer, who needed to be paid for his services. But Saul did not find anything worth bringing as a gift. His servant came to rescue once again, saying, "Look, a quarter of a shekel of silver is in my hand!" (v. 8, my translation). Was this yet another coincidence? What if Kish's donkeys had not wandered off? What if Kish had sent Saul alone? What if the servant that Kish had chosen to accompany Saul had not known of the man of God living in Zuph? Clearly, these are not coincidences, but rather God sent Saul to the man of God (see v. 16).

9:11–14 SAUL MEETS WOMEN AT A WELL

On their way to the city, Saul and his servant meet "young women coming out to draw water" (v. 11). Normally water sources were located outside a city, and it was young women's job to draw water for the day's use. Saul addresses them with a question, "Is the seer here?" The women's answer to this question is unusually long, extending over two full verses (vv. 12–13), and appears repetitive. Although some Jewish rabbis take this as evidence of the talkativeness of girls, Saul's appearance suggests a better explanation for their long-winded and repetitive answer. Verses 12–13 reflect a situation where friendly girls were eager to take turns in answering the question posed by the handsome and tall young man.[5] But this explanation does not fully express the literary significance of the long-winded and repetitive answer of the women at the well. The author of 1 Samuel is certainly drawing the reader's attention by devoting significant space to this scene. The reason may be found in the fact that this scene is a creative variation of the so-called betrothal type-scene.

The betrothal type-scene is made up of a sequence of motifs, such as a man traveling away from home and arriving at a well outside a certain town, where women come out to draw water. There is conversation between the man and women, a banquet at the women's house, followed by a marriage contract. The biblical author uses this type-scene in describing the betrothal of Isaac, Jacob, and Moses, all of whom met their wife, whether face-to-face or through an agent, at a well. The observant reader, familiar with this betrothal type-scene, will immediately be tempted to interpret Saul's encounter with the women at the well as such. Saul, a handsome young man (v. 2), was traveling away from home and arrived at a well outside a city just as women come out to draw water. This naturally led to the conversation. But the ending of this scene is different from other betrothal type-scenes, for Saul did not meet his bride-to-be. Soon after parting with the girls, Saul bumped into Samuel at the city gate. Instead of a wife, Saul found Samuel, his partner in his royal office. The author of 1 Samuel portrays the first encounter between the future king of Israel and the prophet Samuel as a betrothal type-scene to teach that the kingdom that will be established in Israel requires the cooperation of both king and prophet. The relationship between king and prophet can be compared to that of husband and wife.

---

5. Bar-Efrat discerns in the girls' long-winded answer multiple voices of girls, which the author of Samuel put together as if they were said in unison. Bar-Efrat, *Das Erste Buch Samuel*, 157.

THE LUCK OF THE SEA AND THE LUCK OF THE MOUNTAINS IN KOJIKI

The following Japanese story is similar to the betrothal type-scene in the Old Testament.

The Prince followed these instructions, and after he had gone a little way, everything happened just as the God of the Tide had said. He climbed the cassia tree and sat there. When the handmaidens of the daughter of the God of the Sea, bearing jeweled vessels, went to draw water from the well, they saw a light in it. On looking up, they beheld a beautiful young man. They were much amazed. The Prince saw the handmaidens and begged them to give him some water. They at once drew some water, put it into a jeweled vessel, and respectfully offered it to him. Then, without drinking the water, he loosened the jewel at his neck, took it in his mouth, and spat it into the jeweled vessel. The jewel adhered to the vessel so fast that the handmaidens could not get it off. So they took it, with the jewel adhering to it, and presented it to the Princess.

When the Princess saw the jewel, she asked her handmaidens, "Is there perhaps someone outside the gate?" They answered, "There is a very beautiful young man sitting on top of the cassia tree above our well. He is nobler in bearing even than our king. We offered him some water when he asked for it, but instead of drinking the water, he spat this jewel in the cup. We could not separate the jewel from the cup, so we have brought both to you."

The Princess, marveling at this, went out to look and was delighted by what she saw. The Prince and the Princess exchanged glances and then she went to speak to her father. She said, "There is a beautiful person at our gate," and the God of the Sea himself went out to look. "That is Prince Fire-fade," he said and led him inside the palace. He spread out eight layers of rugs of sealskins, and then eight layers of rugs of silk above them, and then had the Prince sit down on top. A great banquet was arranged with a hundred guests and the God of the Sea gave his daughter to the Prince in marriage.[1]

---

1. Donald Keene, ed., *Anthology of Japanese Literature: From the Earliest Era to the Mid-nineteenth Century* (New York City: Grove Press, 1955), 55–56.

The point of the women's long-winded speech to Saul (see vv. 12–13) is simple: "Samuel is here in the city," which is all that Saul needed to hear. He had asked, "Is the seer here?" (v. 11). But other details in the women's replies are prophetic because they emphasize the most important aspect of the afternoon sacrifice for which Samuel returned to the city: a post-sacrificial meal. Thirty men were invited for that meal, and Saul was soon invited by Samuel. In fact, Saul was the guest of honor in the post-sacrificial banquet organized by Samuel.

9:15–17 FLASHBACK: GOD'S REVELATION TO SAMUEL

After parting with the women at the well, Saul and his servant went up to the city. "As they were entering the city they saw Samuel coming out toward them on his way up to the high place" (v. 14). The moment Samuel saw a tall and handsome young man walking toward him, he knew that he was Saul, the future king of Israel – not simply because of his distinct appearance, but because on the previous day, God had revealed to Samuel that he would send a Benjamite for Samuel to anoint as ruler over Israel (v. 16). At the moment of encounter, God told Samuel that this was the man he had spoken to him about (v. 17), which confirms that the hidden but powerful hand of the Lord led Saul to Samuel.

In speaking to Samuel, the Lord defines the essential duty of the king of Israel as saving God's people from the hands of the Philistines (v. 16), which relates to the historical fact that the Philistines were the biggest threat to Israel in those days. Although they began as an immigrant group who settled in the southern coastal strip of Palestine, they quickly assimilated to Canaanite culture. As their population grew, they tried to expand their territory inland, which brought them into constant conflict with the Israelites. It appears that the Philistines succeeded to a certain degree in their infiltration inland, and they made some portion of the Israelite population their slaves (see 4:9). The institution of kingship in Israel must be understood in this context, for one of the qualifications for the king of Israel was his military ability to deliver Israel, particularly from the oppressive hand of the Philistines.

Noteworthy with reference to Saul's rule is the Hebrew word *'atsar*, which the Lord used to refer to Saul's governance: Saul will "restrain" my people (v. 17). This serves as a subtle foreshadowing of the oppressive nature of Saul's rule. Although the NIV makes it palatable by rendering it as, "[Saul will] govern my people," the Hebrew *'atsar* has a negative connotation. Saul's reign will be about limiting the people's freedom, taking things from the people, and eventually reducing them to slaves, as described in 8:11–17.

9:18–25 SAUL ENCOUNTERS SAMUEL

Without recognizing Samuel, Saul asked him where the house of the seer was. Samuel, who recognized Saul through divine revelation, introduced himself as the seer in question and told Saul to go to the high place ahead of him. He adds, "for today you are to eat with me" (v. 19). This post-sacrificial banquet of fellowship had been prepared specifically with Saul, the guest of honor, in mind. One may even say that the sacrifice was an excuse for this meal, for in those days meat could be consumed only after offering the animal to the Lord. Thus the narrator skips over the scene of sacrifice to the scene of the meal in verse 22. As it turns out, thirty guests were also invited to eat with Saul (v. 22). Further, a special order had been placed to the cook for Saul's portion to be "the thigh with what was on it" (v. 2). To put this in perspective, the thigh of a sacrifice animal was usually reserved for the priest (see Lev 7:32). As the host, Samuel was willing to give up his own portion for the guest of honor as a way of showing the highest respect for the future king of Israel.

The purpose of this meeting at the banquet hall was no casual fellowship. Samuel may have wanted an opportunity to observe Saul up close: "Isn't he the one the LORD has chosen as king of Israel, after all?" He wanted to test the water before he anointed him as king. In other words, he wanted to make sure he was the right one. Having said that, the number of invited guests suggests that they were not a haphazard group of people, for thirty was the number for the royal bodyguard of the king of Israel. One might even say that in that banquet hall, the three pillars of the Israelite kingdom were gathered together: the future king, the prophet – his inseparable partner – and the king's elite warriors. But only Samuel knew the real significance of that post-sacrificial meal.

After inviting Saul to the meal, Samuel adds, "And in the morning I will send you on your way and will tell you all that is on your heart" (v. 19). What did Samuel mean by "all that is in your heart?" Since Saul had a particular question in mind when he visited Samuel – the whereabouts of his missing donkeys – the reader may think that Samuel meant to give Saul that information the next morning. But in verse 20 Samuel says to Saul, "they have been found!" The clue to what Samuel meant by "all that is in your heart" may be found in verse 27. For the next morning, Samuel told Saul the message that had come from God the previous day about installing Saul as king over Israel. "All that is in your [Saul's] heart" should be understood in this context. We may infer that Saul, although a Benjamite who was antagonized by other Israelites, had a burden in his heart for his people, who were suffering from foreign oppression. He may have been secretly praying for his role in that darkest age. Samuel saw through it and told Saul that he would tell him "all that was in his heart" the next morning.

This seems to be corroborated by Samuel's rhetorical question in verse 20, "And to whom is all the desire of Israel turned, if not to you and your whole family line?"[6] This has an unmistakable political connotation, which Saul perceives. His reply to Samuel's rhetorical question in verse 21 recalls such political leaders as Moses and Gideon, who demurred the divine calling at first by citing their shortcomings. In particular, Saul's answer is similar to Gideon's, who said, "Pardon me, my lord, but how can I save Israel? My clan is the weakest in Manasseh, and I am the least in my family" (Judg 6:15). All this shows that Saul proved himself as a worthy candidate for king of Israel. He was not perfect, but he was noble in character. He was a man of filial piety and a patriot concerned about the future of his own people.

In this regard, verse 25 is noteworthy: "After they came down from the high place to the town, Samuel talked with Saul on the roof of his house." Some versions render the second half of verse 25 as "a bed was spread for Saul on the roof, and he lay down to sleep" (ESV). But this rendering is based on the Septuagint rather than the Hebrew text. Here it is better to retain the Hebrew reading, according to which Saul and Samuel continued their dialogue at Samuel's house after their common meal at the high place. What did they talk about so late into the night. Most likely Saul and Samuel discussed some common interest, which would have been the matter of kingship. During those hours, Samuel told Saul the way he should take in order to restore peace in Israel, which recalls the servant's suggestion in verse 6: "Let us go there now. Perhaps he will tell us which way to take." The metaphorical nuance of that suggestion was fulfilled during their frank conversation on the roof.

---

6. The Hebrew word *hemdah,* "desire," may also be translated as "wealth." An alternative translation of the statement, "to whom belongs all the wealth of Israel," fits the immediate context, in which Samuel advises Saul not to worry about the lost donkeys. Samuel was saying, in effect, "You and your family are rich. Why worry about a few missing donkeys?"

TALKING ON THE ROOF?

The typical four-pillared house of ancient Israel had a bi-level structure. On the lower level, house chores were conducted during the day and sheep and goats slept in the pen during the night. The upper level provided a living space where family members slept and rested. The roof was also utilized for various purposes. During summer people often slept on the roof to cool off, but more importantly, the roof was recognized as a holy place because the people could see the moon and the stars. Thus the future king of Israel and his prophet discussed the matter of kingship in two holy places: the high place and the roof of Samuel's house.

Saul is referred to as "a young man" in this episode (v. 2), although he was well over thirty at the time.[7] The narrator might have characterized Saul as a young man because of his passion for his people. Living in Gibeah, where there was a Philistine outpost (see 10:5), he saw daily the suffering of his people under the Philistines. Although he was a Benjamite, a *persona non grata* in Israel, Saul's heart became burdened for his people who were in pain. He may have been praying secretly for his role in saving Israel from the hand of the Philistines. In this sense, Saul was indeed a young man who was willing and hoping to serve his country. Then the Lord sent Saul to the prophet Samuel to be anointed as king of Israel.

---

7. The chronology of Saul is difficult, but Saul's son Jonathan served as a general of Saul's army at the beginning of Saul's reign (see ch. 13), which suggests that Saul might have been close to forty years old when he became king – unless he bore Jonathan in his teens.

1 SAMUEL 9:26–10:16

FIRST CYCLE OF THE INSTITUTION OF KINGSHIP: SAUL'S FIRST DISOBEDIENCE

Religious experience does not always translate into authentic living in faith. In a similar vein, one of Confucius' disciples said to his master, "It is not that your Way does not commend itself to me, but that it demands powers I do not possess."[1] We find this so true with Saul in this episode. Although the Lord anointed Saul as the king of Israel through the prophet Samuel and then empowered Saul with his Spirit, Saul did not obey the Lord's commands through Samuel to rise in faith against the Philistines. Instead, he backed off from that faith at the last moment.

9:26–10:1 SAMUEL ANOINTS SAUL: DESIGNATION

Early in the morning at the break of dawn, when people were still asleep, Samuel called out to Saul, who had spent the night on the roof. They went outside together, and Samuel led Saul to the deserted areas of town. These narrative details suggest Samuel's intention to send Saul on a secret mission. As they arrived at the edge of town, Samuel told Saul to make his servant go on ahead of them (v. 27). Left alone with Saul, Samuel took a flask of olive oil and poured it on Saul's head. In ancient Israel, pouring oil on someone's head was a symbolic act of installing him in a public office. Samuel made Saul's office clear by kissing him and saying, "Has not the LORD anointed you ruler over his inheritance?" (10:1). This scene of anointing raises many questions. First, it is not clear why Samuel wanted to make it a secret event. Did not the people of Israel demand a king? Did not God order Samuel to anoint Saul as king over Israel? Yet God did not order Samuel to anoint Saul in secret, so why all the secrecy? One possible reason might be the political situation at that time, when the Philistines maintained military outposts within Israel. The news of Saul's anointing as king would have placed Saul in significant danger, and Samuel may have wanted to keep it secret until Saul had acquired enough power and popular support to defend himself against the Philistines. For that to happen, Samuel needed to do much more than pour olive oil on

---

1. Confucius, *The Analetics*, Book IV, 10.

Saul's head, and so he gave further directions about which way Saul should take as he sent him back to his hometown of Gibeah.

Some scholars note that the container for the anointing oil was not a horn but a flask, which suggests an ominous foreshadowing of Saul's ultimate failure as king of Israel.[2] A horn of oil was used in anointing Davidic kings (see 1 Sam 16:13; 1 Kgs 1:39). Also, Hannah mentioned a horn both at the beginning and the end of her prayer in the context of blessing "his king" or "his anointed" (see 2:10). A flask of oil, on the other hand, was used in anointing King Jehu of northern Israel (see 2 Kgs 9:1). This creates a literary connection between Saul and the kings of northern Israel – many of whom did not build a dynasty but met a similar fate to the first king of Israel. It does seem strange that Samuel made all the necessary preparations for meeting with the future king of Israel yet failed to pour the oil into a horn.

Samuel's words of installation, "Has not the LORD anointed you ruler over his inheritance?" (10:1), also suggest an ominous future for Saul. Although Samuel's words are introduced as the "word of God" (9:27), they do not represent faithfully what God told Samuel: "Anoint him ruler over my people Israel; he will deliver them from the hand of the Philistines. I have looked on my people, for their cry has reached me" (9:16). Samuel's words of installation relay only the first part of the divine revelation and leave out the rest. Further, Samuel rephrased the first part of the revelation as a question, perhaps implying uncertainty. Along with the use of a flask of oil, this question serves as another omen for the fate of King Saul. These literary details establish Saul as a tragic hero, for according to Aristotle, a tragic hero must be doomed from the start.

Finally, in the words of institution, Samuel did not use the word "king," but declared Saul as a ruler over Israel. In fact, the Lord also used the word "ruler" instead of "king" when commanding Samuel to anoint Saul as a "ruler" over the people. For God wanted to give Israel a different kind of king, and the word "ruler" represented a new ideology of kingship that was free from the baggage of a traditional king. The king of Israel was not to imitate his counterparts in neighboring kingdoms, where human kings considered themselves as gods or demigods. Instead, the king of Israel was to be a *nagid*, "ruler." The Hebrew word *nagid* may refer to a man that goes ahead of others, suggesting that the king of Israel was not to boss around the people from behind but rather go before the people through the various ups and downs of life – including

---

2. Peter D. Miscall, *1 Samuel: A Literary Reading*, Indiana Studies in Biblical Literature (Bloomington: Indiana University Press, 1986), 59; Bodner, *1 Samuel*, 92–93.

wars, just as the Lord went before the Israelites in the wilderness. The king of Israel was meant to lead by example.[3] Koreans can easily relate to this ideology of kingship, since Korean kings used to till the land in their small rice fields within the palace in order to set an example for the farmers, who comprised the majority of his people. But this ideology of kingship was totally new to the Israelites and to Saul.

10:2–6 THREE SIGNS

Saul was a farmer from the rejected tribe of Benjamin who suddenly found himself thrown into a life of greatness when he was divinely designated as king over Israel. The text is silent about Saul's response, but we may infer from the subsequent episodes that the experience was surreal for Saul. Although he heard Samuel tell him that God had appointed him as king over Israel, he was not ready to embrace what that might entail. After all, Saul had to start from scratch. The people of Israel had never experienced the rule of kings before. What should Saul do to make the Israelites accept his kingship? Where should he begin? He may have wondered whether the people from other tribes would recognize a Benjamite king. He needed an extra boost to stay on his mission. So Samuel gave Saul three signs to reconfirm his divine calling as king of Israel. If Saul saw all three of these signs fulfilled, he would have faith in God to carry out whatever commands the prophet Samuel would give him.

First, Samuel predicted that Saul would encounter two men near Rachel's tomb at Zelzah in the land of Benjamin as well as what they would say to Saul: "The donkeys you set out to look for have been found. And your father has stopped thinking about them and is worried about you. He is asking, 'What shall I do about my son?'" (v. 2).[4] Second, Samuel predicted that Saul would meet three men under the great tree of Tabor who were on their way to a sanctuary at Bethel (v. 3), and they would give Saul two loaves of bread as a gift (v. 4).[5] Third, Samuel predicted that Saul would turn into "a different person" (v. 6) in his hometown of Gibeah:

---

3. The imagery that best captures this kind of leadership is a shepherd. Glück even attempts to connect the title "ruler" with the term *noqed* "shepherd" (*TDOT*, 191).

4. Note that the two men – who apparently did not belong to Kish's household – had been informed of the most recent news about Kish's missing donkeys. In other words, it appears that the return of Kish's missing donkeys had become "national" news. How much more so when Kish's son Saul returned as king of Israel! It could easily have become national news. That would certainly help Saul consolidate his rule over all Israel.

5. The fact that three men gave gifts to Saul under the great tree of Tabor is another hint about Saul's kingship, as it recalls an enthronement ceremony, in which the people brought gifts to

As you approach the town, you will meet a procession of prophets coming down from the high place with lyres, timbrels, pipes and harps being played before them, and they will be prophesying. The Spirit of the LORD will come powerfully upon you, and you will prophesy with them; and you will be changed into a different person. (vv. 5–6)

As Samuel predicted, the Spirit of the Lord came powerfully upon Saul and turned him into a different person (v. 6), just as the Spirit came upon other great leaders of Israel – Moses (Num 11:29), Joshua (Deut 34:9), Gideon (Judg 6:34), and Samson (Judg 14:6). If Saul had been a man of passivity and inaction, we might assume that he would become a man of initiative and action. But did he?

10:7–8 TWO COMMANDMENTS: DEMONSTRATION AND CONFIRMATION

Verses 7–8 record Samuel's first command to King Saul. The three signs were intended to prepare Samuel emotionally and spiritually for this initial command. But Samuel's command poses many difficulties to interpreters. First, verses 7 and 8 seem to contradict one another. In verse 7, Samuel charged Saul to "do what your hand finds to do, for God is with you." In verse 8, however, Samuel charged Saul to "go down ahead of me to Gilgal . . . you must wait seven days until I come to you and tell you what you are to do." Second, we do not have any record of how those two commandments were carried out, if ever. One may point to 1 Samuel 13:8 as a record – Saul "waited seven days, the time appointed by Saul," but this instance has nothing to do with the two verses in question, because the event in 1 Samuel 13 happened several years after the official installation of Saul as king. This makes Samuel's command in verses 7–8 hang mysteriously unfulfilled. Although some scholars take these inconsistencies in the narrative as a sign of haphazard compilation from different sources, my view is that the final text constitutes a coherent and flowing narrative about Saul's accession to kingship. In order to read Saul's story as a consistent whole, we need to digress for a moment to discuss the process by which kings in early Israel came to power based on the narrator's presentation of this process.

---

the king's house. The open space under the pomegranate tree essentially functioned as Saul's "Oval Office" (see 14:2).

It has been argued that the process by which a man of humble origin came to power seems to have entailed three stages: designation, demonstration, and confirmation.[6] First, an individual should be "designated" as king by God. Second, the designee should "demonstrate" his divine calling through his prowess on the battlefield. Third, the designee should be "confirmed" in royal office officially through an installation ceremony.[7] Those who are called into ministry may relate to this three-stage process. Their calling by the Holy Spirit, which is usually a personal experience and so may be dubbed a "subjective calling," does not enable them to minister immediately. Rather, this subjective calling must be demonstrated in mission fields. The power of God must be manifested through their ministry so that lives are saved. Finally, the minister must be ordained officially by proper ecclesiastical authorities. Only after completing this three-stage process can someone be truly "called" to the ministry. We can say the same thing about Saul, a Benjamite farmer. He was designated as king of Israel when the prophet Samuel poured oil upon his head. But this "subjective" anointing did not make him the king automatically. There remained two more stages. First, Saul had to demonstrate his divine calling as king in battle. Once he did that, he had to be "confirmed" in kingship during an official ceremony. Who would be more qualified to guide Saul through this process than Samuel? His command in verses 7 and 8 concerned the additional two steps that Saul had to take before he could ascend to the throne.

To solve the problem of inconsistency, we need to assume that Samuel's command in verses 7–8 constituted a two-part command, with the second part to go into effect only after the first part was fulfilled.[8] From this, we may argue that the first part of the prophet's command (v. 7) related to Saul's demonstration of his calling through his prowess in the battlefield; the second part of the command (v. 8) related to Saul's confirmation, his official installation as king.

Regarding the first, Samuel commanded Saul to do "what your hand finds to do" (v. 7). This Hebrew idiom means to do whatever you think is right to do as king. In the context of Samuel's speech (10:1–8), this action must be an attack against the Philistine outpost at Gibeah, Saul's hometown (v. 5). Note that in this verse, Samuel referred to Saul's town as "Gibeah of God," instead of simply Gibeah when he gave Saul the third sign for his assurance. Samuel could have simply said "Gibeah," but he wanted to remind Saul that Gibeah

---

6. Iain Provan, V. Phillip Long, and Tremper Longman III, *A Biblical History of Israel* (Louisville: Westminster/John Knox Press, 2003), 210.
7. Ibid.
8. Ibid.

belonged to God. Further Samuel added a digressive note about a Philistine outpost in Gibeah of God, which was intended to remind Saul that Gibeah was under the oppressive rule of the Philistines. In those days, the Philistines had apparently infiltrated deep into Israelite territory and installed their base for looting operations in Gibeah. It would not be an exaggeration to say that the Israelites had become slaves to the Philistines (see 4:9). Saul had grown up watching all this and must have been frustrated by this humiliating fate for his proud tribe. He was genuinely concerned and regularly prayed for God's intervention. Now, the very God to whom he had prayed had designated him as king of Israel and spoke through his prophet to do whatever he judged was right to do as king. What would have crossed Saul's mind first was undoubtedly an attack of the Philistine post in his hometown. Defeating the Philistines would serve as an effective demonstration of his divine calling as king.

So why didn't Samuel simply say, "Attack the Philistine outpost at Gibeah"? Apparently, he wanted Saul to figure out the Lord's will, based on the wisdom he had acquired through his life experience and rational judgment. This suggests that obeying the Lord involves first understanding God's will and then seeking to live that out in faith.

The second part of Samuel's command would only go into effect if Saul obeyed the first part by defeating the Philistine outpost in Gibeah. Yet Saul's surprise attack would have provoked the Philistines into an all-out war, and so the second part of Samuel's charge responded to this challenge: "Go down ahead of me to Gilgal. I will surely come down to you to sacrifice burnt offerings and fellowship offerings, but you must wait seven days until I come to you and tell you what you are to do" (v. 8). At this point, Samuel would not only officiate Saul's installation with proper sacrifices – thereby fulfilling the confirmation stage – but he would also tell Saul how to vanquish the Philistines out of Israel permanently. Understood in this way, verses 7 and 8 are not contradictory, but rather constitute two parts of the initial command that Samuel gave to King Saul. Unfortunately, Saul failed to obey the first part of Samuel's command, and therefore the second part of the command could never transpire.

10:9–16 SAUL'S FIRST FAILURE TO OBEY

The narrator skips the first two signs that Samuel predicted would happen and devotes verses 10–13 to describing in detail how the third sign was fulfilled in Gibeah. Further he does not explain how Saul responded to Samuel's first command. To some scholars, this may be evidence for the careless compilation of different sources, but it seems more likely that the narrator intentionally omits this information to communicate a theological message. First we will discuss the narrator's silence about how Saul responded to Samuel's two-part command. Next we will discuss the narrator's purpose in giving prominence to the third sign in describing how Samuel's three signs were fulfilled on Saul's way home.

Regarding the first point, the narrator does not explain how Saul respond-ed to Samuel's command because Saul failed to obey the first part of Samuel's command, which effectively eliminated the opportunity to obey the second part. Saul's disobedience is jarring because he should have had faith in God after seeing all three signs be fulfilled exactly as Samuel had predicted. He should have carried out Samuel's command against all odds, but he did not attack the Philistine outpost at his hometown. The one-night, two-day retreat with Samuel, which culminated in the anointing ceremony, kindled Saul's heart for the nation, and the fulfillment of the three signs assured Saul of his divine calling, but the grim reality outside the holy city of Ramah dampened the Spirit's empowering fires within Saul. Despite the epoch-making event at Ramah, the world apparently remained the same to Saul, still too big for him to take on. Thus his knees weakened, his faith left him, and he failed to obey the Lord's command through Samuel. Had Saul taken a leap of faith and at-tacked the Philistines, he would have experienced a miraculous victory. But the Philistine outpost looked greater in his eyes than the Lord, who had anointed him as king. Saul's failure to obey is made clear by his reaction to his uncle's request, "Tell me what Samuel said to you" (v. 15). Yet rather than telling his uncle about his anointing as king of Israel or Samuel's command to attack the Philistine outpost in Gibeah, Saul talked only about the donkeys. Saul's uncle was the father of Abner, the future commander of Saul's army, who may have been a local warlord with a private army. Had Saul intended to attack the Philistines, his uncle was the first man Saul should have asked for help. But Saul pretended as if nothing significant had happened during his journey.

Regarding the second question raised above, the narrator skips over Samuel's first two signs and then devotes three verses to the third sign about Saul's spirit-filled prophecy:

> When he and his servant arrived at Gibeah, a procession of prophets met him; *the Spirit of God came powerfully upon him, and he joined in their prophesying.* When all those who had for-merly known him saw him prophesying with the prophets, they

asked each other, "What is this that has happened to the son of Kish? *Is Saul also among the prophets?*" A man who lived there answered, "And who is their father?" So it became a saying: *Is Saul also among the prophets?* (vv. 10–12, emphasis added)

There are positive connotations in the narrator's note about the Spirit of the Lord coming powerfully upon Saul, which recalls the endowment of divine gifts to great political or military leaders in ancient Israel, such as Moses (Num 11:29), Joshua (Deut 34:9), Gideon (Judg 6:34), Samson (Judg 14:6), and David (1 Sam 16:13). The literary connotation here is that Saul will also deliver the people of Israel from the hand of foreign oppressors. But we soon realize that the spirit falling upon Saul is more closely tied with his prophesying than with his gifts as a warrior king. The narrator tries to connect the origin of the popular saying, "Is Saul also among the prophets," to this first outpouring of the Spirit on Saul. As a result, Saul's role as a prophet becomes dominant in this section of the narrative. The question is whether the narrator intended the image of Saul as a prophet as something good for Saul. To answer this question, it is important to note that one salient feature in the Israelite ideology of kingship is the division of roles between king and prophet. The role of the prophet is an independent institution set up by God to ensure that the Israelite kings listen to the True King in heaven. Unlike pagan kings, an Israelite king should not attempt to manipulate prophets at whim, nor should he shut them down by force. In general, pagan prophets or diviners spoke only what their king wanted to hear because they were on his payroll. But Israelite prophets were messengers of God, directly reporting to the Lord. They were the Lord's hire, not the king's. One may even argue that God allowed a human king in Israel only on the condition that he listened to the prophet. The repeated motif of Saul prophesying seems to fly in the face of such a division of the roles in an Israelite monarchy. It also bodes ill for Saul's career as king. This is confirmed by the fact that later incidences of Saul's prophesying occur always in a negative context. When possessed by the evil spirit, Saul prophesied (see 18:10). Also, when he went to Ramah to capture David, he was overpowered by the spirit and prophesied against his will (19:23). In prophetic ecstasy, he fell on the ground and stripped off his royal clothes (19:24).

Recently, more scholars consider Saul's rejection unfair.[9] What wrong did Saul commit to deserve such damnation? In their estimation, David committed

9. See Steve B. Chapman, *1 Samuel as Christian Scripture: A Theological Commentary* (Grand Rapids, MI: Eerdmans, 2016), 123.

more serious crimes than Saul. Yet David was promised an eternal dynasty, not Saul. We have to remember that disobedience was no small matter in choosing the king of Israel. A king of Israel may have had many shortcomings, but he could still remain on the throne. But when he failed to obey the Lord, he could not remain king. This absolute demand of obedience for kings of Israel is owing to Israel's unique ideology of kingship. The king of Israel was a vassal to the Lord who ruled the Lord's people on the Lord's behalf. This required the king to rule in obedience to the Lord's words as delivered by his prophet. Samuel's first command to Saul was designed to test his suitability as king of Israel, a king unlike those of other nations. Saul's failure to obey the prophetic command cannot be overstated, as it demonstrated his fundamental inaptitude for the position of king of Israel. As we will see, by repeating this same error over and over again, Saul proved himself unsuitable to rule over Israel as a vassal of the True King.

1 SAMUEL 10:17–11:15

SECOND CYCLE OF INSTITUTION

OF KINGSHIP

King Saul failed to obey Samuel's command to deliver Gibeah from the hand of the Philistines because the towering outpost of the Philistines may have seemed bigger to him than the prophet's words. Like all of us, Saul succumbed to the intimidating appearance of the godless world. Yet God gave him a second chance. He brought him out of his hiding place and declared him as king of Israel anew. What a grace! From this place of confirmation, Saul went on to achieve a stunning victory against the Ammonites and delivered his people from humiliating oppression. Further he extended forgiveness to those who had opposed his kingship, just as he had been forgiven by God. In this episode, Saul had his moment to shine, but it began with God's willingness to give him another chance. Some people say, "Fortune knocks three times at everyone's door," which is often interpreted to mean that we only have a limited number of chances after a certain number of failures. But the grace of our Lord has no end, for he is a God of innumerable chances.

10:17–19 SAMUEL'S SPEECH AT MIZPAH

Samuel called the people of Israel together at Mizpah (v. 17). At the previous gathering at Mizpah, God's kingship had been affirmed through the agency of Judge Samuel (see 7:8), but at this gathering Samuel called the Israelites together so that God could give them a human king because they had rejected God as king. Speaking through Samuel, the Lord reminded the Israelites of their redemptive history as a people. Since the Exodus, the Lord had continually delivered Israel out of all the kingdoms that had oppressed them (v. 18). In other words, the direct rule of the Lord had ensured Israel's well-being.

Then Samuel rebuked Israel's demand for a human ruler as an ungrateful act of treason (v. 19). Although Samuel spoke on behalf of God, he took their rejection personally as well. He had been ministering faithfully to the people of Israel for the past twenty years and after all those years of hard work and service, he received a demand for his replacement rather than appreciation. He must have felt betrayed and heartbroken.

To select a human king, Samuel employed a process of elimination that recalls the way in which Joshua ferreted out a criminal among the Israelite community (see Josh 7:14–18). This intimates that the Israelites were being given a human king as punishment for rejecting God as their divine king. This makes Samuel's rebuke of Israel's sin before casting lots even more appropriate.

Nevertheless, obeying the Lord's command (see 8:22), Samuel designated Saul as king of Israel again, thus launching a new cycle of designation, demonstration, and confirmation for kingship in Israel. In contrast to Saul's previous secret designation by anointing with oil, this designation was public, for Samuel told the people, "So now present yourselves before the Lord by your tribes and clans" (v. 19).

10:20–27 SAUL DESIGNATED AS KING AGAIN

Samuel cast lots to choose the king through a process of elimination. From twelve tribes, the tribe of Benjamin was taken by lot. From the Benjamite clans, Matri's clan was taken. Finally, from the men of Matri's clan, Saul was taken. Although the word "by lot" (v. 20) does not appear in the Hebrew text, the context makes it clear that Samuel casts lots to identify "God's chosen one" (see v. 24) among the Israelites. Unfortunately, the exact mechanism for casting lots is not known. But the Hebrew word *hilāqēd* ("taken by lot"), which is rendered literally as "was captured," is used here as in Joshua 7:14, where the same word is used for ferreting out a criminal among the Israelites. The author appears to frame the scene of choosing the Israelite king in terms that strongly recall the scene of hunting down a criminal, which intimates that their demand for a human king was sinful and that Saul, who was chosen by lot, was also a sinner because he failed to obey Samuel's command to demonstrate his calling as king by attacking the garrison of the Philistines at Gibeah.

Meanwhile, Saul might have wanted to avoid a confrontation with Samuel, because he did not show up at the general assembly. So when the lot fell to Saul, he was hiding himself among the supplies, and Samuel had to send people to find him. By hiding himself among the supplies, it seems clear that Saul was trying to run away from his divine calling. He might have thought that being king was beyond his capabilities, for he had already failed once. We do not know whether he wanted a second chance, but God gave him one! God does not want a sinner to perish but to repent and be saved. When Saul stood face-to-face before Samuel once again, he knew very clearly that he had been chosen by God to be king over Israel. Saul was given a second chance, and every Israelite witnessed his confirmation. He could no longer run away from his calling.

In the eyes of the public, Saul was an ideal candidate for king. He was not only "a head taller than any of the others" (v. 23) but he also had good character traits, including filial piety, humility, compassion for the people, and tolerance for those who opposed him. No wonder Samuel said, "There is no one like him among the people" (v. 24). Further, Saul was chosen by God (v. 24). As an ancient Chinese proverb says, "Heaven picks king." Without proof of divine favor, Saul could not have claimed kingship.

Having said this, however, Samuel's words about Saul being the chosen one of God must be read with caution – both because they were spoken in the context of presenting King Saul to the Israelites and also because Saul was only named king in response to the people's request. In a sense, Saul was the embodiment of the people's desire for a better life – namely, the prosperity of neighboring kingdoms. So when the people shouted, "Long live the king!" (v. 24), Samuel replied by explaining the rights and duties of kingship (v. 25) – as he did in 8:11–17 – which were mostly negative. He wrote these rights and duties down in a scroll and deposited it in a sanctuary as if it were a contract between God and the people regarding Saul's kingship.

This event signaled a big change – and much controversy – for the Israelites had never had a king before. Though the elders demanded a king, the people must have had conflicting opinions. The narrator notes that there were "some scoundrels" who despised Saul and brought him no gifts (v. 27). He also mentions "valiant men whose hearts God had touched" who supported Saul's kingship (v. 26). These valiant men accompanied Saul to his home in Gibeah and, one may assume, served as Saul's bodyguards. In the midst of this conflict, Saul did not harm those who opposed him. Although one could argue that Saul's tolerance was politically calculated, it might not have been necessarily so. One could also argue that Saul made sincere efforts to embrace them as his people, because he was also given a second chance by a gracious God.

11:1–3 NAHASH ATTACKS JABESH-GILEAD

Once designated as king, Saul had to demonstrate his worthiness through a military feat, and Nahash's attack on Jabesh-Gilead gave Saul such an opportunity. Saul gathered an army from every Israelite tribe, defeated Nahash king of Ammon, and delivered the people of Jabesh. By so doing, Saul demonstrated his calling as king of Israel. Soon after the victory, Samuel officiated sacrifices for Saul's installation at Gilgal and confirmed Saul into the royal office. Thus Saul successfully completed the three-stage process for ascending to the throne after failing in his first attempt.

The story of Saul's victory over the Ammonites began with Nahash the Ammonite king besieging Jabesh in Gilead.[1] Gilead refers to the Transjordan area between the Jordan and the city of Amman, covering forty kilometers from east to west and 160 kilometers from north to south. This area boasted of fertile soil that made farming a profitable industry. More noteworthy, however, the King's Highway went through this area. The King's Highway ran from the Gulf of Akiba to Damascus and was one of the two major roads in Palestine that connected Mesopotamia to Greece and Africa. Nahash oversaw a stretch of this highway and made a fortune by providing paid conveniences to travelers. His hostility against the Israelites in Gilead may have had something to do with their looting merchants who traveled the King's Highway under Ammonite control (see Judg 5:6). This explains why Nahash wanted to gouge out the right eye of every Israelite man (v. 2). Nahash's intention was not to annihilate the Israelites, but to incapacitate them from looting merchants any more. The Israelites might have continued to live as shepherds or as farmers without their right eyes, but the loss of the right eye would have put them to great disadvantage on the battlefield, since one cannot aim correctly with one eye. Further, since losing one's ability to fight was as humiliating as losing one's sexual organ, Nahash could have "killed two birds with one stone," so to speak. By gouging out the right eye of every Israelite, he could also bring disgrace on all of Israel (v. 2).

When the elders of Jabesh proposed a peace treaty, Nahash rejected it because he was determined to gouge out the right eye of every Israelite man. Left with no alternative, the elders requested a period of seven days so that they could enlist help from their compatriots on the other side of the Jordan. If they failed, they would surrender themselves to the hand of Nahash king of Ammon (v. 3).

Nahash granted their request and gave them seven days. Why did he give them the opportunity to get help from other Israelites? He may have reasoned that it was a sure way to bring disgrace upon all Israel – not just the people of Jabesh – because Israel was known as a divided country. If the Israelites on the other side of the Jordan refused to help their brothers in Jabesh-Gilead,

---

1. According to LXX and the Dead Sea Scrolls, about one month after Saul was chosen as king at Mizpah, Nahash king of Ammon threatened to gouge out the right eye of every Israelite man in Gilead. Seven thousand Israelite men escaped and took refuge in the city of Jabesh.

whether out of fear or lack of love, that would bring disgrace on the whole nation of Israel known as a people chosen by God. Even if they came to rescue their beleaguered brothers in Jabesh, Nahash king of Ammon was confident that his professional army could deal with a ragtag band of amateur soldiers. Further, by defeating the combined forces of the Israelite tribes, he could bring all Israel under his rule. In either case, there was nothing for Nahash to lose.

But Nahash did not take into consideration the fact that Israel now had a king. Under the leadership of judges, getting the tribes to agree on a common agenda was a time-consuming, complicated, and often unsuccessful process. A judge's call for war was often ignored because tribes were under no legal obligation to respond to the call. On the contrary, kings could impose forceful punishment on those who did not answer a call for war. The people could not disobey the king's call to arms without risking their own lives. Thus the tribes became more united under a king. Saul, recently designated as king, wanted to demonstrate his ability, and so he raised an army to deliver his brothers in Jabesh-Gilead from the Ammonites. He was willing to use force, if necessary, against any people who refused to follow him into battle. Nahash king of Ammon did not factor King Saul into his formula for success.

11:4–8 SAUL'S CALL FOR WAR

When the messengers came to Gibeah, Saul's hometown, and reported the matter in the ears of the people of Gibeah, they all wept aloud (v. 4). The messengers were sent to Gibeah to plead for help because Gibeah was the royal city of Israel. But even more significantly, the people of Jabesh-Gilead had maintained a good relationship with the people of Gibeah. When all the other tribes of Israel had gone to war against the tribe of Benjamin for the atrocity committed by the people of Gibeah against a Levite's concubine from Ephraim (Judg 19:1–21), Jabesh-Gilead refused to join forces with the other tribes in their retaliatory war against the Benjamite people in Gibeah. Further, the people of Jabesh-Gilead, including women and children, were killed as a punishment for failing to go to war against Gibeah. Only four hundred virgin daughters of Jabesh-Gilead were spared and given in marriage to the Benjamites who survived the civil war (Judg 21:1–14). Thus, had it not been for Jabesh-Gilead, the Benjamites in Gibeah would have gone extinct. Now it was Gibeah's turn to return the favor to Jabesh.

For Saul, this plea for help from Jabesh-Gilead provided a second opportunity for him to demonstrate his worthiness as the Lord's anointed. He had already failed at his first opportunity, but he would not repeat the same mistake. In contrast to his secret anointing at Ramah, Samuel declared Saul as the king chosen by God in the assembly of all Israel at Mizpah. Everyone knew that Saul was the chosen king, and so he had to behave as a king. The eyes of the Israelites were on Saul, who must demonstrate his divine calling as king in this war against the Ammonites.

Interestingly, verse 5 notes that Saul was on his way home from the field when he noticed commotion among his people. It appears that Saul was plowing the field like an ordinary farmer, though he had been designated as king just one month before, and "men of valor" had accompanied him to Gibeah as bodyguards. So how do we explain the fact that Saul still tilled his land? Although some scholars argue that this story was originally an independent story about Saul's rise to the throne with nothing to do with similar stories in chapters 9–10,[2] it can also be read as a harmonious sequel to the previous stories. As the saying goes, "Rome was not built in a day," and it takes generations for a group of tribes to organize themselves into a bureaucratic kingdom. Though Israel had just received her king about a month earlier, he had not been officially installed. The assembly at Mizpah designated Saul as a king, but he was not coronated there. There was no system of administration in place to run the state, and so the institution of kingship did not affect people's lives – including Saul – until an external threat appeared. Having said that, one must also note that agriculture was the most important industry for urbanization, so any king would have done everything in his power to encourage it. Farming was worthy of royal attention, which is why Korean kings also engaged in agricultural labor in their small rice fields within the palace.

But when foreign enemies invaded, kings dropped the plough and picked up weapons. When Saul heard about what the Ammonites had done to Jabesh, he "took a pair of oxen, cut them into pieces and sent the pieces by messengers throughout Israel, proclaiming, 'This is what will be done to the oxen of anyone who does not follow Saul and Samuel'" (v. 7).[3] Unlike judges, King Saul resorted to violence to round up his army, threatening the people of Israel into obeying his command to arms. Sending parts of a carcass around towns in the nation was a well-known strategy for instilling fear in the people's mind.

---

2. See J. Kugel, *How to Read the Bible: A Guide to Scripture Then and Now* (New York: Free Press, 2007), 443–447.

3. The way Saul terrorized the people into obedience recalls the crime committed by the people of Gibeah (see Judg 19:1–21). The narrator makes the connection explicit by calling the town "Gibeah of Saul" (v. 4).

Zimri-Lim king of Mari (1779–1745) is said to have recruited an army by sending a decapitated head on a tour of his cities. Though the Israelite tribes had been able to reject the judge's call for war and get away with it, disobeying Saul's command would cost them their oxen, which were very expensive.[4] As the narrator notes, a great terror ("the terror of the LORD," NIV) came upon the people, and they all marshaled at Bezek,[5] as many as 330,000. The narrator divides the number into 300,000 men from Israel and 30,000 from Judah (v. 8), a ratio that approximately reflects ten northern tribes to one southern tribe. The point was that all the Israelite tribes were united under Saul's leadership to go to war against foreign oppressors, which was unprecedented.

Saul's positive character traits are apparent in this passage. First, Saul proved himself to be a man of compassion and initiative when he sacrificed his two oxen to save his troubled compatriots on the other side of the Jordan. Second, Saul was a man of the Spirit. The narrator connects Saul's dismembering the oxen with a prompting of the Spirit. Although sending body parts on tour was a method of rounding up an army that was not uncommon in the ancient Near East, the narrator articulates that Saul did it while carried away with the Spirit. Interesting to note in this regard is that the phrase "the terror of the LORD" in verse 7 may simply be an idiom for great terror, but the narrator used it to demonstrate the Lord's powerful presence with King Saul. This is corroborated by the fact that Saul positioned Samuel next to himself in his recruitment speech: "This is what will be done to the oxen of anyone who does not follow Saul and *Samuel*" (v. 7, italics added). This implies that Samuel the prophet had been with Saul in his decision-making since he returned to Gibeah as the designated king of Israel.

---

4. Although it is very difficult to know the exact value of an ox in those days, one may safely assume that it was very expensive. According to one Mari letter (ca. 1800–1750 BCE), only a few villages, with no mention of individuals, owned oxen for plowing. Most villages had to rent them from the central government.

5. The modern location of Bezek is not certain. One hint for its approximate location is that Saul was able to move his army from there to Jabesh-Gilead overnight. It may be argued that Bezek was located somewhere on the way from Gibeah to the Jordan valley, twenty to thirty kilometers away from Jabesh. Thus scholars note Khirbet Ibzik as a promising candidate for the biblical Bezek. See Adam Zertal, "Bezek" in *ABD*, 718.

11:9–11 SAUL DEFEATS NAHASH KING OF AMMON: "DEMONSTRATION"

Having mustered an army at Bezek, Saul sent the messengers back to Jabesh-Gilead with a message: "By the time the sun is hot tomorrow, you will be rescued" (v. 9). The people of Jabesh, encouraged by Saul's message, played their part and lied to the Ammonites: "Tomorrow we will surrender to you" (v. 10). By so doing, they tried to keep the Ammonites off guard until Saul launched a surprise attack. In this sense, one may discern a double meaning in their words, "Tomorrow, we will surrender to you." The Hebrew original is rendered literally, "Tomorrow, we will go out to you," which could easily be interpreted as, "We will attack you," because the Hebrew *yatsa'*, "to go out," may connote going out either for capitulation or attack.

While the people of Jabesh-Gilead deceived Nahash, Saul's army moved stealthily overnight in order to attack the unsuspecting king of Ammon. Upon arriving at the scene, Saul divided his army into three companies and then attacked the Ammonite camp's front and flank simultaneously. Taken by surprise, the Ammonite soldiers were not able to fight back effectively. Saul's army continued to slaughter the Ammonites until noon. Those who survived ran for their lives. The narrator gives a hyperbolic touch to this scene by adding "no two of them were left together" (v. 11).

11:12–15 SAUL OFFICIALLY BECOMES KING OF ISRAEL: "CONFIRMATION"

Elated by Saul's victory, his supporters suggested that the scoundrels who had failed to recognize Saul as king by bringing him gifts should be purged (v. 12). Curiously, they brought this matter to the prophet Samuel rather than King Saul. They might have been threatening Samuel or testing his loyalty by pushing him to punish the scoundrels, since Samuel had been strongly opposed to the kingship at first. But Saul intervened and resolved the tension by granting political pardon to those who had been charged with treason (v. 13) and ascribing all the glory for the victory to the Lord (v. 13). This accentuates Saul's virtuous traits, for he not only had compassion on his people in need, but he also forgave those who had opposed him. This may be derived from his experience of being forgiven and given a second chance by the Lord. In any case, he demonstrated his worthiness as king and his right to rule. One may even argue that this initial period of his reign was the highest point in

Saul's royal career. For in this scene, the narrator portrays Saul in more heroic, virtuous, and pious terms than he does anywhere else.

At last, Saul could be officially installed as king at Gilgal. The prophet Samuel took initiative in confirming Saul into the royal office by saying, "Come, let us go to Gilgal and there renew the kingship" (v. 14). Responding to the prophet's call, all Israel gathered to watch the birth of monarchy in Israel. When the ceremony reached its climax with fellowship offerings, all those who gathered, including Saul, "had a great celebration" (v. 15). And on this happy note, the chapter ends.

Although Saul successfully demonstrated his divine calling as king by defeating the Ammonites and then the prophet Samuel confirmed his kingship before the Lord and all Israel, the three-staged process to the throne was not ideal in terms of the broader perspective of the narrative. First, the main threat to Israel's security was the Philistines, and God specified that the king's job was to deliver the Israelites from the hand of the Philistines (see 9:16). Samuel's first command to King Saul in 10:7 is best understood in terms of this Philistine threat, and so one may argue that Saul's victory against the Ammonites did not fully demonstrate his ability to be king of Israel.

Second, during the confirmation at Gilgal in verse 15, Saul and all the Israelites rejoiced, but Samuel is not mentioned. Rather, the people "went" to Gilgal, "made" Saul king, "sacrificed" the fellowship offering, and "had a great celebration" (v. 15). Samuel's absence in this scene can be contrasted with his presence in Saul's call for war (v. 7). Saul mentioned Samuel's name while rounding up an army, where the prophet's role was not clear at all, but Samuel's name was missing during the enthronement ceremony when his role was crucial. This implies that the prophet gave only tacit support for Saul's enthronement, even though he was physically present, officiating the ceremony. This is yet another ominous foreshadowing for King Saul's future.[6]

---

6. For more details on the three-staged process of Saul's rise to kingship, see Provan, Long, and Longman III, *A Biblical History of Israel*, 211–215.

1 SAMUEL 12:1–25

SAMUEL'S GILGAL SPEECH

Chapter 12 is known as Samuel's farewell speech, but this title is misleading for several reasons. First, Samuel did not say goodbye to the people in chapter 12. His speech had two purposes: to accuse the people of requesting a king when the Lord was their king and to show them the way forward now that they had a king. Samuel urged the Israelites and their new king to fear and obey the Lord or else they would perish. Second, Samuel did not declare his retirement but redefined his role in Israel's community. From here on, he told the people that he would focus on praying for them and teaching them "the way that is good and right" (see v. 23). Third, Samuel does not disappear from the narrative, but appears again in chapters 13, 15, 16, 19, and so on, where we see him executing his prophetic role of pronouncing divine judgment on Saul. In fact, he made his presence felt to Saul even after his death (see ch. 28). Chapter 12, however, describes the most critical turning point in Samuel's career, when he yielded his political leadership to King Saul, whose enthronement ceremony he officiated at Gilgal. From here on, King Saul rather than Judge Samuel ruled Israel, officially ending the period of the judges.

12:1–2 SAMUEL DECLARES THE INAUGURATION OF THE KINGDOM

Samuel's speech was delivered during Saul's enthronement ceremony at Gilgal, which is indicated by the clause that Samuel "said to all people" (v. 1). Since there is no textual hint for a change in time or place, one may assume that Samuel's speech in chapter 12 was delivered to those who had gathered in Gilgal to celebrate the official inauguration of King Saul (see 11:14–15). To be more specific, Samuel may have begun his speech right after the loud cheering of the crowd naturally tapered off (see 11:15). Samuel's absence in that cheering crowd anticipates the generally negative tone of his speech.

Samuel began his speech by declaring the transfer of his power to Saul: "Behold, the king walks before you . . . I have walked before you from my youth until this day" (v. 2, my translation).[1] These words are performative,

---

1. "Now you have a king as your leader . . . I have been your leader from my youth until this day" (v. 2, NIV).

like those of a judge in a wedding ceremony. By uttering those words, Samuel inaugurated the kingdom in Israel – another sign that Samuel's speech was delivered to the cheering crowds gathered at Gilgal to celebrate Saul's inauguration. Further, Samuel makes it very clear that he installed King Saul at the demand of the people: "I have listened to everything you said to me and have set a king over you" (v. 1). These words imply that Saul was not the king that God had originally planned to give to the people of Israel, but was conceded because of their demands. Because Saul was the king that the people had asked for and chosen for themselves,[2] Saul's kingship was the embodiment of their desire to become like other nations by having a god-like king.

Regarding the idiom *hithalek lipney,* "(for a king) to walk before (the people)," some scholars connect this to the act of a military general leading his army in and out of a city gate. But the Hebrew *hithalek,* "to walk," may apply to all areas of human activity, not only military action. The phrase "(for a leader) to walk before (the people)" may denote the general actions of the head of the state. The NIV's translation, "Now you have a king as your leader," reflects this meaning. Further, by using this idiom to refer to the general actions of the head of state, the narrator underscores that the king of Israel should be a shepherd king who will be held accountable by the people for his acts. Numbers 27:16–17 says that "a man over the congregation . . . shall go out before them and come in before them, who shall lead them out and bring them in, that the congregation of the Lord may not be as sheep that have no shepherd." Here the idea of walking before the people is connected to shepherding a flock. The king of Israel should imitate a good shepherd, who abandons his life to save his sheep from the claws of wild beasts.

12:3–5 SAMUEL ADVOCATES HIS INNOCENCE

Having declared the inauguration of a kingdom in Israel, Samuel advocated his innocence – and possibly his sons' innocence[3] – before reviewing Israel's history of redemption. Under the judgeship of Samuel's family, he argued, no

---

2. Note that the subject of all verbs in 11:15 is "the people": they "went . . . made Saul king . . . sacrificed fellowship offerings . . . held a great celebration."

3. The phrase, "my sons are with you" (v. 2), appears in the context of Samuel's defense of his own rule and the institution of judges. But it is puzzling because Samuel's two sons were known to pervert justice by taking bribes (8:3). Why then did Samuel mention his two sons in defending the rule by judges? Although some scholars attribute this to Samuel's old age, it is more plausible to postulate that Samuel did not regard his two sons' misbehavior so serious as to abandon the institution of judges in favor of a monarchy.

one was oppressed or treated unfairly in Israel. He made his point by having the people answer a series of quasi-rhetorical questions. Then he called on the Lord and his "anointed" (v. 3) to bear witness to the people's admission that Samuel's rule was just and good.[4] The purpose of Samuel's self-defense was to assert that the inauguration of the kingship was not owing to his moral failures, nor the Lord's failure, but to Israel's ungrateful rebellion against the Lord, who had never failed in his duty as king of Israel.

Samuel's rhetorical questions repeatedly use the verb "to take" (*laqah*) – "Whose ox have I *taken*? Or whose donkey have I *taken*? Whom have I cheated? Whom have I oppressed? From whose hand have I *taken* a bribe to make me shut my eyes?" (v. 3, italics added).[5] These questions echo "the ways of the king" outlined in 8:11–17, which state that a king by profession makes a point of "taking" things from his people, such as silver, fields, time, labor, and so on. By posing these questions in terms that are reminiscent of the demerits of kingship, Samuel differentiated his good judgeship from the potentially oppressive rule of king. The Korean proverb, "The previous *Sato* is better than the newly appointed *Sato*,"[6] which means, "Oldies but Goodies," or, "You don't know what you've got until it's gone," mirrors Samuel's sentiments in this speech.

12:6–13 AN OVERVIEW OF REDEMPTIVE HISTORY

After defending his rule as a judge, Samuel gave a quick survey of Israel's redemptive history from Exodus through the period of Judges to the institution of kingship. There are some hints that suggest his speech was extemporaneous. First, he repeated the story of Moses and Aaron without obvious purpose (vv. 6, 8). Also, he enumerated Israel's enemies in verse 9 and the judges who defeated them in verse 11, but they do not match. Although Moab is mentioned as Israel's enemy in verse 9, Judge Ehud – who defeated Eglon, the Moabite king – is not mentioned in the list of heroic judges in verse 11. Also, verse 9 does not mention Median and Ammon, Israel's enemies during the period of the judges, but verse 11 mentions Gideon and Jephthah, who defeated them.

---

4. "The anointed" no doubt refers to Saul, who had just been declared as king over Israel. Calling Saul by his title rather than his name implies that Samuel's anti-monarchic tirade took place at the enthronement ceremony at Gilgal. Although Saul was the new king of Israel, he had to hear out Samuel's unpleasant and long-winded speech, probably sitting or standing close to the speaker.

5. NIV: "accept a bribe."

6. *Sato* refers to a district magistrate in ancient Korea.

In a manner of speaking, Samuel's speech may be compared to improvized jazz rather than an orchestrated symphony.

This survey of the history of redemption demonstrated that Israel's request for a king was an idolatrous sin, a rebellion against the Lord as king. Samuel made this point by saying that God had never failed to send a deliverer to the troubled Israelites even though they had repeatedly rebelled against God. Whenever they cried out to the Lord for help, he had compassion and saved them. Whether or not they repented sincerely, the Lord was faithful to his covenant and never abandoned his people for the sake of his great name (see v. 22). For instance, God heard the cry of his people in Egypt and chose Moses and Aaron to bring the Israelites out of slavery and settle them in the land flowing with milk and honey. But they "forgot the Lord their god" as soon as their lives became comfortable in settled societies in Canaan, and so he sold them into the hands of various enemies, such as Sisera – the commander of an army of Hazor – the Philistines, and the king of Moab (v. 9). Whenever Israel cried out to the Lord, however, God sent deliverers (Jerub-Baal,[7] Barak, Jephthah, and Samuel) to save them from oppression, and they lived in peace again. Then Samuel asked, why would Israel want to have a human king when Nahash, the king of Ammon, had attacked them? Was Nahash, the king of Ammon any different from the Philistines, the Canaanites, or the Moabites? In fact, the Ammonites may have been the least threatening of all Israel's enemies at that time.

According to Samuel, the threat from Nahash was an excuse to have a king (see 8:1–3). The real reason they had asked for a king was that they desired to become like other nations who had god-like kings. At that time, Israel was an underdeveloped country in the ancient Near East, where the people lived at a subsistence level, scattered throughout the mountains in the central highlands of Canaan. But their pagan neighbors in Egypt, Babylon, and Assyria lived in safety and prosperity, building irrigation canals, palaces, public buildings, theaters, stadiums, libraries, and temples. Stores in their markets were full of exotic goods. Their strong armies regularly went on expeditions to bring in timber, exotic animals, gold, slaves, and so on. What made them so prosperous was the king, who was regarded as divine. Entrusted with absolute power, the king commanded human and material resources to build cities as high as his pride. From the desire to become rich and prosperous like their neighbors,

7. Literally, this means, "Let Baal contend with him," which was another name for Gideon. For the origin of this name, see Judges 6:25–31.

the people of Israel made excuses to have a god-like king, although it meant rejecting the Lord as their king. But Samuel saw through the people's sinful desire and accused them of rebelling against their Lord. He would have rejected their request for a king, but it was God's will to concede to their desire for a king. Even though God had allowed them to have a king, their request was not righteous, for they had rejected the Lord as their king. Saul, whom the Lord allowed to rule over them, is characterized by Samuel as "the king you have chosen, the one you asked for" (v. 13). This description is a foil for "the king the LORD has chosen" or "the king after God's heart." In a sense, Saul's kingship was the embodiment of the people's desire to declare independence from the Lord.

12:14–15 CONDITION FOR COEXISTENCE OF HUMAN AND DIVINE KINGS

We have seen that Samuel preferred the divine rule of judges over the rule of human kings, but here he revealed how divine and human kings could coexist in Israel. To be more precise, Samuel taught that the Lord would allow a human king and his people to remain under God's protective rule and last long in *shalom* if – and only if – they "fear the LORD and serve and obey him and do not rebel against his commands" (v. 14). This point is made clearer when we read the second half of verse 14 as the main clause of a conditional sentence, as in the following translation: "*If* you [the people] fear the LORD . . . and do not rebel against his commands, *then* both you and the king . . . will remain under the rule of the LORD your God" (my translation). The NIV places the word "good!" at the end of verse 14, but this is not in the original, although the NIV adds it for good reason. In biblical Hebrew, there is no syntactic marker – no Hebrew equivalent to the English construction, "if . . . then . . ." – to distinguish the clause that expresses the condition from the main clause of a conditional sentence. Both are expressed as the Hebrew *waw*. Since the context is the only way to interpret a conditional sentence, ambiguity may occur. Verse 14 has such ambiguity. The NIV assumes that there is no main clause expressing result in verse 14, and so they supplied "good" to finish the thought. But there is a possibility that the second half of verse 14 may serve as the main clause, which can be translated literally as, "You, as well as your king who reigns over you, are after the LORD your God." The idiom, "Be after someone," sometimes refers to the king-subject relationship. For instance, 2 Samuel 2:10 reads, "Ish-Bosheth son of Saul was forty years old when he became king over Israel, and he reigned two years. The tribe of Judah, however, *was after David*." Here Ish-Bosheth's kingship over Israel is contrasted with David's kingship over Judah, the latter of which is couched in the idiom "be after someone."[8] If this interpretation holds (see my translation of v. 14 above), then verse 14 clearly presents the condition – fearing and obeying the Lord – upon which the divine king allows a human king and his people to remain under his blessing and protection.

Samuel reinforced this message by warning Israel of the divine judgment that her disobedience and rebellion would incur. If Israel did not obey the Lord's command, "his hand will be against" her. Interestingly, Samuel mentioned God's hand being against Israel instead of saying that the Lord would sell them into the hand of the enemy. In the past, the Lord's judging hand had appeared to the Egyptians or the Philistines and was a metaphor for the Lord's judgment of the pagans. But here Samuel mentioned God's hand in the context of divine judgment against Israel, as if to warn Saul and the people that if they did not obey the Lord, the Lord would treat them like pagans and drive them out of his kingdom. As long as Saul and the Israelites obeyed, however, God would remain their king.

12:16–22 THE LORD PLEASED TO MAKE ISRAEL HIS OWN

In this section, Samuel tried to demonstrate through wonders that his message had come from the Lord himself. He told the people that he would call on the Lord on that day, the day of the wheat harvest, to send thunder and rain. Thunder and rain would have been disastrous on that day, as farmers had been working hard throughout the year, looking forward to this day of harvest. Wheat fields, like other grain fields, need good sun as harvest approaches, because the grain inside the husk becomes full and ripe during the short period right before harvest. Thunder and rain during the harvest season significantly reduce the amount and quality of the grain, squandering farmers' year-round efforts. Samuel's sign in nature was, therefore, an object lesson about divine judgment to the Israelites, who had rebelled against the Lord's commands. Interesting to note in this regard is that the phrase, "Stand still and see" (v. 16), is an idiom mostly used in the context of the Lord's judgment against the pagans (see Exod 14:13; 2 Chr 20:17). Further, thunder is used as an image of divine judgment several times in 1 Samuel. In Hannah's prayer,

---

8. See also 1 Kings 12:20.

we are told, "the Most High will thunder from heaven; the LORD will judge the ends of the earth" (2:10). When the Philistines approached to attack the worshipping Israelites at Mizpah, God thundered against the Philistines and routed them before the Israelites (7:10).

Then Samuel called upon the Lord, and the Lord sent thunder and rain. Terrified by the thunder and rain, the people confessed their sin of asking for a king and turned to Samuel to ask him to pray for God to have mercy on them. Although they had been justifying their request for a king with various excuses, their hearts were idolatrous (see v. 21), for they had wanted to take off the yoke of God's rule and worship a human king as a god who would make them as rich and prosperous as the people around them. Filled with compassion, Samuel encouraged them not to be afraid. Samuel's compassion toward repentant sinners reflects the heart of the Lord. When sinners repent, God's heart melts. Samuel also had a shepherd heart, and though he had been betrayed and hurt by the people, he ministered words of comfort to the penitent Israelites: "You have done all this evil; yet do not turn away from the LORD, but serve the LORD with all your heart . . . For the sake of his great name the LORD will not reject his people, because the LORD was pleased to make you his own" (v. 20).

A profound pastoral message is concentrated in these words. Pastors should expect to minister to sinners. People, whether they are saved or not, have sinned, are sinning, and will sin. Many Christians continue to struggle with sin. The first message that Christians need hear is, "yet do not turn away from the LORD!" (12:20). Satan lies to us that we are hopeless and helpless sinners who are unworthy of any purpose in life and estranged from the Lord. But Christians should stick to the Lord no matter what. Sticking together is what covenant is all about. But in order not to sin anymore, we need to love the Lord *with all our heart.* This also means that we should continue to do good works, despite our shortcomings. What enables us to do these good works is the Lord's faithfulness. He put his own reputation on the line and said he would never abandon us. Further, the Lord desires to make us his own people!

Returning to the story of Saul, why is God so concerned about having a human king who obeys? Certainly, God is the true King and a human king is a mere servant. But more profoundly, God wants to make us his own people. God's people are those who obey God. The role of an obedient king is to lead his brothers and sisters into a life of obedience to the Lord. The role of such a king can be compared to that of a womb out of which God's obedient people are born. Only from an obedient king of Israel will there become an obedient people of God. This is the ultimate reason that God keeps looking for a king after his own heart.

12:23–25 SAMUEL'S NEW ROLE

Once Saul officially became king of Israel, Samuel had to redefine his role among the community. Previously, he had played a triple role as judge, priest, and prophet, but now he had to yield his political leadership to King Saul and limit his role in the community to that of a priest praying for a king and the people and a prophet teaching them "the way that is good and right." If King Saul and the people of Israel obeyed the good and right way that Samuel taught, Samuel would pray that the Lord would bless them. But if they rebelled against the good and right way, Samuel would call on the Lord to send judgment against them. In a sense, the role of Samuel continued to be both political and religious. Though this may violate modern sentiments concerning separation of the state and religion, there is nothing in the Bible against Christians who engage the world of politics and economics with the good and right way of the Lord.

Samuel concluded his speech by repeating what he had already said: "Be sure to fear the LORD and serve him faithfully with all your heart; consider what great things he has done for you. Yet if you persist in doing evil, both you and your king will perish" (vv. 24–25; compare vv. 14–15). Though this may sound as if Samuel is belaboring the point, this fundamental truth certainly bears repetition. Israel's faithful walk with God boils down to fearing and obeying the Lord, which should be a voluntary response to the grace he showed to them in the past. Likewise, if we think about what God has done for us, we will want to serve him with all our heart. Samuel's last words during Saul's enthronement ceremony, however, must have been particularly painful to Saul. For rather than congratulating and blessing the new king, Samuel ended his speech by declaring that King Saul would perish if he did not change his ways (v. 25). The fact that Saul's enthronement ceremony ended with Samuel mentioning Saul's doom serves as a subtle foreshadowing of Saul's ultimate failure to establish a dynasty of his own.

1 SAMUEL 13:1–22

SAUL'S SECOND DISOBEDIENCE

Saul officially began his reign at Gilgal, where Samuel offered sacrifices for him and installed him as king of Israel. Chapters 13 through 15 deal with Saul's tenure as king under the aegis of the Lord, the true King of Israel. Most of the text is devoted to narrating two episodes, both of which revolve around Israel's battle against foreign enemies. The narrator's focus, however, is not on Saul's achievements as a military leader, but rather on his failure as the king of Israel to listen to the voice of the Lord as relayed to him through the prophet Samuel. Ironically, Gilgal is where Samuel confirmed Saul into royal office, but it is also where Samuel declared the Lord's rejection of him as king. The narrator put these two events almost back to back, giving the impression that Saul was "fired" as soon as he came into office. It is no coincidence that Samuel's last word to the joyous crowd during Saul's inauguration was "both you and your king will perish" (11:25).

What fault of Saul led Samuel to foretell his doom? Many people point to the fact that Saul overstepped his bounds and took the priestly prerogative to himself by offering sacrifices. Some Korean pastors even use this story as a warning to lay people who might presume to "trespass" their pastor's prerogatives, arguing that David's ethical failures may be forgiven but Saul's violation of priestly prerogatives cannot be forgiven. But the text certainly does not suggest this reading. As we will discuss below, Saul was rejected as king because he failed to obey the Lord's commands through the prophet Samuel.

The episode in this chapter reveals what it means to obey the Lord's command – not through blind obedience nor obedience to the letter of the law, but rather by seeking to know the Lord's will.

13:1–2 SAUL'S REIGN

The narrator of the book of Samuel divides the careers of King Saul and later King David into two periods before and after their accession to the throne, using a regnal formula that gives chronological data, such as their age at the time of accession and the period of their rule. David's regnal formula appears in 2 Samuel 5:4. However, the exact numerical data on Saul's reign, whose regnal formula appears in 1 Samuel 13:1, is lost forever. The Hebrew original may be literally translated as follows: "Saul was X years old when he became king, and he reigned over Israel X-two years" (v. 1, my translation).[1] Thus translators fill in the blank to make sense of the verse. The NIV's "thirty years old" is based on a few manuscripts of the Septuagint, and "forty-two years" is based on Acts 13:21, which ascribe forty years to Saul's reign. But both suggestions are not without a problem. First, if Saul became king at the age of thirty, one cannot explain how Jonathan could become his chief general shortly after Saul's accession as verse 2 implies. For Jonathan to play such a prominent role in Saul's army, he must have been at least twenty years old. This would suggest that Saul had become a father at the age of ten, which is very unlikely. As the Korean Revised Version translates it, forty years would be more proper to Saul's age at the time of accession. If this were the case, Jonathan would have been twenty years old when Saul became king. Second, Acts 13:21 does not specify Saul's reign as lasting for forty years. The Greek text only says "forty years" without the words "who ruled," and "forty years" may include both the period of Samuel and Saul. Thus we don't need to be bound by Acts 13:21 in determining the period of Saul's reign. Considering that David and Jonathan are about ten years apart and David became king at the age of forty (contra NIV "thirty"), we may conclude that Saul ruled over Israel no more than twenty years.[2]

One of the changes that came with the inauguration of the kingdom was a standing army. In the period of the judges, there were no professional soldiers. Whenever foreign enemies invaded, judges would call on farmers and shepherds to bear arms for the country. But then they went back to their homes once the threat was gone. After the battle at Jabesh-Gilead, not all soldiers went back to their homes. Saul selected three thousand men to serve him as professional soldiers. They were stationed in military outposts to reconnoiter and watch important passes for possible enemy attacks. Saul stationed two thousand under his command at Mikmash and Bethel, about ten kilometers north of Mikmash. These are the last bastions protecting the hill country of Benjamin and Judah against Philistine attacks from the north. Jonathan commanded another thousand soldiers at Gibeah of Benjamin. His role may have

---

1. This translation assumes missing numbers, but some scholars would translate this verse more literally as "Saul was (one) year-old when he became king, and he reigned over Israel two years." Iain Provan, V. Philips Long, Tremper Longman III, *A Biblical History of Israel* (Louisville, KY: Westminster/John Knox Press, 2015), 200.
2. Jonathan's younger brother, Ish-Boshet, and David are five years apart, since David was thirty-seven years old when Ish-Boshet died at the age of forty-two (see 2 Sam 2:10; 5:4–5). Since Jonathan was the eldest brother, and there are two or three brothers between Jonathan and Ish-Boshet, we can say that Jonathan and David are at least ten years apart.

been to spy on the enemy's movements at the Philistine outpost (see 10:5). Although Saul vanquished the Ammonites from Jabesh-Gilead, he failed to deliver the Israelites from the Philistine threat. The Philistines had already infiltrated deep inland and installed a military outpost in Saul's hometown at Gibeah to launch raiding parties to plunder villages in Benjamin. Yet Saul did nothing about the Philistine threat until Jonathan took initiative.

13:3–7 JONATHAN ATTACKS THE PHILISTINE OUTPOST AT GIBEAH

Jonathan succeeded where his father failed: "He attacked the Philistine outpost in Geba." Geba is an alternative spelling for Gibeah, Saul's hometown.[3] Jonathan carried out the overdue command that Samuel had given to his father: "Once these signs are fulfilled, do whatever your hand finds to do" (see my commentary on 10:7). This is the first time the narrator introduces Jonathan, Saul's first born, into the narrative. Judging from his role in Saul's army, he must have been at least twenty years old (see my commentary above on vv. 1–2). He appears to have had the wisdom to discern the Lord's will and the faith to obey it – even if it meant yielding the right of succession to David. Even still, he took the initiative in carrying out the overdue attack against the Philistine outpost in Gibeah.

When the Philistines heard that their garrison in Gibeah had been attacked, they retaliated with full force against Saul's army in order to regain their foothold in the hill country of Benjamin. In response, Saul issued a full mobilization order by having the trumpet blown throughout the land. The narrator preserves Saul's speech as it was distributed among all Israel to encourage the people of Israel to bear arms for King Saul: "Let the Hebrews hear. Saul has attacked the Philistine outpost, and now Israel has become obnoxious to the Philistines." This speech was calculated to stir up Israel's anger against the Philistines and to raise their hope for breaking free from Philistine oppression. First, Saul called the Israelites "the Hebrews." Foreigners such as the Philistines mostly used this term to refer to Israel in a pejorative sense. By using a term that recalled their foreign oppression, Saul stirred up the people out of their passive stupor. Second, he deliberately took the credit for attacking the Philistine outpost at Gibeah in order to present himself as a hero king in

---

3. The narrator refers to the town in various ways: Gibeah of God (10:5), Gibeah of Saul (11:14), Gibeah of Benjamin (v. 2), Geba of Benjamin (v. 16 "Gibeah in Benjamin," NIV).

whom the people could place their hope. Third, the idiom "become obnoxious to the Philistines" expresses irreconcilable animosity (see 27:12). The people might have sensed firm confidence in Saul's words as if he were saying, "it is no problem that we have become obnoxious to the Philistines." Encouraged by Saul's speech, the people left their homes to join Saul in Gilgal, which was not only farthest from the Philistine land but also spacious enough to serve as a marshalling area.

Meanwhile, the Philistines camped "at Mikmash, east of Beth Aven." Since Beth Aven, "the house of iniquity," was a nickname for Bethel (see Hos 4:5), one may infer that Saul's two thousand strong army had already abandoned their posts at Bethel and Mikmash and retreated to Gilgal to reorganize themselves for the battle. As for the Philistine army, the narrator uses hyperbole to emphasize the overwhelming power of the Philistines over Saul's army. The Philistines, we are told, had thirty thousand chariots ("three thousand," NIV) and six thousand charioteers, whereas Saul's army had neither chariot nor charioteer. Thirty thousand chariots are an obvious exaggeration. The anti-Assyrian allies of twelve kings could mobilize only five thousand chariots in the battle of Qarqar (853 BC). Thus many scholars correct the number to three thousand following the Septuagint.[4] Also, the Philistine foot soldiers were said to be "as numerous as the sand on the shore" (v. 5), whereas Saul's army dwindled to "about six hundred" (v. 15). This hyperbole reflects the psychology of the Israelites, who were overwhelmingly frightened at the sight of the Philistine army. In the eyes of the panic-stricken Israelites, the Philistines looked not only numerous as the sand on the shore but also as invincible as the descendants of the legendary giant Nephilim.

The intimidating presence of the Philistines at Mikmash made the people of Israel forget Saul's war speech and run for their lives. Some of them hid in "caves and thickets, among the rocks, and in pits and cisterns," while "some Hebrews even crossed the Jordan to the land of Gad and Gilead" (v. 6). By piling up words denoting various hideouts, the narrator underscores their desperation; for instance, they tried to hide in thickets that could barely cover their body. Further, the narrator cynically refers to those who crossed the Jordan to flee as "the Hebrews." Those who made it to Gilgal, however, were also in great fear. Of particular note, the phrase "all the troops *with him* [Saul] were quaking with fear" may also be translated as "all the troops were quaking

---

4. David T. Tsumura, *The First Book of Samuel*, NICOT (Grand Rapids, MI: Eerdmans, 2007), 338.

with fear *after Saul*" (v. 7). In this case, King Saul was no less afraid of the Philistines than before he had become king.

13:8–15 SAUL OFFERS SACRIFICES; SAMUEL REBUKES SAUL

"Saul remained at Gilgal" (v. 7) without moving his troops to the battlefield at the pass of Mikmash while waiting for Samuel to come down to Gilgal to offer sacrifices to the Lord. Offering sacrifices before war was a well-known practice in the ancient Near East, including ancient Israel (see 7:10), both for garnering divine favor in the upcoming battle and for boosting the morale of fighters by giving them meat and drink. Ancient Chinese also gave a feast to their fighters before seeing them off to the battlefield. No wonder Saul ordered his men to bring him the burnt offering to gain divine favor and the fellowship offerings to encourage his fighters. Yet Samuel did not come at the appointed time. Saul could not wait any longer, because his men were losing their will to fight and running away, and so he took the liberty to offer up sacrifices without Samuel. Just as he had finished making the burnt offering – yet before he had offered up the fellowship offerings – Samuel arrived to stop Saul and rebuked him, saying, "What have you done?"

Notice that Saul came out to "greet" Samuel (v. 10). Although he was king of Israel, Saul paid highest respect to his prophet by coming out to greet him. It appears that he undertook to offer sacrifice because he felt he had no other choice – not out of arrogance nor intent to overstep his bounds and violate Samuel's prerogatives. In fact, he himself said, "So I felt compelled to offer the burnt offering" (v. 12). But Samuel rebuked Saul without greeting him. From an Asian perspective, Samuel's act of skipping this formality is unforgivable. In ancient Chinese or Korean court, you may be forgiven for speaking plainly to your king, but you are never forgiven for skipping the formality in approaching your king. Even when you insist on an opinion that is against the king's, the formality reminds everyone in court who is in charge.

In Saul's estimation, Samuel did not have a good reason for skipping the formality in approaching the king. His long defense to Samuel's rebuke conveys this (see vv. 11–12). First, Samuel did not come at the appointed time, which he had set. Saul drove this point home by using the emphatic personal pronoun "you", *atta lo-bata:* "It is you who did not come [at the set time]" (v. 11, my translation). The narrator confirms this point: "he [Saul] waited seven days, the time set by Samuel; but Samuel did not come to Gilgal" (v. 8). In a sense, Saul obeyed Samuel's command to the letter. Second, Saul argued that his action was out of necessity rather than arrogance, for Saul's men were scattering as the Philistines were assembling at Mikmash. Note that Saul couches the verbs "scattering" and "assembling" in the participle form, as if they were still happening at the time of speaking. He also sandwiches his accusation against Samuel between these two simultaneous events. His logic is that he made the difficult but necessary decision to offer up sacrifices without Samuel because further delay would have led to a disaster in the battle against the Philistines.

Samuel, however, did not agree: "You have done a foolish thing" (v. 13). Samuel's accusation was not about the fact that Saul offered up sacrifices without him, for Samuel said nothing about Saul's violation of priestly prerogatives. Rather, Samuel pointed to Saul's failure to obey the Lord's command at both ends of his rebuke: "You have not kept the command the LORD your God gave you . . . you have not kept the LORD's command" (vv. 13–14). So what was the Lord's command that Saul did not obey? Since the narrator does not mention anything of this nature in chapter 13 or since the beginning of Saul's official tenure as king, many people assume that the Lord's command concerns the Mosaic Law, which stipulates that offering up sacrifices is a priestly prerogative. But the Old Testament attests to many other cases when the king "offered up" sacrifices, which suggests that Saul did not violate any priestly prerogative. For instance, David offered up the burnt offerings and fellowship offerings (2 Sam 6:17–18). Solomon also "offered a sacrifice of fellowship offerings to the LORD" (1 Kgs 8:62).[5] But neither David nor Solomon were accused of disobeying the Lords command. There are two reasons for this. First, saying that Saul "offered up" sacrifices does not necessarily mean that Saul made the offering himself, just as the text might say that David "built" his palace, even though David did not actually do any of the manual labor. Second, many other priests other than Samuel would have been willing to officiate sacrifices. For instance, the high priest Ahijah served Saul, wearing an ephod (see 14:3). Thus Samuel accuses Saul for failing to obey the Lord's command – not for overstepping his bounds. In fact, Saul did everything within his power to meet the daunting challenge he confronted.

The Lord's command that Saul failed to keep is literarily related to the command that Samuel gave to Saul right after anointing him as king the first time:

> Once these signs are fulfilled, do whatever your hand finds to
> do, for God is with you. Go down ahead of me to Gilgal. I will

---

5. See also 2 Kgs 16:13 and 2 Chr 26:16.

surely come down to you to sacrifice burnt offerings and fellow-ship offerings, *but you must wait seven days until I come to you and tell you what you are to do.* (Italics added: 10:7–8)

Yet the chronology does not match. Several years may have passed since Samuel issued this order to Saul. Further, Saul's failure to carry out the first part of the command – attacking the Philistine outpost in Gibeah – had already made the second part obsolete. But the narrator constructs the episode in chapter 13 in terms that recall Saul's first failure to obey the Lord's command through the prophet Samuel in chapter 10. The all-out war with the Philistines started with Jonathan's attack against the Philistine outpost in Gibeah, something Saul should have done a long time before. It seems that Jonathan's belated obedience to the first part of Samuel's command made the second part return from obsolescence. Now, the command goes, Saul should wait seven days in Gilgal until Samuel comes to him and tells him what to do next. The spirit of this command dictates that Saul should wait for Samuel's further instructions in Gilgal. In this case, the Lord's command that Saul did not keep refers to the Lord's command through the prophet Samuel. Some scholars may regard Samuel as a control freak wanting to boss around Saul, but the narrator regards Saul's failure to obey Samuel as a grave sin that costs Saul his dynasty. In this way, the narrator underscores the unique ideology of Israelite kingship: the *raison d'etre* of a king in Israel was to realize God's rule among the Israelites, which was only possible when the king listened to the voice of the messenger of the Lord.

In a sense, Saul may have argued that he had in fact obeyed the Lord's command by waiting seven days for Samuel. The narrator confirms Saul's assertion, despite some scholars' efforts to make it otherwise.[6] The point here is that keeping the law to the letter is not obedience. Rather, true obedience starts with our efforts to discern the will of the Lord and then to live in accordance with it. To put this more simply, true obedience refers to living out the spirit of the law. Saul was right in waiting seven days, but he did not understand the will of the Lord behind this command. The Lord wanted him to obey his further instructions through Samuel concerning the battle with the Philistines. After all, considering the difference in number and power of both armies, Saul did not stand any chance of winning the battle, even if he launched an attack at the time he wanted in the way he wanted. Only the Lord could deliver Israel

---

6. Some argue that Saul did not wait seven full days and that Samuel arrived on the seventh day, but this is not borne out by the text (see 13:8).

out of the hand of the Philistines. But Saul did not understand that "nothing can hinder the Lord from saving, whether by many or by few" (14:6).

After establishing Saul's sin, Samuel declared the Lord's judgment as well:

> If you had [kept the command the Lord your God gave you],
> he would have established your kingdom over Israel for all time.
> But now your kingdom will not endure; the Lord has sought
> out a man after his own heart and appointed [or "commanded"]
> him ruler of his people. (vv. 13–14)

The sin of disobedience cost Saul his dynasty.[7] But if Saul had obeyed, the Lord would have established his kingdom, and we would have had a different history of salvation. Although the narrator constructs his narrative to imply that Saul's doom was predetermined, that is a later reflection on Israel's history. It is more consistent with biblical principles to believe that if Saul had obeyed, his life would have been different. Yet this is the second time that Saul failed to obey because of fear. Later in the story, he will have another chance to prove himself as an obedient king of Israel. God does not take pleasure in the destruction of sinners, but waits for them to repent and be saved. Although Samuel declared Saul's doom, and proclaimed another as the chosen one of the Lord, God would have honored Saul if he had obeyed the Lord's command through Samuel.

The phrase, "A man after his own heart," does not mean a man of God's selection, as many people would think. Rather, it means a man who subjugates himself under the rule of God's pleasing will. In other words, it refers to a man who strives to understand what the Lord's will is and to live up to it against all odds. In short, God sought out a man of obedience for the position of Israel's king. David will be such a king, but he was not a man of obedience from birth. As we will see later, God put him through many tribulations in order to mold him into a man of obedience.

The first part of verse 15 is difficult: Why did Samuel go up to Gibeah of Benjamin after declaring Saul's doom? Since we find Saul in Gibeah of Benjamin facing the Philistines in Mikmash in verse 16, it is better to follow the Septuagint and read it as follows: "And Samuel arose and departed from Gilgal on his way. And the rest of the people went up after Saul from Gilgal to Gibeah of Benjamin, to meet behind the people of his army." According

---

7. This is shown by the narrator's clever use of the verb "to command," which he used both to refer to Saul's failure and also to David's appointment.

to this reading, Samuel did not play any role in the upcoming battle against the Philistines, which gives Jonathan his moment to shine.

13:16–23 ISRAEL WITHOUT WEAPONS

Although Saul could not hold his position at Mikmash, his son Jonathan maintained his hold on Gibeah, and so Saul's six-hundred strong army went up to Gibeah to join Jonathan to face the Philistines across the pass of Mikmash. Meanwhile the Philistines continued to dispatch raiding parties to adjacent villages to accumulate more provisions in preparation for the battle. They sent raiding parties in three detachments from Mikmash, one north (Ophrah), another east (Beth Horon), and the third southeast (Valley of Zeboyim), thus everywhere except to the southwest in the direction of Gibeah (v. 17). Another party, however, was sent in the direction of Gibeah to the pass at Mikmash, not only to watch the movements of Saul's army, but to increase tension at the front (v. 23).

To emphasize the overwhelming power of the Philistines against Saul's army, the narrator mentions Israel's lack of iron weapons. "On the day of the battle not a soldier with Saul and Jonathan had a sword or spear in his hand" (v. 22) because the Philistines had monopolized the knowledge of smelting iron for fear that the Israelites would "make swords or spears" (v. 19). The Israelites had to depend on the Philistines for sharpening their plough wares, and it was as expensive as any monopolized merchandize would be: "two-thirds of a shekel for sharpening plow points and mattocks, and a third of a shekel for sharpening forks and axis and for repointing goads" (v. 21). To put this in perspective, it was a half-shekel for a poll tax in Israel (see Exod 30:13) and an annual income of a Levite hired by Micah was ten shekels (Judg 17:10). Thus sharpening tools would have been a significant drain on Israelite farmers' finance.

Chapter 13 ends on an ominous note: "Now a detachment of Philistine had gone out to the pass at Mikmash." This expedition was not for plunder but for reconnaissance and provocation. The Israelites, on the other hand, kept their ground, unwilling to come out for battle. Saul and his army remained in fearful silence. Who would act as Israel's champion? This is the subject of the next chapter.

1 SAMUEL 14:1–52

SAUL AND JONATHAN

One can be very observant without actually obeying the will of God. Saul is a case in point. He failed to obey the Lord's command through Samuel. Yet ironically, he resorted to various cultic practices, such as making an oath by the name of the Lord, inquiring of the Lord through the ephod, throwing lots to find a criminal, building an altar, and so forth. Saul did not understand that true obedience entailed earnestly seeking to understand God's will and to live it out faithfully. In this episode, Saul's son Jonathan embodies true obedience. He bravely enacted a plan to achieve what he believed was the Lord's pleasing will. He adjusted his course of action according to the concrete needs on the ground. Most importantly he acted in faith, trusting that the Lord was capable of saving Israel, whether by many or few. As the people proclaim in verse 45, Jonathan worked with the Lord, although he never resorted to cultic practices. In this sense, Jonathan is the hero of this episode. His worthiness as a leader underscores Saul's failed leadership. Yet the narrator's portrayal of Saul is not completely negative. His achievements are enumerated fairly; he was a successful military general, he had a good eye for warriors, and he defeated Israel's enemies all around.

For Asians, filial piety is the most basic virtue. Loyalty to superiors in the community is explained in terms similar to filial duty. One of the concrete expressions of the virtue of filial piety is blind obedience. Asians show respect to authority figures by never saying "no" to them. This sentiment has affected the way Asian Christians think of their relationship with God, as they tend to take blind obedience to God's words as virtuous. But Jonathan's behavior in this episode may give Asian Christians a counterpoint for this paradigm. Thinking and judging rationally goes hand in hand with faithful obedience to the Lord.

14:1–5 BACKGROUND

Verses 1 and 2 set the tone for the whole chapter, throughout which the narrator constantly plays Jonathan against Saul. Jonathan took initiative in attacking the Philistines while Saul sat under a pomegranate tree near Gibeah. Jonathan's first recorded words, "Come, let's go over to the Philistine outpost" (v. 1), establish his characterization as active, positive, and initiative-taking. This contrasts with Saul's first recorded words, "Come, let's go back" (9:5). The two brief notes about miscommunication at the end of both verse 1 and verse 2 foreshadow the conflict between Jonathan and Saul later in the narrative.

Saul stayed on the outskirts of Gibeah, afraid to attack the Philistines because his army of six hundred men was no match for the innumerable Philistine army. He appears to have held a council of war under a tree in Migron.[1] Ahijah, who was wearing an ephod, attended the hopeless meeting, suggesting that Saul was trying to turn a legitimate means of seeking the Lord's will into a divination prop as if to manipulate fate. But the high priest belonged to the Elide family, whom God had already judged into doom. Thus Saul was holding onto a rotten rope instead of trusting in the Lord.

Meanwhile, Jonathan planned a surprise attack against the Philistines. The two cliffs on each side of the pass between Geba and Mikmash were steep, like teeth jutting to the sky, and their surface was too treacherous to climb, as implied by their names, Bozez ("Slippery") and Seneh ("thorny"). This topography would have made it nearly impossible for Jonathan to go down one cliff to the gorge and then up the other cliff to reach the Philistine outpost at Mikmash. The narrator gives this topographical information to emphasize Jonathan's audacity and shrewdness in planning a surprise attack through this route.

14:6–14 JONATHAN SURPRISES THE PHILISTINES

Jonathan's bravery came from his faith in the Lord. By calling the Philistines "those uncircumcised men," Jonathan defined this war as a punishment against covenant breakers (see v. 48), not simply as the vanquishment of a foreign enemy.[2] Further, he trusted in the Lord who would act mightily on behalf of his people: "Nothing can hinder the LORD from saving, whether by many or by few" (v. 6). The size of the army was no issue for faithful Jonathan, whereas fearful Saul judged that his six hundred men could not stand up to the Philistines.

Jonathan not only trusted in the Lord but also took initiative in developing a strategy to carry out the Lord's will. Trusting in the Lord did not mean doing nothing or acting on superstitious beliefs. Rather, he devised a plan to test the readiness of the Philistine guards at the Mikmash outpost. How they reacted to Jonathan and his armor-bearer when they showed themselves in the

---

1. Most likely, Saul did not have a proper palace at this time.
2. Circumcision is a sign of covenant; by going under circumcision, the Israelites pledged allegiance to the Lord.

pass would gauge how vulnerable the Philistines were to a surprise attack. If they said, "Wait there until we come down to you," it would show that they were ready to fight. But if they said, "Come up to us," it would mean that they had no intention to fight, since their assumption in this case was that it would be impossible for the Israelites to climb up the steep and treacherous surface of a cliff to attack their post. So if the Philistines said, "Come up to us," Jonathan discerned that he and his armor bearer would have a reasonable chance to succeed in their risky venture, and so he decided to take this response as a divine "sign that the Lord has given them into our hands" (v. 10). This strategy was not a superstitious act that left everything up to chance. Rather, Jonathan courageously mapped out his plan of attack and asked for the Lord's help in executing that plan. This is how people of faith should meet everyday challenges, big or small. Further, Jonathan was a visionary. When the Philistines saw him and his armor bearer and said, "Come up to us and we'll teach you a lesson," he took it as the Lord's promise that he would give the Philistines into the "hand of Israel" (v. 12) – not simply into "our hands," as he declared in verse 10. He trusted that his surprise attack at the Philistine outpost would succeed, and then he declared in faith that the initial success would lead to Israel's final victory over the Philistines.

In executing his plan, he took the hardest route up the cliff so as not to be seen by the Philistines – "Jonathan climbed up using his hands and feet" (v. 3) – thus maximizing the element of surprise in his attack. Jonathan and his armor-bearer achieved an important victory over the Philistines. In their first attack, we are told that they killed "some twenty men in an area of about half an acre" (v. 14). Though they did not kill many Philistines in number, and the area they recovered was not large in size, their victory did lead to the victory of Israel. However small and insignificant our lives may seem, we should live them out faithfully. For God is able, and he can use our small acts of faith to change the world around us.

Before we move to the next section, a few comments are in order about Jonathan's armor bearer. Although he was not even named, he was Jonathan's indispensable partner. His role went far beyond carrying Jonathan's armor, for he fought the Philistines at Jonathan's side. Further, the narrator describes his relationship with Jonathan in terms that recall the friendship of David and Jonathan. Just as Jonathan "became one in spirit with David" (see 18:1), the anonymous armor bearer becomes one in heart with Jonathan (v. 7). Jonathan could not have succeeded without his armor-bearer, just as David could not have succeeded without Jonathan. The Lord may honor the anonymous armor bearer even more than Jonathan and David, because he worked hard for the Lord without a name. In a shame-based culture, leaving a good name for posterity is considered the ultimate goal of life. Many strive their whole lives to accumulate fame in this world. But we should remember that God's judgment is different from human judgment. What matters is God's judgment, and so Christians should live in pursuit of truth, not fame.

14:15–23 ISRAEL DEFEATS THE PHILISTINES

As Jonathan declared, his small victory was only the beginning of Israel's great victory over the Philistines. The Lord used Jonathan and his armor bearer's faith to deliver the Israelites from the oppressive hand of the Philistines. This is shown by the fact that the Philistines were defeated not by the swords of the Israelites – after all, Saul had only six hundred soldiers – but by the sword of God. God took what little commotion Jonathan's attack may have incurred among the Philistines and inflated it into panic and confusion of cosmic proportions. The narrator uses the Hebrew root *hadar,* "panic," three times in verse 15, each time in different forms, the third of which is "the panic sent by God." He also uses hyperbole to express the cosmic scope of the panic: "the ground shook." So the Philistines killed each other in great panic and confusion.

While Jonathan was working with God in the Philistine camp, Saul remained in Gibeah. Rather than taking part in God's act of redemption, he moved with his troops to the battlefield "to see" the Philistines striking each other with their swords in great confusion (v. 21). The narrator emphasizes that the Lord saved Israel on that day (v. 23). But when Saul learned that the great confusion in the Philistine camps was caused by Jonathan and his armor bearer, he asked the priest Ahijah to bring the ark of God (v. 18). To understand the significance of this act, one should note that the Septuagint reads "the ephod" instead of the ark of God. Some scholars argue that "the ephod" is more proper to the context than "the ark of God,"[3] but I believe that the use of the ark of God in the Hebrew text is intentional, for it recalls the earlier Israel-Philistine war at Ebenezer, when Eli's two sons brought the ark of the Lord to the battlefield. Moreover, Saul asked Ahijah, another Elide priest, to bring the ark of the Lord into the middle of another war with the Philistines. By incorporating these details into the narrative, the narrator criticizes Saul for manipulating the Lord for his own purposes. Then Saul stopped Ahijah

3. MacCarter, *1 Samuel,* 233.

by saying, "Withdraw your hand," and rallied the troops that were with him to enter the battle. Yet this call to arms appears to have nothing to do with his respect for the ark of God. Rather, when Saul saw the great confusion in the Philistine camp, he realized that it was no longer necessary to consult the ark of the Lord. In other words, his dependence on God was neither sincere nor absolute. He manipulated God for his purposes and then withdrew from him when he felt no need for him.

What the Lord did for Israel in this battle turned the hearts of those who had left Israel for one or another reason (see Ruth 1:6). First, the Hebrews who had defected to the Philistines as mercenaries returned to the army of Saul and Jonathan.[4] Second, the Israelite soldiers who had hidden in the hill country of Ephraim came out of the caves to join the battle against the Philistines. Now, Saul's increased army was in hot pursuit of the Philistine remnant. The battlefront expanded from Mikmash to beyond Beth Aven.

14:24–30 JONATHAN BREAKS SAUL'S OATH

In spite of this victory, the morale of the Israelites suddenly changed: "Now the Israelites were in distress that day" (v. 24). This comes as a surprise, because the previous verse ended on a happy note, with the augmented Israelite army pursuing the routed Philistines. Further, the phrase, "Now the Israelites were in distress [niggas]," recalls the condition of Saul's army before Jonathan's attack against the Philistine outpost at Mikmash: "the army was hard-pressed [niggas]" (13:6). So what returned Israel's army to their desperate condition? Saul had rashly banned his entire army from eating until the battle was over, and he had sworn the ban under curse: "Cursed be anyone who eats food before evening comes, before I have avenged myself on my enemies!" (v. 24). So his soldiers, fearing Saul's curse, ate nothing at all and became faint from hunger that day (v. 28).[5] As a result, the victory over the Philistines was not complete, and many of them returned to their land (v. 46). Why did Saul command a fast under the curse of death? Did he not know that hungry soldiers could never win the war? Saul's rash oath reflects his tendency to bypass reason and to resort to superstitious arts of magic and divination. He lacked not only the

---

4. This may provide a historical backdrop against which to understand David's defection to the Philistines (see 27:1–2). Some Israelites appear to have hired themselves out to the Philistines as mercenaries.
5. Verses 25–26 underscore how great the temptation would have been to Saul's soldiers by repeating the same information twice, one from the narrator's perspective and another from the soldiers' perspective.

good judgment that was expected of a commander in chief, but also the faith that was expected of the king of Israel.

When Jonathan breaks the oath, the narrator introduces another counterpoint into the narrative. The narrator defends Jonathan for breaking the oath in verse 27 by pointing out several attenuating circumstances: first, his ignorance of the oath; second, the small amount of honey that he ate (see also v. 43); third, the positive effect of honey consumption on Jonathan's body.[6] This prepares the reader for a later development in the story. Be that as it may, Jonathan protested against his father publicly: "My father has made trouble for the country" (v. 29). He goes on to argue that if the Israelites had eaten proper meals, their victory against the Philistines would have been greater. His argument begins with what a little honey did to him and extrapolates to what a proper meal would have done for Israel's army. This particular manner of argumentation is a well-known rhetoric called *qal-wa-homer* among the Jews. In other words, he appealed to something that rational Israelites could relate to with the intent of persuading the people to his way. In this regard Jonathan is portrayed differently from Saul, who threatened the people to follow his way, either because of his political authority or the religious authority he arrogated to himself from Ahijah.

14:31–35 SAUL'S OATH MAKES ISRAEL SIN AGAINST THE LORD

With empty stomachs, the Israelites fought hard and advanced about twenty-five kilometers, striking down the defeated Philistines from Beth Aven to Aijalon. No wonder they were "exhausted" (v. 31) at the end of day. That evening, when the curse was lifted, they "pounced on the plunder" like birds of prey "and, taking sheep, cattle and calves, they butchered them on the ground and ate them, together with the blood" (v. 32). Yet eating blood was strictly forbidden in the law (see Lev 19:26; Deut 12:23) and was considered a sin against the Lord, as an anonymous soldier told Saul (v. 33). When Saul heard about it, he installed a makeshift altar on which to slaughter the animals for consumption (v. 35).

At first glance, this paragraph paints Saul in a positive way. He stopped the people from sinning against the Lord by quickly building an altar. Further the

---

6. "His eyes brightened" (v. 27). The Hebrew words that the narrator uses for "cursed" and "brightened" sound similar to each other, thus forming a pun: 'arur and 'oru (taro'na). The deliberate pun underscores the irony that despite Saul's curse, breaking the oath leads to life rather than death.

narrator implies that Saul built many more altars after this (v. 35). Put differently, he sponsored many altars in Israel. This is comparable to Korean missionaries sponsoring church building projects in other parts of Asia. Building altars would be something in which Saul could take pride. Also, the Israelite soldiers should have known better than to eat meat with blood. These details seem to paint Saul as a hero and hold the Israelites responsible for their sin. In fact, Saul accused the people directly: "You have broken faith" (v. 33). But on a closer examination, Saul knew that he was partly responsible for the people's sin because of his foolish oath, and then he used the people's sin to cover for his failed leadership. This is intimated by the fact that Saul did not punish anyone for eating blood.

Saul's rash oath that prohibited his army from eating anything put his entire army in danger of losing their combative power and dying from exhaustion on the battlefield. The soldiers' breach of the law about blood consumption was inevitable, because Saul did not take the initiative to restore life to the soldiers who were exhausted from long hours of battle. When he said, "cursed be anyone who eats food before evening comes, before I have avenged myself on my enemies" (v. 24) it wasn't clear what the Israelites were supposed to do if the Philistines were still running away after evening came. As Jonathan suggested, Saul's army could have vanquished the Philistines completely by evening if they had been allowed to eat properly. Saul also knew that his oath did not achieve his hopes, for once evening came, he either had to lift the ban or force his soldiers to pursue the Philistines. The latter was no real option, but he did not take the initiative to lift the ban either. Instead, he let the soldiers decide the matter. Once the people started to eat meat together with the blood, he was forced to take measures to prevent them from sinning. Rather than admitting that his strategy of making an oath had failed, the people's sin gave him the opportunity to cover up his failure and to act as a hero by building an altar and helping his soldiers have proper meals without sinning against the Lord.

14:36–46 THE PEOPLE RECUE JONATHAN

Even then, Saul did not give up his goal, for he wanted to continue his pursuit of the Philistines into the night. So he proposed an incentive to his men: "Let us . . . plunder them till dawn, and let us not leave one of them alive" (v. 36). His goal was to finish off the Philistines, and the incentive for his soldiers was the plunder. The people agreed rather enthusiastically: "Do *whatever* seems best to you" (v. 36, italics added). At that moment, the priest stopped Saul and suggested that he inquire of the Lord, which was customary.[7] But God did not answer Saul's inquiry that night, and so he could not continue his pursuit. The defeated Philistines returned home in safety.

On a surface level, it appears that the pious Saul then tried to bring to justice the one who had sinned against the Lord. But on a deeper level, he was simply finding a scapegoat so he could shift blame for his less than perfect victory over the Philistines. His religious zeal was only a cover-up for his failure as leader. Immediately, Saul summoned the leaders of his army to announce his plan to search by lot for the criminal who would account for the Lord's silence. He even swore by the Lord that he would kill his son Jonathan if he were found guilty (v. 39). When Jonathan was taken by lot, he swore again by the Lord that Jonathan should die (v. 44). Without the people's intervention, Jonathan would have been killed for "tasting a little honey with the end of my [Jonathan's] staff" (v. 43). But the people of Israel rebelled against Saul's command to kill Jonathan by saying, "Should Jonathan die – he who has brought about this great deliverance in Israel? Never!" (v. 45). Notice the subtle contrast between "a little honey" and "this great deliverance." They saw clearly what Saul had not been able to see from the beginning: "for he worked with the LORD this very day" (v. 45, my translation).[8] Saul was immensely occupied with rituals and frequently swore by the Lord, inquired of the Lord, fasted, and cast lots. But unlike Jonathan, he did not trust the Lord. Unlike Jonathan, he did not take initiative in attacking the Philistines in spite of the odds. Though the people knew that Jonathan had brought about great deliverance in Israel, Saul did not understand this.

This episode assumes that breaking an oath is a sin that must be punished. The Lord did not answer Saul's inquiry about continuing the pursuit of the Philistines through the night, but he did answer Saul's inquiry about who was responsible for the Lord's silence. This suggests that the Lord's silence was due to the sin of breaking the oath. Further, as the narrator notes, the people "redeemed" Jonathan (v. 45: "rescue," NIV). The Hebrew *padah*, "to redeem," assumes a debt or a sin on the part of the one who is "redeemed." If breaking

---

7. Saul's question to the Lord consists of two questions: the first concerns what he should do, the second what would happen. Both questions are formulated in such a way that they could be answered in a binary fashion: correct/yes or incorrect/no. This is related to the fact that priests could get only two answers from the ephod, *Urim*, "Incorrect/No," or *Thummim*, "Correct/Yes."

8. NIV: "for he did this today with God's help."

an oath was a sin, why was Jonathan redeemed? The narrator tries to show that there are more important things in life than simply observing ritual obligations. Although Jonathan broke an oath, he saved Israel and acted as the Lord's partner in delivering the Israelites. In other words, the narrator teaches that the Lord delights in saving people's lives, and the work of salvation is more important than following the letter of the law.

14:47–52 OTHER ACHIEVEMENTS OF KING SAUL

The victory over the Philistines at Mikmash helped Saul consolidate his rule over Israel. During his reign, he continued to fight against foreign invaders and had some success:[9] Ammon and Moab in the east, Edom and Amalek in the south, Zoba in the north, the Philistines in the west. The narrator notes two enemies in particular who will figure prominently in the subsequent narrative: the Amalekites and the Philistines. The Amalekites represent all the enemies who invaded Israel for plunder – thus the narrator calls the Amalekites, "its plunderer" (*shosehu,* v. 48)[10] – but the Amalekites are the worst of them, because they killed innocents such as infants and women in their plunder operations. The Philistines, however, wanted to expand their territory inland due to an increase in their population. Instead of going back to their land after plundering, the Philistines tended to remain and lay claim to some cities (see 7:14). For this reason, defeating the Philistines was more important for the king of Israel than defeating any other enemies: "All the days of Saul there was a bitter war with the Philistines" (v. 52).

King Saul was more akin to a successful warlord than a king. He had a good eye for warriors: whenever he saw a warrior, he took him into his service (v. 52). He differed from a judge in that he established a kingdom, though to a minimal extent. Saul's sons and relatives may have served as court officials along with the Elide priests, and Saul appointed his cousin Abner as the commander of his army. All Saul's sons and daughters except Malkishua will have roles in the subsequent narrative of Saul and David.[11] Many scholars argue that Ishvi is an alternate name for Ish-Boshet or Esbaal, the short-lived successor of King Saul (see 1 Chr 8:33).[12]

---

9. The expression "inflicted punishment" suggests that Saul's wars were mostly defensive. Enemies invaded Israel mostly for the plunder.
10. NIV: "those who had plundered them."
11. Malkishua was mentioned as one of Saul's sons who was killed in the Gilboa battle (see 31:2).
12. Tsumura, *The First Book of Samuel,* 384.

1 SAMUEL 15:1−35

SAUL'S THIRD DISOBEDIENCE

Because Saul failed in obedience twice, Samuel pronounced that he was denied a dynasty. Yet God gives Saul another chance to act as king of Israel by carrying out the Lord's command faithfully. The Lord does not take delight in the destruction of sinners but wants them to come back to him with all their heart. So when Saul failed in obedience, God must have grieved for Saul, just as the prophet Samuel did (v. 35). God sorely regretted Saul's disobedience. As the Korean saying, *Eup-Cham-Ma-Sok,* goes, God ordered Saul to be dethroned while shedding tears. But Saul was to blame for being rejected as king, for he repeatedly failed in the most essential aspect of Israel's kingship. Further his repentance was not genuine. The narrator records three occasions when Saul failed to obey the Lord's words through the prophet Samuel. If God had given Saul more chances to obey, the narrative implies that he would have behaved in the same way. Thus Saul's failure was his own responsibility, not because of circumstance.

GOD'S *EUP-CHAM-MA-SOK*

The Lord's grieving for Saul recalls Zhuge Liang's grieving for Ma Su. Zhuge Liang was a famous commander-in-chief in the state of Shu Han. In accordance with the desire of his deceased king Liu Bei, he launched an expedition to conquer the state of Wei in the north. The most important thing for his success was to secure the store city of Jieting from the hand of Sima Yi, a renounced general of Wei. While Zhuge Liang was wondering who the most suitable person would be to protect Jieting, Ma Su volunteered: "Lifelong study of military science has given me a good understanding of warfare . . . If anything goes wrong, you can put my whole family to the sword."[1] At these words, Zhuge Liang gave strategic orders to Ma Su to protect Jieting through Wang Ping, the adviser to Ma Su: "pitch camp along the main road to prevent the enemy from slipping past." But Ma Su did not obey Zhuge Liang's order and decided to camp out on the nearby mountains, which led him not only to lose Jieting to Sima Yi, but also to lose the war. After retreating to Hanzhong, Zhuge Liang confronted Ma Su: "Had you listened to Wang Ping, you could have avoided this disaster." Although Ma Su was like a son to Zhuge Liang and never failed in battle except at Jieting, Zhuge Liang, shedding tears, ordered Ma Su executed.

1. Roberts, trans., *Three Kingdoms*, 1138.

15:1–3 THE LORD COMMANDS TOTAL DESTRUCTION OF THE AMALEKITES

Before delivering the Lord's last command to King Saul, Samuel reminded Saul that he was the "sent one" by the Lord: Samuel, and no other, was the messenger sent to Saul from the Lord. The fact that he was also the one who made Saul king of Israel sounds like an afterthought. This emphasis on Samuel's role as the Lord's messenger to King Saul is necessitated by Saul's repeated failures to listen to Samuel. Samuel may have suspected that Saul was identifying his words as the Lord's words, and so he prefaced his divine message with the so-called messenger-formula: "This is what the LORD Almighty says" (v. 2). This formulaic phrase, traditionally rendered as "Thus says the LORD," would have made it clear to Saul that Samuel was speaking on behalf of the Lord (see 32:3). Thus Saul should listen, because Samuel's words constituted a message from the Lord.[1] Saul's whole narrative revolves around the idea that the king of Israel should listen to the prophet's voice as coming from the Lord himself. This was not meant to elevate the religious institution over the political one. Rather, this arrangement stemmed from the theocratic constitution of Israel's kingdom. Namely, the kingdom of Israel was the only kingdom in history that the Lord ruled as the King of kings. Therefore, religious leaders in modern states had no biblical warranty to force politicians to listen to them under the threat of divine curse.

Be that as it may, the Lord gave Saul another chance to act as king of Israel. He ordered Saul to destroy the Amalekites completely – to inflict *herem* on them. The Hebrew word *herem*, "devoted things," refers to total destruction

1. In urging Saul to listen to him, Samuel uses a redundant expression, "the voice of the words of the LORD" (v. 1: "The message from the LORD," NIV), to emphasize that Samuel's words are the Lord's. This emphasis is repeated in v. 16.

when used in the context of a holy war.[2] Ancient peoples including the Israelites practiced a holy war. Unlike a regular war, whose main purpose was to take plunder, the soldiers could not take any plunder in a holy war. If someone took anything as plunder, he downgraded the war to a regular war. Although there were some variations of the scope of destruction, a city put under *herem* must be destroyed completely – all the living killed, all things burned, without exception. The total destruction for the Amalekites appears to have been limited to the living, but in killing the living, there should not be any exceptions. The Lord made it clear by enumerating the four pairs of humans and animals by major categories: adults, children, meat animals, riding animals.

The Lord ordered Saul to put the Amalekites under *herem*, or total destruction, because he wanted to make good on his words to the Israelites. The Amalekites were a nomadic people who operated along the desert area in northern Sinai. When the Israelites went through the wilderness after the Exodus, the nomads ambushed them from behind. Instead of fighting with the strongest Israelites, they made a point of attacking and killing the weakest members of the Israelite community. The evil that they had inflicted on the Israelites was so great that the Lord once promised Moses that he would wipe out their name from under heaven (Deut 25:17) and that he would fight them "from generation to generation" (Exod 17:16). Moses' successor, Joshua, not only fought the Amalekites in the wilderness but also inherited the same promise to "completely blot out the name of Amalek from under heaven" (Exod 17:14). By assigning the job to Saul, the Lord gave him the opportunity to serve as God's vessel in fulfilling his prophecy against the Amalekites, the ultimate enemy of the Israelites. If Saul had carried out the Lord's wrath against the Amalekites faithfully, he would have avoided his fate. God would have established an enduring kingdom for Saul, as Samuel once said (see 13:13). This new chance was a real opportunity for Saul.

---

2. John Walton defines *herem* as "to remove from human use." It helps us understand that total destruction is not the goal of *herem* itself, but the purpose is for the preparation of a new order after the destruction. See John H. Walton and J. Harvey Walton, *The Lost World of the Israelite Conquest: Covenant, Retribution, and the Fate of the Canaanites* (Downers Grove: IVP Academic, 2017).

15:4–11 SAUL SPARES AGAG AND SOME ANIMALS

Saul honored the Lord's command by attacking Amalekite cities "all the way from Havilah to Shur, near the eastern border of Egypt" (v. 7),[3] all across the region where the Amalekites wandered around making their living. Yet he did not destroy them completely: he killed all the Amalekites but their king, Agag, and he destroyed all the animals but the best. So the Lord told Samuel that Saul had not "carried out my instruction" (v. 11). Further the Lord mentions his regret about Saul for the first time: "I regret that I have made Saul king" (v. 11). Saul's repeated failure to obey the Lord's words faithfully made the Lord change his mind about Saul. Though he had chosen Saul as king of Israel, now he rejected Saul as king.

Before turning to the extensive conversation between Samuel and Saul that follows, we will discuss two matters: first, the narrator's literary tactics to emphasize the egregiousness of Saul's fault; second, a theological question about whether God changes his mind.

Regarding the first matter, there are some hints in the text that subtly foreshadow Saul's failure. First, there is a significant reduction in the number of Saul's army. For his mission to save Jabesh-Gilead from the hand of the Ammonites, he mustered three hundred thousand men from northern Israel and thirty thousand from Judah at Bezek (see 11:8). But at Telaim (compare "Telem" in Josh 14:24), he mustered only two hundred thousand men from Israel and ten thousand from Judah (v. 7). Given the weight of his mission to embark on a holy war against Israel's eternal enemy the Amalekites, this number was not impressive.[4] Second, Saul's generosity towards the Kenites serves a double purpose. By saving the Kenites who "showed kindness" to the Israelites in the wilderness, Saul made it clear that his *herem* war against the Amalekites was not indiscriminate genocide but a just war to punish the sinners. But at the same time, Saul violated the Lord's command to "totally destroy all that belongs to" the Amalekites by letting the Kenites live (v. 3), since the Kenites living in the city of Amalek were certainly part of all that belonged to the Amalekites. Some Kenites, who were skilled at making and

---

3. The exact location of Havilah is not known, but it is assumed to be somewhere in the Sinai Peninsula. Shur, however, refers to the desert area stretching along northern Sinai. Two major highways ran through this area from Egypt to Syria: one is the way of the sea and the other is the way of Shur.
4. The translators of LXX expand the number to four hundred thousand men from Israel and thirty thousand men for Judah. This number would have been more proper to Saul's mission. But the number in the Hebrew text should be preferred as the narrator's subtle foreshadowing of Saul's failure.

repairing tools, must have settled there to work for the Amalekites. After all, the Lord did not tell Saul to save the Kenites, and so this was an independent act on Saul's part. This has been the pattern of Saul's "obedience," where he changes the Lord's commands according to his changing circumstances. Third, the narrator exaggerated the animals that the people spared, implying that there was a significant number and that the people only killed the "despised and weak" animals (v. 9). As it becomes clear later, the number of spared animals was small enough to be burned in one sacrifice offering (see commentary on vv. 21–23 below). However, the narrator's exaggeration underscores the egregiousness of Saul's sin of rebellion against the Lord.

Regarding the second matter, the Lord's regret in the narrative does not create a theological problem. The narrator uses human language and human concepts to express who God is, and the language expressing God's attributes are essentially metaphorical. For instance, the statement, "God regrets or envies," is just as metaphorical as the statement, "God's hand is strong." These statements derive from our experience, whether direct or indirect, and metaphors can conflict with one another. This does not suggest that God is contradictory but that our imperfect language cannot grasp the fullness of God. In chapter 15, we can observe contradictory statements about God: God regrets in verses 11 and 35, but verse 29 says that God never regrets as humans do. When the biblical narrator mentions divine regret, we should understand that the focus is not on God's mistake but on his future new act. In other words, when God regrets, God starts a new thing. If God did not regret, his decree would be final and never changing (see Ezek 24:14; Zech 8:14).

When God told Samuel about his regret over Saul, Samuel "was angry, and cried out to the LORD all that night" (v. 11). Was Samuel angry at Saul or God? Most likely, Samuel was angry with both – Saul because he had not learned to obey the Lord faithfully, despite the Lord's grace in giving him multiple chances, and the Lord because God changed his mind too quickly. Samuel was also gripped with emotion because his fate was closely intertwined with Saul's. Just as Saul could only be king of Israel with Samuel as his prophet, Samuel could only remain a prophet if Saul was king. When the Lord sent Saul to Samuel's hometown of Ramah, Samuel submitted, although reluctantly, to God's will to anoint Saul. Further, after he anointed Saul as king, he may have dreamt about working in cooperation with Saul, hoping to establish a theocratic monarchy in the land of Israel. The divine regret over Saul shattered such visions for Samuel. So he cried out to the Lord all night long. We can only speculate about his prayers, but Samuel clearly did not take delight in Saul's failure, because his failure was connected to the failure of the whole people of Israel who had asked for "a king to lead us such as all the nations have" (8:4). Furthermore, Samuel's feelings may have reflected the Lord's, who was also heavy-hearted about having to remove Saul from the throne. But the Lord had to dethrone Saul, because he lacked the most essential trait for a king of Israel. The statement, "he . . . has not carried out [*heqim*] my instructions" (v. 11), refers both to Saul's failure to obey the Lord and also his failure to "establish" [*heqim*] God's will on earth. As the Korean saying goes, "Whatever hunts a pheasant deserves calling a falcon." Saul could only reign as king of Israel to establish the Lord's kingdom on earth by obeying God faithfully. Just as a falcon who cannot hunt a pheasant is not a falcon, a king of Israel who fails to obey God is not king of Israel. Saul could not remain as king any longer. Shedding tears, God rejected him.

THE ETERNAL ENEMY OF ISRAEL, THE AMALEKITES

The Lord's wrath against the Amalekites has a special place in the history of Israel, for it is ubiquitous in space and never-ending in time. God promised the people of Israel that he would not only blot out the name of Amalek "from under heaven" but also fight against the Amalekites "from generation to generation" (Exod 17:16). This raises the question, what makes the Amalekites unique among other nations? While the people of Israel were wandering in the wilderness, they attacked "all who were lagging behind," namely, those women and children who were the weakest members of Israel's community (see Deut 25:17). Killing innocent people is a heinous crime against humanity and against the Lord. God said of the Amalekites, "They had no fear of God" (Deut 25:17). In other words, the Amalekites had no fear of God in committing crimes against humanity, and so the Lord continues to fight against "Amalekites" everywhere and always. Christians should be godly in fighting against those who kill innocent people for their own political, economic, or religious agenda. The kingdom of God begins with caring for one single soul.

15:12–23 SAMUEL CONFRONTS SAUL

As the Lord revealed to Samuel his regret over Saul, and as Samuel angrily cried out to the Lord, Saul went to Carmel, south of Hebron, to "set up a monument in his own honor" and then moved down to Gilgal to prepare sacrifices (v. 12). As they say, ignorance is bliss. Without knowing about God's regret, Saul tried to publicize his victory over the Amalekites, glorifying himself before the people by setting up a monument in Carmel and offering sacrifices with the animals from the plunder.[5] When Samuel caught up with Saul at Gilgal, Saul came out to greet him, just as he did in chapter 13 (see 13:10). But there was no sign of humility in Saul's greeting, for he needed Samuel to offer thanksgiving sacrifices and to re-confirm his kingship before the people of Israel. Saul boasted to Samuel that he had "carried out the LORD's instructions" (v. 13). Although this squarely contradicts what God said in verse 11, it is likely that Saul genuinely believed what he was saying.

Then Samuel asked, "What then is this bleating [qol] of sheep in my ears? What is this lowing [qol] of cattle that I hear [shama']?" (v. 14). The Hebrew words qol, "voice or sound," and shama', "to hear," in Samuel's question recalls his exhortation to "listen to the message" (shama' le qol) from the Lord (v. 1). The sound that Samuel hears from the animals debunks Saul's claim that he listened to the message of the Lord. So Saul shifted blame to the people for sparing "the best of the sheep and cattle" and then defended them by saying that they did it "to sacrifice to the LORD your God" (v. 15). Then he added, "but we totally destroyed the rest," though he does not admit that "the rest" were all despised and weak.

Samuel interrupted, as if to say Saul's words and excuses made no sense, and delivered God's verdict in the form of a question: "Why did you not obey the LORD? Why did you pounce on the plunder and do evil in the eyes of the LORD?" (v. 19).[6] Nevertheless, Saul insisted that he obeyed the Lord. In fact, Saul had good reasons to plead innocence. In the ancient Near East, war began and ended with sacrifices. Kings offered sacrifices to the gods before they headed to the battlefield and again when they returned triumphantly from the battlefield. In Saul's estimation, the war was not over until the last sacrifice was offered to the Lord. Saul killed all the Amalekites except their king and

---

5. Setting up a monument was one way of making his name last eternally. People would see the monument that Saul established and remember his name. Absalom, who had no children, set up a monument in the King's Tomb so that his name would be remembered after his death. Usually children carried their father's name through generations, so having children was also a way to live eternally.

6. The language "pounce" recalls the sin of the Israelite soldiers in the Mikmash battle against the Philistines. Out of exhaustion from hunger, they "pounced on the plunder . . . ate them, together with the blood" (see 14:32–33). Just as Saul did not finish off the Philistines because of his own sin, he also could not wipe out the Amalekites. Thus Saul failed in his missions against the two most intractable enemies of Israel.

destroyed all that belonged to them except the best animals. Saul planned to kill Agag and the animals during the sacrifices, which would effectively devote all the Amalekites to the Lord. In fact, Saul calls the animals that the people spared from the plunder "the first of *herem*" (v. 21),[7] as if to recall the law about the firstlings and first fruits. Further, when Samuel summoned Agag, the king of Amalek thought that he might live. If Saul had summoned him, he would have assumed otherwise. Thus Saul actually thought that he had obeyed the Lord.

But Samuel did not buy into Saul's argument, because God, who knew Saul's heart inside out, had pronounced that Saul was guilty of rebellious disobedience. Saul could have completed "total destruction" to the letter of the law at the time of sacrifice by killing Agag and burning the spared animals on the altar, but Saul could not deceive God. Samuel's accusation comes in the form of poetry in verses 22–23. By putting Samuel's words in poetry, the narrator gives them eternal significance, applying them to everyone in every age, not only to Saul. The theme that the Lord delights in an obedient life – namely, a life of justice and compassion – more than sacrifices is repeated again and again in the books of the prophets. Conversely, a rebellious life is as hateful to God as the sin of idolatry. The Lord's verdict for Saul is based on the principle of retribution: "Because you have *rejected* the word of the LORD, he has *rejected* you as king" (v. 23). This reminds us that sinners perish because of their sin.

15:24–35 SAMUEL KILLS AGAG AND PARTS WAYS WITH SAUL

The spiritual authority with which Samuel spoke to Saul helped debunk Saul's pretense of innocence. Although he tried to cover-up his inner secret with logic, Saul may have felt himself exposed by the words of the prophet. For he confessed his sins, saying, "I violated the LORD's command and your instructions" (v. 24), finally acknowledging Samuel's words as the Lord's. He also revealed his innermost thoughts: "I was afraid of the men and so I gave in to them" (v. 24). Rather than shifting blame to the people, Saul was honest about his motivation to spare Agag and some sacrificial animals because of his fear of the people. Earlier, his authority as king was compromised when he was rejected by the prophet Samuel (see 13:13–14) and again when the people rejected him by rebelling against his order to kill Jonathan (see 14:45). Feeling threatened, Saul realized that he might lose his kingship, and the Lord's

---

7. NIV: "the best of what was devoted to God."

command to destroy the Amalekites completely gave him the opportunity to consolidate his rule over the people in public. Therefore Saul tried to use the war against the Amalekites as an opportunity for self-glorification and self-service. He and his people knew well Balaam's prophecy about Israel's kings: "Their [Israel's] kings will be greater than Agag; their kingdom will be exalted" (Num 24:70). Although the Agag in Balaam's prophecy was different from Agag, king of Amalek, Saul could have publicized himself as the king of Israel who the pagan prophet had said would be greater than Agag by killing the namesake king of Amalek himself. Technically he did not have to compromise the Lord's commands while appropriating them to his own glory. As long as he killed Agag and the spared animals during the sacrifices that would officially end Saul's mission, he could claim to have fulfilled the Lord's command for total destruction. This would be, as the Koreans would say, catching two birds with one stone. But God saw through Saul's sinful plan. Saul did not obey the Lord's command wholeheartedly, because he wanted to glorify himself before the people while pretending to serve the Lord.

Though Saul realized and confessed his sin in public, he did not turn away from pursuing his own glory. Saul's confession of sin was a convenient tool that enabled him to follow through with his original plan. He may have thought that if he confessed his sins, Samuel would forgive him and officiate the sacrifice for him. After the sacrifice, Saul planned to kill Agag while the people were watching, which would legitimize his kingship before the people of Israel. Although rejected as king by God, he might be able to hold onto his power for the time being.

Samuel saw through Saul's plan and refused to go with him. Saul insisted by grabbing hold of the hem of Samuel's robe. When it tore, Samuel interpreted it as a sign from the Lord: "The Lord has torn the kingdom of Israel from you today and has given it to one of your neighbors – to one better than you" (v. 28). "Today" does not mean that Saul would lose his power immediately, but that God would soon appoint another man for king of Israel. The focus of the subsequent narrative is all about Saul's prophesied replacement. God's decision to tear Saul's kingship from him in order to give it to his neighbor was final. Thus the narrator calls God "Everlasting of Israel" (v. 29),[8] underscoring the Lord's constancy and consistency. Saul's efforts to take Samuel with him to the sacrifice led to yet another prophetic pronouncement of Saul's rejection as king.

---

8. NIV: "Glory of Israel."

A second time, Saul confessed his sin, but his confession was immediately followed by a request to Samuel to "please honor me before the elders of my people and before Israel" (v. 30). This proves that Saul's repeated confessions were simply a convenient tool for him to push through the plan designed for his own glorification. But Samuel did not officiate the sacrifices, and so he did not justify Saul's kingship before the people by serving as his priest and prophet. However, the text is ambiguous, saying, "So Samuel went *after* him, and Saul worshipped the LORD" (v. 31, italics mine). There are two ways of reading it to imply that Samuel did not return with Saul to officiate the final sacrifice. First, one may amend the Hebrew text to say, "Samuel went away from (*min aharey*) Saul." Second, one may take "after" in a temporal sense. Then Samuel went sometime after Saul had gone. In either case, Samuel arrived after Saul sacrificed animals as a burnt offering and before he could execute Agag in the presence of the people. This recalls a similar situation in chapter 13, where Samuel appeared right after Saul had sacrificed a burnt offering (see vv. 10–11).

Then Samuel ordered Agag to be brought before him and put to death "before the Lord" at Gilgal. Thus Samuel subverted Saul's plan to kill Agag "before the public." Although Saul was pretending that he wanted to "devote" (*herem*) Agag, king of Amalek, to the Lord, he intended to glorify his royalty before the people. But Samuel did not allow this to happen by taking the matter into his own hands. Before killing Agag, however, he justified it by reminding the people that Agag was a cold-blooded murderer of innocent people (v. 33). The narrator gives this justification eternal significance by putting it in poetry, as he did with Samuel's rebuke of Saul (see v. 33): "As your sword has made women childless, so will your mother be childless among women." A human life is so precious that only a human life can atone for it. Earlier, Samuel defined Saul's mission as "destroying those wicked people, the Amalekites" (v. 18). In the prophet's opinion, the Amalekites were killed not only for the sins of their ancestors in the time of Moses but also for their own sins. God's command to destroy the Amalekites was meant to teach that God never tolerates crimes against humanity, although God's command to *herem* the Amalekites would have only made sense in the ancient cognitive environment, where the law of talion[9] was widely applied.[10]

---

9. The law of talion is a translation of Latin *lex talionis*, which refers to the law in which the punishment corresponds in kind and degree to the injury.
10. For the metaphoric significance of Amalek in the history of Israel, see Yoram Hazony, *God and Politics in Esther* (Cambridge: Cambridge University Press, 2016), 62–69.

Samuel and Saul then parted and went their separate ways (v. 34). Although Gibeah and Ramah were close to each other, Samuel never saw Saul again (v. 35). For him, King Saul was dead, and so Samuel "mourned for him" (v. 35). The narrator ends chapter 15 by repeating the Lord's regret over Saul. This not only points to the Lord's *Eup-Cham-Ma-Sok*, his sore heart over Saul's doom, but it also foreshadows the new search for a king after God's own heart.

1 SAMUEL 16:1–23

SAMUEL ANOINTS DAVID

Chapter 16 begins a new narrative describing how David arose from lowly status to become king of Israel. This narrative continues through 2 Samuel 5:3. Some scholars entitle this narrative the "History of David's Rise" and take it as an apologetic work defending David against slanderous charges of killing his way to the throne.[1] One should remember, however, that the message of this narrative focuses on proving that David was a so-called "man after God's heart" rather than defending David against alleged murder charges. This change in subject matter is implied by the prophet Samuel's judgment against Saul in the previous chapter: "The LORD . . . has torn the kingdom of Israel from you today and has given it *to one of your neighbors – to one better than you*" (15:28, emphasis added). Chapter 16 introduces this neighbor who is better than Saul, the one to whom God gave the kingdom of Israel.

16:1–3 THE LORD SENDS SAMUEL TO BETHLEHEM

The Lord's regret about Saul is mentioned three times in chapter 15 (vv. 11, 29, 35). As explained earlier, the divine regret in the Old Testament points us to the Lord's new act rather than the past wrong. The fact that the previous chapter ends with the reference to the Lord's regret creates an expectation at the beginning of chapter 16 for what his new work will be. The chapter begins with the Lord scolding Samuel for staying in grief too long and sending him to anoint the future king:

> How long will you mourn for Saul, since I have rejected him as king over Israel? Fill your horn with oil and be on your way; I am sending you to Jesse of Bethlehem. I have chosen one of his sons to be king. (v. 1)

Saul had neither obeyed the Lord's command through Samuel nor repented sincerely, and so the Lord had rejected him. So why was Samuel mourning for Saul? Samuel's feelings here were ambiguous and complex, but Saul and Samuel were bound together by a common destiny. The rejection of Saul as king also meant the end of Samuel's role as a prophet to the people, teaching

---

1. MacCarter, *1 Samuel,* 27–30.

them "what is good and right" (see 12:23). This is confirmed by the fact that Samuel did not serve David in the way he had served Saul. His public career ended with the anointing of the new king, and the role of a prophet for David was given over to other prophets while Samuel was still alive.

In ancient China, the relationship between a king and his chief adviser was similar to that of a king and a prophet in early Israel. Sages who had political ambitions sought to work for a good king. If they could not find a good king, they did not enter court politics. For example, despite Zhuge Liang's worldwide fame for wisdom, he secluded himself in the mountains until he finally met Liu Bei, who was worthy of Zhuge Liang's service. One may say that Zhuge Liang did not want to experience what Samuel went through in mourning over Saul's failure as king. But the Lord did not want Samuel to stay melancholic about Saul's tragic destiny and reminded him that it is "I" the Lord who rejected Saul and who gave Samuel his final mission to anoint one of Jesse's sons as king over Israel. In a similar manner, Christians should not despair because of non-Christians, because our hope is not in people but in God. Even though we may fall into despair because of people, we must not stay in despair but trust that God will never let us down.

Samuel demurred, saying, "How can I go? If Saul hears about it, he will kill me" (v. 2). Although God had rejected Saul as king over Israel, he still sat upon the throne, with the authority to kill anyone who dared to rebel against him. Further, he was surrounded by loyal servants who would willingly murder at Saul's command. If Saul heard that Samuel, the king-maker, visited Bethlehem with a horn of oil in hand, Samuel would certainly be charged with and executed for rebellion. After all, Samuel had insulted him publicly in front of the people and had taken from him the honor of killing Agag, the captured king of the Amalekites. Thus Samuel was not exaggerating the danger of the mission to anoint one of Jesse's sons. Koreans like to say, "A noble man should not tie his shoe strings in a cucumber field, nor should he adjust his head gear under a plum tree," which means that a wise man should act preemptively to avoid unnecessary accusation by staying away from sources of misunderstanding. Though the Lord commands Samuel to act in a way that contradicts this conventional wisdom, he offers a safety measure.

The Lord proposes a cover-up story to justify Samuel's visit to Bethlehem in the eyes of potential accusers. Samuel is instructed to declare his purpose as religious by offering a sacrifice and inviting Jesse and his sons to attend the sacrifice. From there, God says that he will tell Samuel what to do next. Thus God will direct Samuel step by step regarding David's anointing. Notice how this differs from Saul's anointing, where God did not give detailed instructions except to command Samuel to anoint Saul as king over Israel. For instance, he did not specify the type of container to use for the oil, as with David's anointing ("fill your horn with oil"). Samuel could maneuver independently in Saul's anointing, but God directs Samuel in David's anointing as king over Israel. This narrative detail suggests that David and his kingdom will be different from Saul and his kingdom.

16:4–5 ELDERS GREET SAMUEL IN FEAR

The elders of Bethlehem had reason to fear Samuel's visit to their town. Rumors of his conflict with the reigning king may have gotten around by then. Since Bethlehem belonged to the tribe of Judah, a rival tribe to Benjamin, Samuel's visit to the Judahite town could implicate the Bethlehemites in potential charges of rebellion, thereby putting them in danger of Saul's retaliation. One may even discern fear in their greeting: "Do you come in peace?" Samuel assures them that his visit is not political but religious and invites them to the sacrifice: "I have come to sacrifice to the LORD. Consecrate yourselves and come to the sacrifice with me" (v. 5).

Note here that the invitation to the sacrifice was given to all the elders who came out to welcome Samuel. Since the scene of David's anointing follows this invitation to sacrifice, many people believe that the anointing took place during the sacrifice. If that had been the case, however, it would defeat the purpose of the cover-up story given by the Lord. The sacrifice was meant to create a circumstance where Samuel could anoint a new king without generating much publicity. Moreover, the narrator makes it clear that David's anointing took place "in the presence of his brothers" (v. 13), which suggests a private setting. So how can we reconcile this private setting for David's anointing with Samuel's general invitation to the elders to join him at the sacrifice? The text is short on details, leaving much to be filled in by the reader, but we can come up with the following scenario as one possible solution.

Jesse was one of the elders who greeted Samuel at the city gate, and he provided lodging for the visiting prophet. Samuel stayed in Jesse's house during his stay in Bethlehem, which would have given him a natural opportunity to observe Jesse's sons for himself to find out which one the Lord had chosen as king of Israel. Because Samuel was staying with Jesse's family, it would have been natural for him to consecrate Jesse and his sons and invite them to the sacrifice. The narrator then omits the sacrifice scene and moves to the scene of anointing (see vv. 6–13). The anointing took place in Jesse's house after they returned from the sacrifice – not in a sanctuary during the sacrifice. Jesse's house provided a perfect place for Samuel to anoint a new king without attracting unnecessary public attention.

This scenario reconciles Samuel's public invitation to the sacrifice with the private setting for his anointing of David. It also has a few advantages over the traditional understanding, which is that upon arriving at Bethlehem, Samuel took the elders of town to a local sanctuary, offered a sacrifice, and then anointed David as king of Israel, either during or immediately after the sacrifice. This traditional understanding cannot explain Samuel's words, "we will not sit down until he [David] arrives," which convey that they were at a meal. However, the meal in question could not be the post-sacrificial meal, because all of the elders would have participated, and the narrator makes it clear that only Jesse's family participated in the meal, and the elders did not witness the anointing (v. 13). Thus one may argue that David's anointing took place during the private family meal in Jesse's house. Moreover, the traditional understanding cannot account for how Samuel's command for consecration was observed. The law requires participants in a sacrifice to be ritually clean, and it would take days for an unclean person to become ritually pure. Samuel must have stayed in Bethlehem at least several days in order to officiate the town sacrifice at a local sanctuary and to find some time to anoint a new king in Jesse's house.

16:6–7 THE LORD LOOKS AT THE HEART

This section shows how the Lord's promise in verse 3 ("I will show you [Samuel] what to do") was fulfilled as Samuel sought to anoint a new king. The narrator depicts Samuel as communicating with God directly in real time, implying that the process of David's anointing was completely controlled by the Lord himself. When Eliab, Jesse's firstborn, who was handsome and tall like Saul, passed before the prophet, Samuel immediately felt drawn to him, saying, "Surely the LORD's anointed stands here before the LORD" (v. 6). It is not clear whether he said this aloud or inwardly, but we know that Samuel's judgment was wrong, because the Lord "rejected" Eliab by telling Samuel not to be deceived by "his appearance and his height" (v. 7). The vocabulary here recalls Saul and his tragic fate, for Eliab is "rejected." When Eliab reappears later in the narrative, he sounds very much like Saul when he persecutes David (see 17:28). After "rejecting" Eliab, the Lord uttered what has become the most famous verse in 1 Samuel:

> The LORD does not look at the things people look at. People look
> at the outward appearance, but the LORD looks at the heart. (v. 7)

This famous quote seems to pit the outward appearance against the invisible heart. But if God looks only at the heart, David's handsome features are hard to explain. Verse 7 may be better translated as follows: "The LORD does not judge as people judge. People judge by eyes, but the LORD judges by reason" (my translation). This alternative translation pits a myopic and partial judgment over against a rational and comprehensive judgment. This translation accounts for David's good looks later (see v. 12) – because divine judgment does not exclude appearance from the makings of an ideal leader. Furthermore, it makes God's judgment something attainable to men – because we as God's image-bearers are endowed with the ability to "think God's thoughts after him."[2]

That said, people are easily deceived by appearances. Pang Tong in *Three Kingdoms* was known to be extraordinarily wise and learned in politics and military strategies. Yet he spent most of his life without public office because of his ugly looks. Even prudent Lui Bei was misled by Pang Tong's appearance and gave him a low-ranking administrative job despite his high performance on the civil service examination. Christians are no exception in this regard. We often fall into the trap of judging others by appearance, but we should imitate God in his judgment.

16:8–13 SAMUEL ANOINTS DAVID

Eliab, Abinadab and Shammah each passed in front of Samuel, but after each one, Samuel said to Jesse, "The LORD has not chosen this one either" (vv. 8–9). The verdict was the same with seven of Jesse's sons. Due to the conception of seven as a perfect number, the impression is that there is no other son left. Yet the Lord had told Samuel that he had chosen one of Jesse's sons as king over Israel, so Samuel asked Jesse if he had any other children (v. 11).

Jesse admitted that he had one more son, but his description of his youngest son intimates that Jesse thought of David as the least promising: "There is still the youngest . . . He is tending the sheep" (v. 11). The Hebrew phrase *haqatan* ("the youngest") literally means "the small one." This may refer first to his short height, as the author does not say anything about David's stature

---

2. See Cornelius Van Til, *An Introduction to Systematic Theology* (Phillipsburg, NJ: P & R Publishing), especially ch. 14.

when he describes his appearance using several superlatives ("ruddy . . . beautiful . . . handsome") in verse 12. But "the small one" also reflects Jesse's low expectations for David. He must have put more hope in his first three sons, who were all named in the text, but he did not bother to mention his youngest son's name when answering Samuel. Interestingly, David remains nameless until he is anointed with oil and the spirit (v. 13). Further, David's job as a shepherd corroborates Jesse's low expectations, for in those days shepherding was neither a romantic nor a respectful job. Since shepherding required little learned skills, the job was usually given to boys or women. More promising sons were sent to war to make their names through bravery, or they were sent to cities to pursue professional careers, whereas the least promising had to stay with the parents at home, tending the sheep and running the parents' errands. The fact that David was not only the smallest of all the brothers, but also tending the sheep – in contrast to Saul, who was the biggest of Israel and a professional farmer – paint him as the least likely of all Jesse's sons to be great in the world.

On hearing Jesse's reply, Samuel insisted on seeing the youngest son for himself, because he intuited that this was the one God had chosen as king over Israel. When David was brought in from the field, the text says, "He was glowing with health and had fine appearance and handsome features" (v. 12). David's good appearance (Hebrew *tov roi*) may have puzzled Samuel, but he faithfully obeyed the Lord's command and anointed David king of Israel. Immediately, "the spirit of the LORD came powerfully upon David" (v. 13).

David's anointing bears similarities to Saul's anointing. Both Saul and David were anointed by Samuel. Both were anointed in private settings away from the public eye. After being anointed, the spirit came down upon both of them. But these similarities only belie the fundamental differences between the two kings. First, Samuel took many initiatives as a king-maker in anointing Saul (see ch. 10). But in anointing David, he passively followed detailed instructions given by the Lord. In other words, the Lord took more initiative to anoint David than Saul.[3] This intimates that David will be obedient to the Lord, contrasting with Saul's disobedience. Second, Samuel was the only witness to Saul's anointing, but Jesse's whole family witnessed David's anointing. This foreshadows each king's path to the throne, for Saul's personal relationship with Samuel was crucial to the fate of his kingdom, whereas Samuel

---

3. For example, God instructed Samuel to prepare a horn of oil for David, whereas Samuel used a flask of oil for Saul.

disappeared from David's life after anointing him. David's road to the throne was aided by those around him who firmly believed in him as the anointed one of the Lord. Finally, the Spirit's presence in Saul was sporadic, as with the charismatic judges, whereas the Spirit stayed with David consistently after his anointing. Verse 13 uses the Hebrew phrase, *mehayom hahu wama'ala*, which means "from the day on" to describe the Spirit's presence upon David. This suggests that David will be a king who will always be led by the Holy Spirit in contrast with Saul, who suffered from sporadic possession by an evil spirit.

The episode of David's anointing teaches us that God's judgment may be different from people's. First, one who is small in people's eyes may turn out to be great in God's eyes. Thus we should not judge people by external factors such as looks, houses, jobs, or savings. God can use the least of us for his kingdom. Liu Bei's ugly adviser in *Three Kingdoms* ended up rendering the greatest service for his country by sacrificing his own life. Second, Christians should fear God's judgment more than people's. Greatness can be achieved only when we live up to the truth – not to people's expectations. The first king of the Wei Kingdom, Cao Cao, left the following words when he died: "Yesterday, the people in the world had a wrong idea about me. Today, the people in the world have still got me wrong. It is very possible that even tomorrow they will misunderstand me. But I am who I am no matter what they say about me. I am not afraid of being misunderstood by the world." Although Cao Cao was a usurper, his unwavering belief in his own principles enabled him to ascend to the throne from a lowly position. The world under Satan's rule will hate Christians, especially when they think differently and act differently from worldly people. Let us not become weary in doing good works for the Lord (Gal 6:9).

16:14–18 DAVID RECOMMENDED AS A COURT MUSICIAN

The spirit of the Lord departed from Saul (v. 14) the moment it came upon David. The narrator implies this by juxtaposing these two events after one another and by placing the spirit's departure from Saul in a Hebrew syntax that warrants translating it in a pluperfect tense ("had departed," NIV). Now "an evil spirit from the LORD" (v. 14) entered Saul's heart and controlled him thereafter. How can an evil spirit come from the Lord? How is it different from Satan, the arch-enemy of the Lord? This is a difficult question, but many scholars agree that the idea of Satan developed relatively late in the history of the Israelite religion.[4] In the Old Testament, there are only three episodes where Satan figures prominently, and all of them are late in its composition.[5] Two of these episodes portray Satan as one of the attendants in the Lord's heavenly court (see Job 1–2; Zech 3:2). The idea of an evil spirit from the Lord may be a transitional concept in that it is similar to Satan in its function as an accuser, tormenter, and liar, but different from Satan in that it works for the Lord. For instance, the spirit of the Lord empowers David to do what he was called to do, whereas "an evil spirit from the LORD" debilitated and tormented Saul to destruction.

We do not know exactly what the evil spirit did to Saul. Court officials' reactions suggest some symptoms that signify mental imbalance. The Hebrew *biat*, which is translated as "torment" in the NIV, occurs frequently in Job, connoting Job's theological confusion and psychological breakdown caused by disasters, ill health, friends' accusations, and so on (see Job 7:14; 9:34; 13:11; 15:24; 18:11; 33:7). Since insanity was often attributed to an evil spirit, Saul's servants suggested that the king should hire someone skilled at playing the lyre to alleviate his symptoms. Music was used in ancient Israel to help prophets commune with the spirit. For instance, Elisha prophesied for king Ahab while the harpist was playing (2 Kgs 3:14–15). But this is the only place in the Bible where music was used specifically for exorcism. East Asians are familiar with this practice. Korean traditional instrumental music called *Nongak* originated in an exorcistic ritual.

Immediately Saul ordered his servants to search for someone who could play the lyre well (v. 17). One of his servants recommended "a son of Jesse of Bethlehem," who was a good lyre player, a man of virtue,[6] a warrior, an eloquent speaker, and a fine-looking man (v. 18). To top it off, the Lord was with him. The servant's answer seems strange, because he recommended David the moment Saul issued the order! In those days, it would have taken days or even months to search for someone to fill any position of importance. Further, David was the youngest of Jesse's sons, too obscure for the servant within the palace to know so well. Furthermore, David had never gone to war before this conversation, so how could he be called "a warrior" (literally, "a man of war"), a term that was usually reserved for someone with a lot of experience

---

4. See Victor P. Hamilton, "Satan," in *ABD*, 985–989.
5. See 1 Chr 21:1; Job 1–2; Zech 3:2.
6. Hebrew *gibbor hayil* which NIV translates as "a brave man" may refer to an ideal man in a non-military setting: it is better translated as "a man of virtue" here, because the idea of bravery is already assumed under the title "a warrior."

in battles? We may never be able to answer these questions satisfactorily, but David is clearly presented not only as a good musician, but also as an ideal king. Interestingly, the anonymous servant used the same expression in his recommendation of David as the Lord: "I have seen" the son of Jesse! (vv. 1, 18).[7] This subtly hints to the fact that David's role in Saul's court will not be limited to playing the lyre for a sick king, for David will replace Saul as king of Israel.

The five traits that the anonymous servant attributed to David may also apply to an ideal king in ancient China and Korea. Two in particular were considered crucial: a man of virtue and piety. Liu Bei, the founder of the Shu Han state, is widely recognized as a paragon for a king in China and Korea because he acted always for the cause of humanity and tried to uphold the will of Heaven. David was also a man of virtue and a man of God. He tried never to kill innocent people in his endeavor to the throne, even though that would have expedited his enthronement. Further, he tried to do the will of God instead of pursuing his own ambitions (see 1 Sam 13:4). Many Asians have suffered from a lack of good leadership. Good leaders are not those who make their nations rich and strong at the expense of the people, but those who do the will of Heaven by putting the people first in their policy making.

16:19–23 DAVID IN SAUL'S SERVICE

Saul sent messengers to Jesse to summon David for a tryout: "Send me your son David, who is with your sheep" (v. 19). It was natural for Saul to communicate with Jesse rather than David, since the patriarch had absolute power over his household. Similarly, when Saul decided to keep David in his service, he had to send messengers to Jesse to close the deal. Yet in his first message to Jesse, Saul identified David as a shepherd rather than an excellent lyre player. This may have something to do with the fact that shepherding was a traditional metaphor for an ideal king in the ancient Near East. For instance, Hammurabi, king of Babylon, identified himself as a shepherd king who would take care of the lowly and underprivileged. By having Saul call David a shepherd in the context of David's entry into court as a musician, the narrator foreshadows David becoming much more than a musician in Saul's court. It is

---

7. NIV: "I have chosen" (v. 1).

no coincidence that Saul was immediately fond of David and promoted him to "one of his armor-bearers" (v. 21).[8]

It is interesting to consider how Jesse might have felt about Saul's request for David. He may have associated it with the recent event of Samuel's anointing of David. If David was destined to rise to the throne, Saul's call might be the first step towards that fate. So Jesse sent his son to the king with hefty gifts of a donkey loaded with bread, a skin of wine, and a young goat, just as Asians bring gifts when they visit someone they respect highly.

Significantly, the narrator concludes the chapter about Samuel anointing David by saying, "whenever David would take up his lyre and play . . . the evil spirit would leave him [Saul]" (v. 23). This describes David as overpowering the evil spirit that possessed Saul, suggesting that Saul will ultimately give way to David. Thus chapter 16 is not only concerned with David's anointing as a king but also signals David's inevitable victory over Saul.

ARMOR-BEARERS

Saul, Jonathan, Joab, and Goliath are said to have used armor-bearers in battle. We even know one of Joab's armor-bearer by name: "Naharai the Beerothite" (2 Sam 23:37), who was appointed as one of David's thirty bodyguards. Even unnamed armor-bearers play significant roles in the narrative. For instance, Jonathan's armor-bearer helped his master vanquish the Philistines in the battle of Mikmash. This shows that armor-bearers were chosen among one's bravest and most loyal warriors. The most famous armor-bearer in China is Zhou Cang, who was Guan Yu's bodyguard and carried the Green Dragon Crescent Blade, which weighed about 50 kilograms. Even more challenging than the weight of Guan Yu's weapon was the speed of his horse, Red Hare, which was said to travel 417 kilometers per day without stopping. Since armor-bearers of that time always moved on foot, Zhou Cang had to run at top speed. According to one legend, Zhou Cang had wings on his feet that helped him run so fast.

---

8. One may explain this promotion by Saul's penchant for taking mighty or brave men into his service (14:52). But it reveals more about David than Saul, because David is both lovable and capable. First, David was loved by everyone in court. Saul said, "I am pleased with him" (v. 22) when he negotiated a longer contract with Jesse. In fact, Saul is the first person to have loved David (v. 21: "liked," NIV). His family members, his court attendants, and all the people in the streets will eventually love David as well. It is no coincidence that the name "David" means the "one who is loved." Second, David was capable of doing what he was called to do. "Whenever the Spirit from God came on Saul, David would take up his lyre and play. Then relief would come to Saul; he would feel better, and the evil spirit would leave him" (v. 23).

1 SAMUEL 17:1–58

DAVID AND GOLIATH

Saul's calling as king of Israel was to deliver the Israelites from the hand of the Philistines (see 9:16). As chapter 14 shows, he fulfilled this calling to some degree when he and Jonathan defeated the Philistines at the battle of Mikmash. But Saul's imprudent command to fast during that battle compromised Israel's victory, because many remnants of the defeated Philistine army escaped to their land during the night. At the beginning of chapter 17, we see the Philistines gathering their forces in the Valley of Elah for another war with Israel, no doubt reminding Saul of his failure to destroy the Philistines in the previous battle. Just as Jonathan was the true hero in the battle of Mikmash, David will outshine Saul by killing Goliath in the battle of Elah. Though David was characterized as *haqatan*, "the small one," by his father Jesse (see 16:11), he renders the biggest contribution in the battle of Elah. As Koreans would say, "a small chili is hot."

17:1–11 SETTING: PHILISTINE CRISIS

The battle line was drawn up in the valley plain of Elah in western Judah. Having passed Azeka, the Philistine army gathered their forces at Sokoh, a gate city to the Judean hill country (v. 1). In response, Saul's army camped at one hillside of the Valley of Elah to stop the Philistines from advancing further inland (v. 2). The location of Ephes Dammin, where the Philistines pitched camp, has not been identified yet. Notably, the Philistines did not attack the armies of Israel at once, which may be explained by the power equilibrium that had been reached between the two armies since Israel's victory at Mikmash. Had the Philistine army surpassed its enemy in power, they would have launched a full attack without delay. Instead, while camped at Ephes Dammin, the Philistines commanded Goliath to act as "a champion" for their army. They did not engage in battle for forty days.

The narrator introduces Goliath as "a champion . . . from Gath" (v. 4). A champion referred to a soldier who fought a duel on behalf of the whole army. The purpose of this duel varied from battle to battle: it could be the determining factor of a war to avoid shedding too much blood, or it could be to boost the morale of soldiers before an all-out engagement. The duel between two or multiple champions was a well-known practice in ancient warfare (see 2 Sam 2:14). For instance, the duel between Zhang Fei, the third oath brother, and

Machau, a warrior in the northwest of ancient China, became a legend: they exchanged blows with their spears hundreds of times without resolution, and their fight continued even after night fell, under torch light.

Gath, Goliath's hometown, was reputed to produce giant warriors (see Josh 11:22). Even David employed the Gittites as his bodyguard (2 Sam 15:16). The stature of Goliath from Gath was "six cubits and a span," or about three meters (v. 4). Some scholars who find the number unrealistic prefer the Septuagint's reading of "four cubits and a span," or about two meters. In either case, Goliath's stature was big enough to intimidate anyone by ancient standards. After noting his height, the narrator describes Goliath's arms and armor in detail (vv. 5–6). Scholars agree that Goliath dressed like a typical Greek soldier,[1] which supports the idea that the Philistines originally migrated from Aegean Greece. Be that as it may, he thoroughly wrapped himself with armor from head to toe so as to leave no part of his body unprotected. The detailed description of his outfit increases the suspense of the subsequent duel by slowing down the flow of narrative. It also belies the weakness of the Philistine champion, for he left his face uncovered!

As for weaponry, Goliath carried a bronze spear behind his back. Its shaft had a loop of cord attached to it like a weaver's rod to maximize speed and accuracy, and it had an impressive iron head that weighed six hundred shekels, or about seven kilograms (v. 7). This spear eventually became part of Goliath's epithet, for he is later called "Goliath the Gittite, who had a spear with a shaft like a weaver's rod" (see 2 Sam 21:19). This recalls a similar practice in ancient Chinese literature, wherein a warrior is identified with his characteristic weapon. For instance, Gwan Yu, the second oath brother, is always identified as the owner of a legendary weapon called the "Green Dragon Crescent Blade." Yet the author deliberately fails to mention Goliath's sword here, possibly because his sword will soon be wielded by a new owner.

Goliath insultingly challenges the Israelites to a duel. In his speech, he introduces himself as "a Philistine," a free citizen of his land, and denounces the Israelites for being "the servants of Saul" (v. 8). He attempts to hurt the pride of the Israelites even more by adding that the Israelites will become the servants of the Philistines if he wins the duel. The ethos of Goliath's speech recalls that of an anonymous Philistine officer's speech for his dispirited soldiers: "Be strong, Philistines! Be men, or you will be servants to the Hebrews, as they have been to you" (see 4:9, my translation). In contrast to the Philistines, who

---

1. See MacCarter, *1 Samuel*, 292.

fought bravely so that they would not become servants to Israel in the battle of Ebenezer, the Israelites could not conjure up the courage to fight Goliath. No one was willing to take up the challenge as King Saul and all Israel hunkered down in extreme fear. This set the stage for the real hero's debut.

17:12–24 DAVID RUNS ERRANDS TO HIS BROTHERS

The narrator introduces David to the narrative as if for the first time (vv. 12–14). This apparently redundant introduction to the Israelite champion may have been necessitated by the long introduction to his Philistine counterpart. He is introduced as the youngest (literally, "the smallest") of Jesse's eight sons (v. 14), who stayed with his father while some of Jesse's older sons went out to fight the Philistines. The mention of Jesse's advanced age (v. 12) appears to explain why his three sons, rather than Jesse, were drafted for military service. It also explains why David "went back and forth" from Saul to Jesse (v. 15). The aged father would have given David a legitimate excuse to "commute," at least in the opinion of ancient readers. Further, the author presents David as a shepherd who tended his old father's sheep (v. 15) rather than being Saul's armor-bearer (see 16:21). This may foreshadow David's unconventional way of fighting a duel with an experienced warrior who was heavily armed with formidable weapons.

Jesse sent David on an errand to deliver provisions to his soldier brothers, to see if they are well, and to bring back some assurance from them. The most important thing for victory in war was a constant supply of provisions, since ancient wars often extended for weeks and months. This battle between the Israelites and the Philistines had dragged on for forty days (v. 16). Although a king was responsible for provisions during a war, Saul's administration may not have been well-organized enough to pull together resources in a timely manner, thereby necessitating that Jesse send private provisions to his sons. Roasted grain and bread were staple foods for David's brothers, whereas ten cheeses were intended as a gift for the unit commander to make things go smoothly for David.

When David arrived at the camp, the army had already gone out to the valley in battle formations. So after leaving his things to the keeper of supplies, he hurried to the battle lines to make sure that his brothers were well. This would have concluded David's mission from his father, but then he saw and heard Goliath: "Goliath, the Philistine champion from Gath, stepped out from his lines and shouted his usual defiance, and David heard it" (v. 23). The Hebrew word *heref* ("defy") connotes insult and shame. It was commonplace in ancient battles to exchange curses before a physical fight in order to draw an enemy army out of their defensive positions. For instance, Liu Bei's army was not able to capture a castle on Irung Mountain because the enemy within the castle would not come out of the gate to fight. The enemy's strategy was to hole themselves up in a castle and block the passage of Liu Bei's army. Liu Bei had to capture the castle in order to further his military expedition against the Riverland, and so he placed a unit of professional cursers in front of the army and had them throw taunts at those within the castle. Eventually, after cursing the enemy in a loud voice all day every day, the hot-blooded young general, Son, came out with his men, violating the order not to engage a battle under any circumstances. He was defeated by Liu Bei's army and lost his castle, showing that it can be a virtue to ignore the enemy's taunts, especially when holding ground that has strategic advantages. But the reason for silence in the Israelite camp was not strategic, but simply because they were all in great fear.

17:25–31 DAVID'S STRATEGY TO GAIN AN AUDIENCE WITH SAUL

Upon hearing Goliath's taunts, David decided to take up his challenge to fight. But David was only a shepherd boy – not an experienced warrior – and people would not take him seriously if he volunteered to fight. Moreover, if the boy was defeated and killed, it would bring more shame on the Israelite army, for they would become the servants of the Philistines (v. 9). This was a legitimate concern, because when Goliath saw a boy approaching him, he laughed, not only mocking David but also the whole army that David represented. Guan Yu, when he still had no official position, volunteered to fight Hua Xion. But Yuan Shao, a war ruler, did not permit Guan Yu to fight even though no other general had dared to volunteer, saying, "Are you trying to insult us? A mere archer! Have we no more commanders? What nonsense! Get him out of here." Even when Cao Cao tried to help Guan Yu, Yuan Shao insisted and added, "Hua Xion will laugh in his sleeves!"[2] Under normal circumstances there would have been no chance for David to become a champion for Israel.

So David devised a stratagem to get an audience with king Saul. Pretending to have interest in the rewards promised by Saul for killing Goliath, he went around the camp inquiring about Saul's rewards (vv. 26–27). Even after his brother Eliab scolded him for being arrogant and overly ambitious, he did not stop (vv. 28–30). On a superficial level, David appeared to have an interest in

---

2. Roberts, *Three Kingdoms*, 65.

getting rich, marrying into the royal family, and having a tax exemption. But on a deeper level, David was trying to generate a loud enough buzz that it would reach Saul. The strategy worked, for "What David said was overheard and reported to Saul, and Saul sent for him" (v. 31). A similar tactic was used by Zhuge Liang, Liu Bei's chief adviser. In order to seal a political alliance through marriage between his lord and the sister of Sun Quan, king of the Riverland, Zhuge Liang directed his generals to go to public markets in the Riverland and buy various wedding gifts in large quantities, so that the rumor about the marriage might spread across the Riverland. He reasoned that Sun Quan could not change his mind about the marriage, because it would publicly shame his sister and his whole family. Likewise, Saul could not ignore the rumor about David, who claimed to have the guts and skill to kill Goliath.

This perspective helps us solve some difficulties in the text. First, David was not "conceited" or "wicked," as Eliab argued (v. 28), for his heart concern was for the reputation of the Lord. This is revealed in the way David changed the wording of Goliath's challenge. Although Goliath challenged "the armies of Israel" (v. 10), David accepted Goliath's challenge because he defied "the armies of the living God" (v. 26). Second, David was not sinfully competing for his father's love or for power over his brothers, unlike young Joseph, who brought evil reports about his brothers to Jacob. David was not ignoring his older brother Eliab when he responded, "Can't I even talk?" (v. 29). Rather, he was carrying out his secret plan. Eliab's accusation confirmed that David's stratagem was working, for he attracted enough attention to gain an audience with Saul. David's good relationship with his brothers is corroborated by the fact that David's brothers, including Eliab, never posed a threat to David during his circuitous journey to the throne. Rather, his brothers became strong supporters when David was in distress (see 22:1).

17:32–40 DAVID VOLUNTEERS TO FIGHT BEFORE SAUL

After gaining an audience with the king, David had to persuade Saul to let him fight on behalf of Israel. He had to convince Saul of his ability to confront and defeat the Philistine champion, for Saul would not risk his own reputation, let alone his army's. David started by sharing his experience as a shepherd, comparing Goliath to the predators from whom he saved his sheep, which he killed when they turned on him (vv. 34–36). Finally, he appealed to have faith in God: "The Lord who rescued me from the paw of the lion and the paw of the bear will rescue me from the hand of this Philistine" (v. 37).

David proved himself as an eloquent speaker (as the anonymous servant said in 16:18). His speech was moving enough to convince Saul, since he gave David a blessing. Perhaps Saul may have reasoned that even if the devout young man was defeated and killed by the monstrous Goliath, he had nothing to lose. He might have felt that the story of David's selfless bravery and faith in God would be an inspiration for other soldiers. Though Saul was moved by David's zeal for the reputation of the Lord and his supreme faith in his salvation, he did not necessarily share that zealous faith with David.

This is intimated by Saul's attempt to arm David with his armor and his sword. Since he doubted that a shepherd boy could defeat an experienced warrior, he tried to make David as warrior-like as possible in order to increase his odds of winning. But the shepherd boy was not used to the heavy armor, and so he took it off, approaching Goliath instead with his pastoral staff, sling, and a pouch of stones. Although Saul tried to make an avatar out of David by symbolically clothing him with his authority and power, David refused to wear Saul's armor as he went out to confront the Philistine champion, indicating that his trust and hope were in the Lord alone.

17:41–47 DAVID AND GOLIATH EXCHANGE TAUNTS

David and Goliath stepped out from their lines and came closer to each other. Goliath donned armor from head to toe and carried three different assault weapons. To top it off, he was accompanied by a shield bearer. David, on the contrary, neither wore armor nor carried any conventional weapons. Ironically, this portrays Goliath as an underdog who needed weapons and protection.

The moment Goliath saw David, he "despised him" (v. 42) and was convinced of his victory. But he also felt insulted for being challenged by a shepherd boy, as his taunts show: "Am I a dog, that you come at me with sticks?" (v. 43). Goliath continued to curse David by invoking his gods, concluding with the usual "carrion" threat (v. 44). David responded to these insults with one of the most famous speeches in the history of war:

> You come against me with sword and spear and javelin, but I come against you in the name of the LORD Almighty, the God of the armies of Israel, whom you have defied. (v. 45)

But what does it mean to "come . . . in the name of the LORD"? First, David contrasts Goliath's weapons with the name of the Lord, which suggests that for David, God was the weapon that would defeat Goliath. The idea of god being a weapon is not uncommon in ancient Near Eastern literature (e.g.

Tiamat's weapons).[3] This appears to be corroborated by David's words in the next verse: "The LORD will deliver you [Goliath] into my hands" (v. 46). Second, the phrase may also refer to the cause for the battle. David was not fighting for his own glory (see v. 26), nor for Saul's army, but for the reputation of the Lord (v. 36). This is corroborated by the conclusion of David's speech: "I will strike you down and cut off your head . . . so that the whole world will know that there is a God in Israel . . . that it is not by word or spear that the LORD saves; for the battle is the LORD's" (vv. 46–47).

David's zeal for the name of God equates with the zeal for truth and righteousness. When Cao Cao attacked Tao Qian, the governor of Xuzhou, under the pretext of avenging his father, few dared to come to Tao Qian's rescue because they were afraid of Cao Cao's massive army. But Liu Bei and his brothers marched their small force against Cao Cao to help Tao Quian. When a soldier asked Liu Bei why he dared to confront Cao Cao with so small a force, Liu Bei answered, *though we are certainly outnumbered by Cao Cao's army by a huge margin, we can defeat it because what Cao Cao has done is simply wrong. Righteousness is immortal and great cause is eternal.* Then Liu Bei sent his soldiers off to battle by shouting, "Righteousness is immortal and great cause is eternal." David's fight for the name of God teaches us that faith can overcome power when we fight for truth and righteousness in this fallen world.

17:48–54 DAVID KILLS GOLIATH

David ran quickly to engage Goliath in a duel, but Goliath was more cautious (v. 48). Although David vowed that he would cut off Goliath's head, he was carrying no sword. Even the sticks he carried only served as a distraction, for he did not use them in actual battle. The sight of an unarmed shepherd boy would have lowered Goliath's guard. At that moment, David took a stone out of his shepherd pouch and slung it, striking Goliath right on the forehead (v. 49). When Goliath fell, David ran to his body and cut off his head, using Goliath's own sword. Encouraged by David's heroic victory, Saul's army defeated the Philistines and chased them back to their land.

David's victory was a miracle that was made possible by the Lord's help and David's strategic planning. Along with being a man of great faith, David

---

3. In *Enuma Elish*, the Mesopotamian creation story, Marduk engages in a cosmic battle with the opponent god of the sea, Tiamat. In preparation for the battle, Tiamat fashions various divine monsters – the Viper, the Dragon, the Sphinx, the Great-Lion, the Mad-Dog, the Scorpion-Man – so that they march at the side of Tiamat. See ANET 62.

was brave and clever. He wore neither armor nor weapons, and he used sticks to distract the enemy from his secret weapon. David also used a medium-range weapon (a sling), which violated the convention of using a short-range weapon (e.g. a sword, spear, or javelin) in a duel. In the *Iliad*, Paris is hated by almost everyone because his choice of weapon, the bow, was regarded as a cowardly form of combat. Yet in a duel with Menelaus, he did not use the bow. In the *Three Kingdoms*, Pangde was remembered as a scoundrel because he wounded Guan Yu in a duel by using a bow. These two extra biblical examples show that David's tactic was an unconventional, but wise and perhaps inevitable, means for a shepherd boy to defeat a Philistine warrior.

17:55–58 SAUL WANTS TO KNOW WHOSE SON IS DAVID

In this passage, Saul asked the same question twice: once to Abner, the commander of the army, and again to David when he returned from the duel with Goliath's head in his hand. Saul asked, "whose son is he . . . whose son are you?" (v. 55, 58). This passage has puzzled many readers, because it seems to suggest that Saul did not know David, even though David had been in Saul's service for some time. If Saul loved David enough to promote him to be his armor-bearer (16:21), how could Saul not know who David was? Further, he interviewed David right before the duel and gave him his armor.

The solution to this puzzle lies in Saul's question itself, for he asked whose son David was – not who David was. Saul already knew that David was his musician and armor-bearer. But having killed Goliath, David would become Saul's son-in-law, and his father's house would have a tax exemption. Thus Saul had an interest in David's family.[4]

David rose to the center of national interest with his crushing victory over the Philistine champion. David delivered the people of Israel from the hand of the Philistines, a duty that had originally been entrusted to king Saul. If David's anointing in chapter 16 "designated" him as a king, his victory over Goliath "demonstrated" his divine designation as a king. But unlike Saul's ascension to the throne, where his kingship was "confirmed" soon after his victory over the Ammonites, David had to endure many years of suffering before his kingship would be confirmed before the whole nation (see 2 Sam 5:3). This season of suffering characterized David's rise to the throne, for David became a man of obedience through suffering, which is an essential trait of an Israelite king.

---

4. See Provan, Long, and Longman III, *A Biblical History of Israel*, 223.

1 SAMUEL 18:1–30

SAUL'S GROWING FEAR OF DAVID

David won the hearts of the people by his successful battles against the Philistines. His success was interpreted as a sign of the Lord's special presence in him. Saul regarded David with fear and hostility. It was not simply due to his jealousy of popular David, but, more importantly, due to his realization that David was "the neighbor" that Samuel had predicted would replace him as king over Israel (see 15:28). After several failed attempts to dampen David's popularity or even kill him, Saul devised a fake marriage proposal to deliver David into the hand of the Philistines. In *Three Kingdoms,* Zhou Yu uses a similar stratagem to seek to entrap Liu Bei: "Turning to Lü Su, Zhou Yu said, 'I have a plan that will deliver Liu Bei and Jingzhou into our hands with no effort at all . . . I am going to propose to our Lord that he send a go-between to Jingzhou and convince Liu Bei to marry into the family. When he bites the bait and comes to Nanxu, he will find himself held prisoner instead of getting married.'"[1] But David outwitted Saul and married into the royal family. The more well-known David became, the more Saul feared him.

18:1–5 DAVID AND JONATHAN

After David's victory over Goliath, Jonathan, Saul's crown prince, made a covenant with David. The text does not articulate the terms of that relationship, but because Jonathan delivered his royal clothes and weapons to David, we can gather that he yielded his right of royal succession to David, the killer of Goliath. In other words, he abdicated the throne to David. This raises the question of why anyone would want to give up such a huge privilege to a virtual stranger. Some scholars conclude that this episode is a fiction created to legitimize David's kingship.[2] Others may appeal to the romantic notion that Jonathan "loved" David (vv. 1, 3) so much that he wanted to give him everything he had. These two answers are not satisfactory because the first has no textual basis of support, and the second anachronistically applies our modern notion of love to the ancient Israelites.

---

1. Roberts, *Three Kingdoms,* 631.
2. Steven L. McKenzie, *King David: A Biography* (Oxford: Oxford University Press, 2000), 84–85.

A better answer is closely related with the reason that Jonathan did not take up Goliath's challenge in the battle of Elah. Judging from the faith and audacity that Jonathan demonstrated in the battle of Mikmash (ch. 14), his silence before the challenge suggests an inner restraint. He may have reasoned that the one who killed Goliath and saved Israel was "the neighbor" who Samuel predicted would replace Saul (see 15:28). In other words, he was waiting for the God-favored neighbor to appear and demonstrate his calling by delivering Israel from the Philistine crisis. When he saw David, a young shepherd without a sword, defeat and kill the three-meter tall Philistine warrior armed with iron weapons, he knew that David was the one sent by God. Thus Jonathan delivered his right of succession to David right after David finished talking with his father, revealing his faith in the Lord's providence rather than his infatuation with a handsome and able shepherd boy.

The statement, "Jonathan became one in spirit with David and loved him as himself" (v. 1), need not be taken as a romantic relationship between David and Jonathan, let alone a homosexual one, but rather a political relationship. The word "love" in ancient treaty documents often refers to the proper relation between a king and a vassal. The Hebrew *niqsherah* ("became one") may also refer to a political alliance. Further, the word "as himself" does not make the relationship less political, for its original Hebrew, *napsho,* may be translated alternatively as "his life." The notion of loving someone as or with one's life is the highest expression of loyalty towards a king. For this reason, loyal subjects were willing to kill themselves after their Lord died in the ancient world.

But this background does not imply that no personal bond existed between David and Jonathan. Their relationship was political because they worked towards the same political goal, which was to establish David's kingdom in Israel. An intimate personal bond may have developed along the way – as a later story implies (see 19:41). Thus one may argue that the covenantal relationship between David and Jonathan was political in essence, but their political "love" may have developed into brotherly love. We see it among the three oath brothers in *Three Kingdoms* when Liu Bei, Guan Yu, and Zhang Fei swear an oath to become brothers in the peach garden:

> We three, though of separate ancestry, join in brotherhood here, combining strength and purpose, to relieve the present crisis. We will perform our duty to the Emperor and protect the common fold of the land. We dare not hope to be together always but hereby vow to die the selfsame day. Let shining Heaven

above and the fruitful land below bear witness to our resolve. May Heaven and man scourge whosoever fails this vow.[3]

As their oath shows, their relationship was not only political – in the sense that they combined strength and purpose to revive the Han dynasty – but also covenantal – in the sense that Liu Bei, the eldest brother, acted as a warlord over the other brothers. They also cared for one another like real brothers, vowing to die on the same day.

David succeeded in winning Saul's heart as well, for Saul is the first in the text "to love" David (16:21: "liked" in NIV). Saul loved David so much that he promoted him to become his armor-bearer. Later, after David's victory over Goliath, Saul kept David constantly in his service and no longer allowed him to return to his father's house (v. 2). Further, after seeing David achieve victory on every battlefield where he was sent, Saul gave him "a high rank in the army" (v. 5), which certainly refers to a rank higher than a "commander over a thousand men" (v. 13), if not the highest rank in the army available to commoners. David's promotion was well received among all the soldiers, for Saul's officers were excited to have David as their commander. Thus David was successful, and everyone appeared to like him. But this changed suddenly because of a folksong innocently chanted by women in the streets.

18:6–9 FOLKSONG, THE GAME-CHANGER

Ancient Chinese and Koreans believed that songs sung spontaneously by women and children in the streets reflected the will of Heaven. So it was not uncommon for a folksong to be written and disseminated among the commoners to legitimize a coup against an incumbent king, as the song would have made the coup appear to be in accordance with the will of Heaven. Wang Yun once wrote such a song as part of his efforts to remove Dong Zhuo, a villain ruler, from power: "The grass is in the meadow looks fresh now and green, but wait but ten days, not a blade will be seen." Dong Zhuo was so dull and self-absorbed that he interpreted the song in his own favor, and soon after he was removed from power by Wang Yun. But Saul was smarter than Dong Zhuo. When Saul heard a folksong sung by women in the streets, he immediately caught its ominous connotation:

Saul has slain his thousands,
and David his tens of thousands. (v. 7)

---

3. Roberts, *Three Kingdoms*, 12–13.

In fact, the song itself may not have been treacherous. The Hebrew poem praises both Saul and David, using a typical numeric parallelism: for example, 3//4, 6//7, or 1,000//10,000. These numbers are not meant to be read literally in Hebrew poetry. Apparently, the women in the streets were simply celebrating the triumphant return of Saul's army led by Saul's loyal servant David. But Saul found the lyric treacherous and reasoned, "They have credited David with tens of thousands . . . but me with only thousands. What more can he get but the kingdom?" (v. 8). East Asians honor a heroic warrior with the title *wan ren zhi di,* "a match for ten thousand enemies." Gyan Yu acquired this title and people later worshipped him as a god. It is no surprise therefore that Saul feared David when he was praised as *wan ren zhi di*!

This was a game-changer in Saul's dealings with David, for Saul realized that David was the neighbor that the prophet Samuel had predicted would replace him as king over Israel. From that time on, "Saul kept a close eye on David" with murderous intention (v. 9). Saul arrogantly rejected the Lord's will revealed through Samuel and then expressed in the spontaneous folksong in the streets. But this hardness of heart is familiar, for only God's grace can restrain our arrogant rebellion and restore us to attend to his words.

18:10–16 SAUL ATTEMPTS TO KILL DAVID

The next day, an evil spirit came upon Saul, and he attempted to kill David as he played the lyre for Saul. The phrase "the next day" makes a clear connection between Saul's murderous anger and the evil spirit that possessed him, since this temporal phrase may create a logical relation between two temporal events. This intimates that Saul's murderous anger was demonic or that the work of the evil spirit was to make Saul go against the Lord's revealed will. The Hebrew *hitnabeh,* which is rendered as Saul's ecstatic "prophesying," may denote a madman's ravings or even froth at his mouth. One cannot be possessed by the Holy Spirit and intend to murder at the same time.

Saul hurled his spear at David twice without success. Some scholars argue that Saul held a spear as a royal symbol without necessarily intending to use it against David.[4] But this interpretation has no textual basis, for the author did not mention Saul's spear in his first therapeutic session with David as he played the lyre (see 16:23). Further, Saul's signature weapon was not a spear but a sword (see 2 Sam 1:22). More plausibly, the spear in Saul's hand

---

4. See Ellicott's *Bible Commentary for English Reader* at http://biblehub.com/commentaries/1_samuel/26-11.htm, accessed on 4 April 2018.

indicated his murderous intention against David. Though Saul hurled the spear at David at close range, he missed him twice. The fact that God protected his chosen one led Saul to fear David even more, because he knew that the Lord was with David.

Saul's next move was to demote David from commander of the army to section commander and then to send him to remote fronts in order to put a damper on his popularity and have him killed by the Philistines. But instead of being killed on the battle front, David "prospered" wherever he went because God was with him. Further, David was loved by "all Israel and Judah," which included those living in the remote areas of the country. As David became more and more famous, whatever Saul tried to do against David was, as Gordon says, "frustrated; the curse is turned into blessing, because God is with David."[5]

18:17–27 DAVID AND MICHAL

As a desperate measure, Saul resorted to *Goyukjichek*, "a stratagem of tricking an enemy by inflicting suffering on friendly forces."[6] Saul feigned to give his daughter's hand to David while plotting to have him killed by the Philistines. His plan was to give him a special mission related to the wedding. Saul expected David to be killed in that mission so that he would not have to be stuck with him as a son-in-law, which would have been a nightmare scenario for Saul. But Saul's deceptive plan entailed putting his own daughter in danger of some physical or emotional frustration, however short that might be.

Saul first offered his older daughter Merab to David as a bride, but David rejected the marriage out of deference. In other words, he would have accepted the offer if Saul had insisted. There is an unwritten law in East Asia that says, one has to reject a position of importance in the court up to three times. Liu Bei declined three times when offered the emperorship of Hanzhong. Even Cao Pi, a usurper, declined the emperor's edict of abdication twice by declaring his virtue as too meager to assume the throne. Thus we may interpret David's words in verse 18 as a formality. But for some unknown reason, Saul changed his mind and gave Merab's hand to Adriel of Meholah, of whom nothing is known except for the fact that his sons born of Merab were killed by the

---

5. Robert P. Gordon, *I & II Samuel: A Commentary*, LBI (Grand Rapids, MI: Zondervan, 1986), 159.
6. This is an East Asian idiom. *Goyukjichek* is a Korean pronunciation of that idiom. This idiom originated in the scheme that Huang Gai and Zhou Yu hatched in order to deceive Cao Cao in *Three Kingdoms*.

Gibeonites sometime during David's reign (2 Sam 21:8). One may gather that Merab, unlike Saul's second daughter Michal (v. 20), did not want to get married to David. The author did not make Merab's dislike of David explicit, because that would counter his argument that David was the favorite of all Israel. Although marriage was not romantic but political in the ancient Near East, the opinion of a bride could not be ignored completely. For instance, Son Quan had to make sure that his sister liked Lui Bei when he implicated her in his plan to trap Lui Bei through a marriage alliance. Either because of Merab's dislike of David or perhaps Merab's love for Adriel, Saul could not press on with his plan and as a result committed a serious social gaffe, a breach of courtesy towards David.

But Saul did not give up. When he was told that his daughter Michal was in love with David, he decided to try *Goyukjichek* with her in the sense that Saul turned Michal's pure love into a means for his political agenda, even though his plan would an take emotional toll on his daughter: "I will give her to him . . . so that she may be a snare to him and so that the hand of the Philistines may be against him" (v. 21). Because Saul had reneged on his word regarding Merab and put David in an awkward and shameful position, he sent now his attendants to win over David again. They spoke to David privately, saying, "look the king likes you, and his attendants all love you; now become his son-in-law" (v. 21). The Chinese word *shuoke* means "a man of persuasive tongue." Ancient kings and warlords in ancient China often sent *shuoke* to an unwilling or indifferent ally to enlist his support through persuasion. *Shuoke* occasionally requested a private audience to maximize the effect of persuasion. Saul's attendants played the role of *shuoke* and had some success.

David initially expressed his frustration in the presence of Saul's attendants, while his language still deferred to the king. Then he said, "I am only a poor man and little known" (v. 23), words that did not reflect reality and sounded open to suggestion. Though David's popularity had reached every corner of the streets of Israel, his father Jesse had eight sons and may have been not rich enough to marry David off to royalty. In some Asian countries, it is still required for a bridegroom to pay a handsome amount of money to the bride's family. No money, no bride! In Israel, there was a similar tradition of paying a price for the bride (*mohar*, see Gen 34:12). It would have been outrageously costly to get a princess as a bride, and so David must have been worried about *mohar*. Knowing this, Saul suggested that David bring a hundred Philistine foreskins as the bride price. Requesting a hundred Philistine foreskins may have been occasioned by David's suggestive words, "I am only poor." Further,

Saul imbued a patriotic significance, which was revenge on the king's enemy. There seemed to be no reason for David to reject Saul's suggestion, because it would honor both David and the country. But Saul's sly scheme was to have David killed by the Philistines. We do not know if David saw through Saul's scheme and then followed along because he had so much confidence in his ability to defeat the Philistines. But the fact that "it was right in David's eyes" (v. 26: "David was pleased," NIV) points towards David's wisdom in this matter, for the expression "to be right in one's eyes" often refers to a human opinion rather than a divine one. In Judges 14:3, Samson insisted on marrying a Philistine woman and said to his parents, "Take her for me, for she was right in my eyes" (my translation).

Frustrating Saul's plan, David paid a bride price of two hundred Philistine foreskins, twice the number Saul had originally asked for, and he delivered them before the set time.[7] Saul had no choice but to give Michal to David in marriage, but as long as David was his son-in-law and living with his family, Saul would have plenty more chances to kill him. In ancient East Asia, a bride normally left her family to live with her husband's family. But occasionally a bridegroom lived with his wife's family. Koreans call such a bridegroom *Derilsawi*. *Derilsawi* provided labor for the wife's family. David was *Derilsawi* in the sense that he lived with his wife's family in Gibeon rather than his hometown of Bethlehem, and he provided labor in the form of military service. Saul may have reasoned that this arrangement would increase David's chances of falling into the hands of the Philistines – his original plan!

18:28–30 SAUL'S GROWING FEAR OF DAVID

Saul failed in his repeated efforts to reduce David in grandeur or to kill him. Every failure reminded him of the Lord's special presence in David, which increased Saul's fear of David, because he knew that David was the neighbor that Samuel had predicted would replace him as king (15:28). But that knowledge did not stop Saul from trying to kill the chosen one of God, for he was under the influence of an evil spirit, willing to rebel against the divine will.

The fact that God was with David does not mean that all David's decisions were wise and good. Rather, if David made a wrong turn at some point in his journey to kingship, God would restore him to the right path. The decision

---

7. LXX has it that David killed "one hundred" Philistines and brought their foreskins. Also, later, when David asked Ish-Bosheth to return Michal, he mentioned that he paid "a hundred Philistine foreskins" (2 Sam 3:14).

to become Saul's son-in-law may have been a wrong turn for David, because God's anointing – rather than the status as Saul's son-in-law – legitimized David's bid for kingship. Further, David did not get to stay in the palace long, for his wife Michal was given to another, and he had no children from her. These narrative details show that God did not want David to have anything to do with Saul's family. Even when we make mistakes, God works out his plan perfectly through imperfect humans. Whenever we hear David's story, we can praise God for his grace even more.

1 SAMUEL 19:1–24

SAUL TRIES TO KILL DAVID

David became a member of the royal family by marrying Saul's daughter, Michal. David may have thought that this marriage was one big step in the right direction towards the throne. As Koreans would say, "In order to catch a tiger, one must go into her lair." After all, it was no small matter for a shepherd boy to become a king's son-in-law – as David himself said in 18:23. Considering David's divine anointing as king, one may argue that he took his royal marriage as God's providence. But David's elevated status did not stop Saul from trying to murder him. In fact, Saul began to publicly seek David's life and issued an execution order to his top commanders. Further, by living with Michal's family, David was placed in even greater danger because he was always under Saul's watch, though with Jonathan and Michal's help, he was able to escape from imminent dangers. But David's privilege as Saul's son-in-law did not last long, and eventually he concluded that he had to leave his wife and become a fugitive in order to survive. David went to Samuel in Ramah, who had anointed David as king over Israel. Samuel symbolized David's first step on his path to kingship. David tried to make his own way to kingship with Saul, but when that path closed, he returned to where he had started. There the Lord stripped Saul of his clothes, which symbolized the divestiture of Saul's kingship.

19:1–7 JONATHAN SAVES DAVID

Prior to this point in the narrative Saul's murderous intention was covert. Saul hatched schemes that would get David killed by the hands of the Philistines, or he tried to kill David during their private sessions so that no one would witness the murder. But in verse 1, Saul publicly displays his murderous intentions towards David: Saul ordered "his son Jonathan" and all the attendants "to kill David." There are two problems with this command, which ultimately thwart Saul's murderous endeavors. First, the Hebrew *hamit* ("to kill") usually refers to execution, particularly killing as a punishment. However, Saul did not articulate any account of David's sin, which implies that David was an innocent and loyal servant. Second, the narrator notes that the execution order was given to "his [Saul's] son Jonathan." Although Jonathan was expected to be loyal to

Saul, the text says that he had "taken a great liking to David" (v. 2). Because of Jonathan's covenant with David (see 18:3), he would not obey Saul's command.

Jonathan not only warned David of imminent danger[1] but also promised David that he would persuade his father to reconcile with David. In his promise to David, Jonathan used the pronoun *ani* ("I") twice for emphasis: "I will go out . . . I will speak to him about you . . . " (v. 3).[2] Further, Jonathan called Saul "his father" three times (vv. 2–3).[3] These narrative details reflect Jonathan's confidence that his father would listen to him. This confidence is also reflected in Jonathan's suggestion that David should remain in hiding until he brought his father to the secret hiding place to reconcile with David.

The argument that killing David was a sin ("wrong," NIV) bookends Jonathan's speech in verses 4–5, with the intervening lines explaining why it was a sin. First, it was a sin because "David has not wronged you" (v. 4). Up to this point, Saul could not specify David's sin, and killing an innocent person is always wrong. Second, "what he [David] has done has benefited you [Saul] greatly" rather than wronged him (v. 4). Then Jonathan gives concrete examples: David killed "the Philistine" (i.e. Goliath) while risking his own life,[4] and the Lord delivered a victory for all Israel through David. Jonathan emphasized David's loyalty by identifying David as "your [Saul's] servant" (v. 4). Finally, he reminded Saul of the good days when he was pleased with David and his victory. Saul was persuaded by Jonathan's reasoning and took an oath not to kill David, although his oath repeatedly turned out to be hollow. After the meeting, Jonathan called David out of his hiding place and brought him to Saul to be reconciled: "David was with Saul as before" (v. 7). David went back into Saul's service both as a warrior and lyre player.

Jonathan's speech was powerful, because it appealed to the general idea of justice: it is wrong to kill an innocent man without reason. Jonathan did not take sides, either with Saul or David. His argument also reveals that Jonathan made a covenant with David because he believed that David was the anointed of the Lord who would bring a just rule to Israel – not because he liked

---

1. Saul had ordered his servant to come and kill David in the morning.
2. Since Hebrew verbs conjugate according to their subject, personal pronouns are usually not used, except for emphasis.
3. NIV translates the third occurrence of "my father" as "him."
4. The expression "to take one's life in one's hands" occurs also in Judg 12:3 and 1 Sam 28:21. Its contextual meaning is clear, but the origin of that idiom is not clear. Bar-Efrat suggests two possibilities. First, what is on one's palm is not protected. Second, the idiom can be alternatively translated as "to take one's throat in one's hands." Shimon Bar-Efrat, *Das Erste Buch Samuel: Ein narratologisch-philologischer Kommentar* BZWANT (Stuttgart, Germany: Kohlhammer, 1996), 263.

David better than Saul. In this regard, Jonathan teaches us what it means to be truly loyal. We tend to think of loyalty in terms of taking sides, but true loyalty leads to serving the truth. Ancient East Asians paid their ultimate loyalty to Heaven. Those who betrayed the will of Heaven were, by definition, disloyal. Thus being loyal to a villainous hero such as Cao Cao was actually an act of disloyalty. Likewise, Christians pledge their ultimate allegiance to the triune God of the Bible. To give an example of what this means, Christian riot policemen should not obey their superiors' evil orders to shoot peaceful demonstrators in the streets because Christians must put their allegiance to biblical truth above their allegiance to a profession.

19:8–17 MICHAL SAVES DAVID

The narrator juxtaposes the report of David's victory over the Philistines (v. 8) with a story about an evil spirit possessing Saul (v. 9) in order to show a cause-and-effect relationship between the two reports. Apparently, just the report of David's success made Saul demonic.[5] Possessed by a demonic spirit, Saul forgot his oath not to kill David and tried to pin him to the wall with a spear as he played the lyre (v. 10). This is the third time that Saul hurled his spear at David at close range. Again, Saul's spear did not find its target and went straight into the wall. David escaped from Saul's palace to his own house. That night Saul laid an ambush around his house, plotting to kill David on his way to work the next morning.[6] This time, Michal took the initiative to save David from imminent danger by helping David escape through the window that night and then playing a trick that would delay Saul's pursuit of David.

What made Michal go to such lengths to save David's life? Verse 11 reveals that Michal was not acting as Saul's daughter but as David's wife. Though she may not have realized that David was the chosen one of God at that time, she certainly loved her husband (see 18:28). This reflects the saying that a wife's love for her husband can be greater than a daughter's love for her own family. In the past, Korean fathers used to call their married daughters *Chulgawein*, which means "a stranger." This is illustrated by Lady Sun's love for Liu Bei in *Three Kingdoms*. Lady Sun married her brother's enemy, Liu Bei, as part of political alliance. But she came to love Liu Bei so sincerely that she helped him

---

5. David's triumphant troops may have been welcomed by the women who sang the song that gave more credit to David than to Saul.
6. "That night" in v. 10 goes better with v. 11, as the Septuagint arranges it.

escape to his country against her brother's will. Like Michal, she told a lie that would secure Liu Bei's safe passage through her brother's territory.

The narrator emphasizes Michal's love for David by filling the passage with her saving acts and speeches. In describing David's escape through a window, Michal is identified as the actor and David as one who is acted upon: "Michal let David down through a window" (v. 11). We can almost feel the weight of love that Michal had to bear in lowering David. But the narrator does not express David's feelings towards Michal in the text. David did not even say goodbye to his wife. He just fled in a hurry. The narrator uses three Hebrew verbs in quick succession to express David's hasty flee: "He went, fled, and escaped" ("He fled and escaped," NIV). This makes us wonder if David loved Michal.[7] But the more important question is why the narrator omits David's farewell to Michal, thereby making David completely passive in this episode. This relates to the fact that David's decision to be part of Saul's family may not have been fully supported by the Lord, as implied in 18:26: "It was right in David's eyes to become the king's son-in-law." In a sense David put himself in harm's way by making a bad decision. By describing David as being completely passive in these episodes, where David is saved first by Jonathan and second by Michal, the author shows that salvation comes from the Lord. David contributed nothing to his salvation, a message that is even reinforced by the next episode, where David was saved by the Lord's spirit!

After letting David escape through a window, Michal played a trick that delayed Saul's pursuit. She took a household idol, which is called a *terapim* in Hebrew, and laid it on the bed. Then she covered it with a blanket and put some goat's hair at the head to make it look like David in bed (v. 13).[8] When Saul sent in his men to arrest David, Michal bought time for David by telling the lie that he was ill. As many scholars argue, the narrator describes Michal here in a way that recalls Rachel, the wife of the Hebrew patriarch Jacob. Both Michal and Rachel helped their husbands escape against their fathers' will. Also, both stories feature a household god: Michal laid it in bed, while Rachel sat on it. Finally, both told a lie to their fathers. Regarding the connections

---

7. Later, when David becomes powerful, he brings Michal back, though this is not necessarily done out of love (2 Sam 3:14–16). It would have been a political strategy to conciliate northern bribes and to claim his legitimacy for his kingship. The general truth is that an ambitious man like David can prioritize his political success over anything, including his wife.
8. *Kebir*, the Hebrew word used here for "goat's hair," is not clear in meaning. In Song of Songs, a man's hair is compared to a goat's hair. *Kebir* may be related to the word *makbir* in 2 Kgs 8:15, which Kimhi translates as "pillow of goat hair." The point is that "goat's hair" looks like David's hair.

between these stories, Dekker insightfully observes that "the narrator wishes to emphasize the similarities between David and Jacob. David is like another patriarch, a founding father of the nation. In making Michal look like Rachel, the narrator is suggesting to us that David is a new Jacob."[9]

Michal lied twice: once to protect David (v. 14) and then to protect herself (v. 17). For when confronted by Saul, she said she was threatened by David. Did Saul believe her, or not? The narrator does not report Saul's response to Michal's lie, but most likely Saul did not believe Michal since her lie did not explain why she had laid a dummy in bed to pretend that David was ill. If she had been forced to help David escape, why did she continue to help him by playing a trick? Though Michal's lie about David's threat seems too transparent to deceive Saul, he did not hold her accountable. It may be that Saul did not want to admit that his children, including Michal, were rebellious. Cao Cao had four children who competed for the crown. The oldest son Cao Pi killed the youngest, his father's favorite, by poisoning. Although Cao Cao had circumstantial evidence to convict Cao Pi as the murderer, he decided not to press charges without direct evidence as long as Cao Pi insisted on his innocence because Cao Cao could not stand the idea that his son had rebelled against him. He wanted to believe Cao Pi's plea of innocence! In a similar way, Saul may have wanted to believe that Michal was loyal to him. But Saul will come into open conflict with his children about David later in the narrative.

19:18–24 SAMUEL SAVES DAVID

Saul's repeated murder attempts and his oath breaking convinced David that his life would be in constant danger in Saul's house, so he decided to become a fugitive. He fled north to Ramah, not far from Saul's hometown of Gibeah, possibly because he wanted to see Samuel, the prophet who had jettisoned David into a life of greatness by anointing him as king. David had failed in his efforts to become king of Israel through marriage. David and the prophet Samuel went to the place called Naioth near Ramah, where Samuel led a band of prophets. This was a perfect place for David to reset his journey towards kingship. Meanwhile, Saul heard a report of David's whereabouts and sent men to capture him. Each time they arrived at Naioth, they were possessed by the spirit of the Lord and "prophesied" like other prophets in Samuel's custody. As a result, they failed to arrest David. After three failed attempts,

9. John Dekker, "May the Lord Make the Woman Like Rachel: Comparing Michal and Rachel," *TB* 64 (2013): 31.

Saul himself went there, but he was overpowered by the spirit of the Lord as well and prophesied like the other prophets. Saul's prophesying was different than that of his men in several respects. First, he began to prophesy on his way from Ramah to Naioth, before he saw the other prophets prophesying under Samuel's watch. Second, at Naioth, he took off his royal garment and prophesied naked in Samuel's presence. Third, his prophesying lasted "all that day and all that night," inducing the people's response: "Is Saul also among the prophets?" (v. 24).

By taking off his royal garments, Saul symbolically gave up his kingdom in front of Samuel, who had given him the kingdom symbolically by anointing him with oil. Noteworthy in this scene is the way that the narrator describes Saul's last meeting with Samuel in a way that recalls their first meeting at Ramah. Just as Saul met a group of girls drawing water at the well and asked for directions to Samuel's house before their first meeting (see 9:11), Saul stopped at a cistern at Seku in Ramah and asked people for information about Samuel's whereabouts at their final meeting (v. 22). Just as Saul prophesied and people responded by saying, "Is Saul also among the prophets?" (see 10:11), in their first meeting, the people responded in the same way to Saul's prophecies in this final encounter (v. 24). By linking Saul and Samuel's last encounter with their first meeting, the narrator gives a sense of closure to their relationship as king and prophet.

This episode concludes a series of episodes where God delivers David out of Saul's murderous hand. David is portrayed in the passive tense (i.e., as someone who is acted upon) in all of these episodes, revealing that David contributed nothing to his salvation, but God alone saved David from the mess that he got himself into by becoming Saul's son-in-law. Whereas God used Jonathan and Michal to save David in the previous two episodes, the spirit of the Lord came to the rescue in this third episode, rendering Saul powerless to carry out his evil intentions towards David. Although David faltered and stumbled on his way to the throne, God was guiding David's life throughout the process. Human imperfections and failures cannot be an obstacle to the Lord as he works out his kingdom on earth.

1 SAMUEL 20:1–42

DAVID AND JONATHAN

David returned to Gibeah, Saul's seat of power, to run a final test regarding Saul's intentions towards him. His return reveals his sense of shock and devastation at being forced out of the palace, Saul's family, and a safe and secure path to the throne. To test Saul's heart, David needed help from Jonathan, because an arrest warrant had been issued for David. So he went to Jonathan, who had pledged allegiance to him, and instructed him about the test. After renewing his covenant with David, Jonathan proposed, in turn, a clever way to inform David of the test result without attracting Saul's suspicion. Everything went as planned. David ascertained that Saul would never change his murderous intentions against him and shared a tearful farewell with Jonathan. Now David officially became a fugitive with Saul in pursuit. Throughout this chapter, David implicitly urged Jonathan to take a side. Ideally speaking, no one can be loyal to two masters who do not recognize each other's right to exist. But ideals do not always teach us how we should behave in this fallen world. Jonathan made the best decision possible between Saul and David. Although he never left Saul for David – if he had done so, he would have been an impious son – he remained loyal to David by refusing to be involved in Saul's hostile acts towards David. One may say in this sense that Jonathan represents an Asian paragon of an ideal hero. In *Three Kingdoms,* when Cao Cao found out that his repeated defeats in battle were due to one wise counselor in the enemy camp, he hatched a scheme that got the wise counselor to enter into his service. Since his old mother then lived in Cao Cao's territory, Cao Cao used her as a hostage to acquire the service of the wise counselor. Being a loyal son, the wise counselor had no choice but to leave his king and defect to Cao Cao's court. But allegedly he did not give Cao Cao any advice that might jeopardize his former king.

20:1–8 DAVID'S FINAL TEST OF SAUL

David left Ramah to return to Jonathan's quarters. After all that happened in chapter 19, David's return to Saul's house might seem extremely strange. David's return to Saul's house should not be explained away by appealing to a clumsy editor who left different and often conflicting sources as they were, for it is better to read the narrative as a complicated but coherent story. The narrative seems to suggest that David still had a lingering hope to ascend the throne through Saul's court, for the court officials loved David, as did Saul's children. David continued to hope that Saul would reconcile with him, the divinely chosen as king of Israel. David probably hoped to be appointed as a legitimate successor to Saul, since Jonathan had already handed over his princely inheritance to David. In countries such as Egypt, a king's son-in-law was eligible to succeed to the throne.[1] Further, rebelling against Saul, let alone killing him, was not an option for David who had high regard for God's anointed. All these considerations may have led David to return to Jonathan to discern Saul's attitude towards him. In a sense, David's dilemma is similar to Liu Bei's struggle in *Three Kingdoms* to deal with Liu Bao, the imperial prefect of Jingzhou. In order for Liu Bei to revive the Han dynasty, which had been shattered by villainous heroes, he had to establish himself at Jingzhou. This required Liu Bei to take the throne from his benefactor and distant relative Liu Bao. Despite Kongmin's advice to this end, Liu Bei resisted and said, "I would rather die than do this dishonorable deed."[2]

DAVID AS THE SECOND MOSES

The author uses the Hebrew *mebaqesh* ("trying to kill") to refer to Saul's intention to kill David (20:1; see 19:2, 10). The same word is also used when Pharaoh tried to kill Moses (see Exod 2:15; 4:19, 24). An interesting analogy emerges out of that observation: just as Pharaoh's attempts to kill Moses sent Moses into the wilderness, Saul's murderous intention to kill David forced David to become a fugitive in the wilderness. Just as Moses came back from the wilderness to lead the Israelites out of Egypt to become a nation, David will return from the desert to create his nation in Israel. In this regard, the author portrays David as the second Moses, just as he portrays him as the second Jacob in chapter 19 (vv. 11–17).

At first Jonathan did not recognize how close to death David had been while he lived in Saul's house. Rather he tried to set David at ease by saying, "You are not going to die!" (v. 2). Then he answered David's question about Saul's murderous intention: "It can't be true! If he did try to kill you, my father

---

1. It appears that in those days, there were no set rules for succession. According to those of ancient Egypt in the New Kingdom period, a king's son-in-law could have the privileged position in the competition for the throne.
2. Roberts, *Three Kingdoms*, 471.

would never hide it from me" (v. 2). Then David explained that Saul would hide his intentions from Jonathan, knowing that his son would grieve for his closest friend. Then David swore an oath: "Yet as surely as the LORD lives . . . there is only a step between me and death" (v. 3). Jonathan's naiveté stands out in this scene, for there are at least two incidents that defeat Jonathan's argument: first, Saul set an ambush around David's house to kill him and second, he went on an expedition to Ramah to kill David. Apparently, Saul did not reveal either to Jonathan and yet Jonathan believed that Saul would reveal any plans to him. Jonathan's naiveté is intentionally exaggerated, for God will use it to advance his plan for David.

David's test for Saul's attitude revolves around two religious festivals: the new moon festival and an annual sacrifice. The new moon festival was prescribed in the Mosaic law (Num 28:11–15) to be held on the day of the new moon and was popular throughout Israelite history.[3] The sacrifice required for this festival was significantly greater than the Sabbath sacrifice. The annual sacrifice, on the other hand, was not mandated in the law and was celebrated on a clan basis at a local sanctuary. Elkanah, Hannah's husband, made an annual pilgrimage to the sanctuary at Shiloh for this very purpose. The annual sacrifice provided an opportunity for a clan or a family to get together to strengthen their familial bond and to nurture faith in God. Since this was an annual event, it may have preceded the new moon festival in priority. In other words, if the two festivals fell on the same day, one would naturally attend the annual sacrifice. So David's test went like this: if Saul burst into anger over David's reasonable decision to attend his clan festival, David would know that Saul was determined to kill him. Since there was not a clear connection between Saul's anger over David's decision to go to his clan festival and his determination to kill David, David seems to have been asking for a sign from the Lord reminiscent of the sign that Jonathan asked for from the Lord in the battle of Mikmash (see 14:8–10).

David concludes by asking Jonathan to show him kindness, appealing to the covenant between them. Interestingly, David calls his covenant with Jonathan "the covenant of the LORD" (*berit YHWH*, v. 8). The NIV translates it, "covenant . . . before the LORD," which may mean that God is the witness to the covenant. But it may also refer to God's providential intervention in David's rise to the throne, in which Jonathan played a very important role. This is corroborated by the way the narrator formulates the "divine witness"

---

3. *Baker Encyclopedia of the Bible*, 784.

refrain: "The LORD is between you and me forever" (v. 23, my translation). The context makes it very clear that David and Jonathan invoked the Lord as a witness to their covenant, but the narrator intentionally omits the word "witness" in order to imply the Lord's intervention in their relationship. In sum, by referring to "the covenant of the LORD," David increases its significance and puts extra pressure on Jonathan to keep it faithfully.

20:9–23 COVENANT BETWEEN JONATHAN AND DAVID

Although David said to Jonathan, "show me kindness" (v. 8), he did not elaborate about his meaning right away. Instead he asserted his innocence with strong and emotional language, thereby inducing Jonathan's voluntary offer of kindness: "If I had the least inkling that my father was determined to harm you, wouldn't I tell you?" (v. 9). Then David asked Jonathan how he would inform him if Saul spoke harshly about his collaboration with his enemy. Jonathan left his quarters and went to a field with David so their conversation would not be overheard by eavesdropping court officials. Then he spelled out his plan for informing David about Saul's intentions without being seen by Saul's attendants. But before he got into any details, he renewed his covenant with David.

The updated covenant consists of two parts. In the first part, Jonathan promised that he would inform David of the result of Saul's test – if Saul was favorably disposed towards David, or not. In the second part of the covenant, Jonathan asked David for "the kindness of the LORD" (*hesed YHWH*, v. 14)[4] while he was alive. Interestingly, Jonathan responded to David's request for "kindness" with his own request for the "kindness of the LORD." Moreover, Jonathan asked for the same kindness to be extended to his descendants after he died.[5] Thus David should not kill Jonathan's descendants after God makes David king. As verse 16 shows, this renewed covenant was made between two houses, with a binding effect on all their descendants.

After having David reconfirm his oath (v. 17), Jonathan spelled out his plan for how he would inform David of the result of Saul's test without being seen by Saul's attendants. Jonathan instructed David to hide himself by the stone Ezel (v. 19). The stone Ezel was a mound that would have served as a natural target for archers. He would shoot three arrows into its side as if to shoot at the target. If his arrows did not reach the target, he would say to his

---

4. NIV: "the unfailing kindness like the LORD's kindness."
5. I prefer reading the Hebrew, *welo' amut,* at the end of v. 14 to go with v. 15.

serving boy, "the arrows are on this side of you," which would mean that Saul was not determined to kill David (v. 21). But if Jonathan's arrows flew beyond the target, he would say to his boy, "the arrows are beyond you," which would mean that David should run (v. 22).

Although some scholars argue that Jonathan's elaborate plan is without a clear purpose, it does provide a ruse to avoid Saul's watchful eyes and ears. First, Jonathan's characteristic weapon was a bow (see 2 Sam 1:22), which he probably practiced with an archery range. Thus it would not attract any attention for Jonathan to go to a target range. Second, it was natural for him to take his servant with him to the archery range, as someone had to stand close to the target to inform the archer if his arrow had landed on target or not. His job also included fetching arrows for his master. Third, a brief meeting with David would not necessarily make Jonathan's secret sign redundant or irrelevant, because the purpose was not to reveal Saul's murderous intentions to David, but to bid farewell to each other.

Jonathan concludes his speech by invoking the Lord as a witness to their covenant: "Behold, the LORD is between you and me forever" (v. 23, my translation). The Hebrew original does not have the word "witness," contrary to the NIV translation. The context makes the NIV translation plausible, but it conceals the possibility that the phrase in question may also refer to the LORD's intervention in the covenantal relationship between David and Jonathan.

20:24–34 CONFRONTATION BETWEEN SAUL AND JONATHAN

The narrator details what happened on the days of the New Moon feast, describing David's empty seat at the king's table as well as where other key figures seated themselves. Significantly, Abner sat next to Saul. Remember that Saul asked Abner to find out whose son had killed Goliath. Saul may have been trying to draw Abner's attention to David, his potential rival. Abner and David would have been competing for the same position in Saul's court if David had remained in Saul's court. After David became a fugitive, Abner's role as the commander of Saul's army became more prominent.

Saul gave David the benefit of the doubt when he did not appear on the first day of the New Moon feast, since anybody could be made impure by accident. But David's absence on the second day of the festival angered Saul, because he would have been clean again and able to attend the feast. So Saul asked Jonathan about David's absence: "Why hasn't the son of Jesse come to the meal [lehem], either yesterday or today?" (v. 27), referring to David not by his name but by his patronymic, "son of Jesse." Although calling someone by his patronymic was not always derogatory, Saul's tone certainly was, especially since Saul later called David the "son of Death" (v. 31, my translation).[6]

Jonathan's answer does not mirror the answer that David entrusted to Jonathan in verse 6. Though the major elements were included – the annual sacrifice held in Bethlehem for the clan, David's request for permission from Jonathan to attend. But Jonathan emphasized the inevitability of David's emergency visit by saying: "He said, '. . . my brother has *ordered* me to be there . . . let me *get away* to see my brothers'" (v. 29, italics added). To Saul, David was not merely choosing which festival was more important – the new moon festival or an annual sacrifice – but rather was revealing his loyalty, whose orders he would obey: Saul's or his brothers'. David's loyalty appeared to lie with his own family rather than Saul's, which filled Saul with rage. A Korean idiom *Mulmunjihwa*, or "a disaster that wipes out a whole family," refers to a punishment dealt to traitors, because treason was considered a family rather than an individual crime. David's prioritizing of his brother's command over Saul's may have been taken as an unmistakable sign of treason. Also, Jonathan's words suggested to Saul that David was not simply visiting his hometown but "getting away" from Saul. The Hebrew phrase *malat* ("get away") that Jonathan used to refer to David's visit to Bethlehem is the same word used to describe David's escape from Saul when he was attempting to kill him (see 19:10, 11, 12, 17, 18). Further, David's visit to Bethlehem recalls Samuel's visit there to anoint David as king, because Samuel used his need to attend an annual sacrifice as a pretext for anointing David as king. Thus the emphasis that Jonathan added in his explanation for David's absence contributed to Saul's burning anger. Jonathan may have been too enthusiastic in defending David, but he was not wise in his choice of words. As the Korean saying goes, "timely words can pay off the debt worth a thousand coins but a single syllable change in speech can make the world upside down." This reminds us of Jonathan's naiveté in appraising Saul's attitudes towards David earlier in this chapter. Jonathan's naiveté in defending his friend before Saul functions as a catalyst in hardening Saul's heart completely against David. In a sense, the Lord used Jonathan's naiveté to drive David into a life in the wilderness, because that was where God wanted him to be.

Saul directed his anger towards Jonathan and even cursed him (v. 30). A Korean saying has it that a sister-in-law who tries to serve as a peacemaker

---

6. NIV: "he must die."

is more loathsome to a woman than her mother-in-law who persecutes her. Jonathan was similarly loathsome to Saul, for he appeared to be a loyal son, but he backstabbed Saul by colluding with David. Saul ranted that Jonathan "chose" (v. 30)[7] David over his father and practically plotted treason with David. But Saul's execution order was issued for David, not Jonathan, who had masterminded the treasonous plot: "Now send someone to bring him [David] to me, for he must die" (v. 31).[8] When Jonathan protested against Saul's order, Saul threw a spear at him. Though Jonathan's protest was legitimate and Saul's suspicion against David had no basis, Saul tried to kill his own son when he stood in his way. Finally Jonathan realized that his father was determined to kill David. His grief at David's fate and his anger at his father's unreasonable animosity towards David drove Jonathan from Saul's presence.[9]

20:35–42 PARTING OF WAYS

The next morning David went out in the field to perform a prearranged act that would reveal Saul's murderous intentions to David. After shooting the arrows much further than the target, way over the stone mound where David hid, Jonathan shouted to his boy and secretly to David, "Isn't the arrow beyond you? Hurry, Go quickly! Don't stop" (v. 37). David knew then for certain that he should leave Saul's court immediately and forever in order to survive and fulfil his divine calling. Interestingly, the narrator describes the boy whom Jonathan brought to the field as "the boy of Jonathan" in verse 38 ("the boy," NIV) and "the boy that belongs to him" in verse 40 ("the boy," NIV). Similarly, Jonathan is called "his [the boy's] master" in verse 38. These details emphasize the boy's loyalty to Jonathan, which is important for the success of Jonathan's plan, because the boy came very close to David's hiding place and might have noticed David's presence. Although the text clarifies the boy's ignorance about the secret arrangements, the implication is that Jonathan would have been able to contain the boy even if he had seen David. These details reveal the lengths to which Jonathan went to ensure the secrecy of his arrangements with David.

After the boy had gone, David came out of the stone mound[10] and prostrated himself before Jonathan three times. Ancient Chinese court officials used

---

7. NIV: "sided with."
8. The Hebrew *ben-mawet*, "son of death," ("he must die," NIV) may play with David's patronymic "son of Jesse," which only Saul uses to refer to David.
9. Jonathan was upset because his heart went out to David, who had to live under the death warrant, and also because his father humiliated him so much (v. 34: contra NIV). Bos, 114.
10. The NIV, "from the south side of the stone," is intelligible. I follow LXX here.

to hit their head on the ground three times when approaching their emperor as a sign of servitude. However, David's prostration to Jonathan expressed more gratitude than servitude, for they kissed each other and grieved for their separation. Interestingly, David is said to have "wept the most" (v. 41). Thus far in the narrative, David has not revealed his inner emotions. We know that Michal and Jonathan loved David, but we do not know how David felt about them. But here David broke down in tears. This farewell scene recalls a similar scene in *Three Kingdoms*, when Liu Bei bade farewell to Zhao Zilong in tears. Although they felt that their souls were connected from the moment that they met, Zhao Zilong could not follow Liu Bei to Pingyuan, because he was in Gongsun Zan's service. The farewell scene is narrated in the following terms: "They held each other's hands a long time, their eyes streaming with tears, and could not tear them apart . . . . Both men wept freely as they separated."[11] In contrast to Zhao Zilong, who became Liu Bei's blood brother and served him, Jonathan never left his father Saul for David. As they parted ways in tears, Jonathan called the Lord as a witness to their covenantal relationship: "The LORD is witness between you and me and between your descendants and my descendants forever" (v. 42).

It is important to recognize that Jonathan did not play an important role in Saul's court after David became a fugitive. Instead, we hear more about Abner as Saul's handyman. It may be that this was the best course Jonathan could take within Saul's court so that he did not betray the covenant he had made with David. One should not judge Jonathan for not leaving Saul for David. Though one can talk about ideals, they do not necessarily teach us how we should act in a less-than-ideal world. Jonathan's decision to stay in Saul's court may reflect our own moral and spiritual dilemma of living in this fallen world as bearers of a heavenly covenant, which is never simple or straightforward.

---

11. *Three Kingdoms*, ch. 7.

ARCHERY, AN ARROW BOY, AND A TARGET

Archery was an important martial skill for ancient Koreans, along with swordsmanship. They went out in the field to shoot for recreation and practice. The ancient Korean bow was a composite bow called *Gukgung*, which could send an arrow far into the distance. Archers usually aimed the tip of an arrow to the sky so that it could reach the target in the distance, which was usually about 125 meters, if not longer. Since the distance to the target was great, a man was deployed close to the target with a standard in hand. His role was twofold: to signal the archer if the target was hit or not and to fetch arrows for the archer. Jonathan's bow was likely a composite one with a long range. The target may have been installed on a "stone mound," a natural rock formation in the field. The "stone mound" would have made a perfect hideout for David.

1 SAMUEL 21:1–15

DAVID ATTEMPTS TO DEFECT TO GATH

David was now officially on the run, unable to return to Saul. Uncertain where to go or whom to trust, David unwisely decided to defect to Gath, Goliath's hometown. He may have reasoned that no place in Israel was safe as long as Saul was in power. Yet David's decision to seek asylum at Gath was not simply a matter of political convenience, for it reflected the nadir in his spiritual journey.

Filled with the spirit of the Lord when anointed as king, David defeated Goliath, the Philistine champion by using a sling and a stone. Saul, his family and court attendants, along with the commoners in the streets all loved David, confirming God's favor. At this spiritual height, David made an important mistake by allowing himself to become Saul's son-in-law. The text describes David's decision as something that was right in his own eyes – not a decision for which he sought God's counsel. David may have thought it was the most natural way for a commoner such as himself to inherit the throne, but David's troubles began with his marriage to Saul's daughter. Several times, Saul attempted to assassinate David, and before long he was forced out of Saul's court and became a fugitive, with Saul in constant pursuit. Without divine intervention, David would have been murdered.

Though David may have thought he would be safe from Saul in Gath, he did not seek God's will when he made the decision to defect. The text emphasizes this failure by giving a detailed description of the location of Goliath's sword in the sanctuary at Nob, where David met with Ahimelech the priest, who told him that the sword was placed "behind the ephod" (v. 9). David could have sought God's will through Ahimelech and the ephod, but he did not. David's humiliation before the Philistines may have been his clever choice for survival, but it was also a divine punishment, for among the Philistines he would have to compromise his religious principles and be pressured to convert to the pagan religion.

21:1–9 DAVID VISITS NOB

Nob is about five kilometers southeast of Gibeah. Considering its location, it appears that David went out of his way to stop at Nob before heading to Gath in the west. As the narrative reveals, his purpose in stopping at Nob was to retrieve Goliath's sword, which had been deposited in the sanctuary at Nob, so that David might give it to the king of Gath as a gift. When the high priest Ahimelech came out to meet David, he expressed his fear and surprise by asking parallel questions: "Why are you alone? Why is no one with you?" (v. 1). Ahimelech must have noticed that David was on the run from Saul, though he feigned ignorance. Ahimelech's fear related to the general recognition that Saul would kill anyone, even his own son, who tried to help David, his most wanted criminal (see 18:28).

David then invented a lie about being on a secret mission for Saul. To explain his being alone on this mission, David made up another lie about a future rendezvous with his troops "at a certain place" (v. 2), but he did not provide any evidence to back up his story. In fact, there would have been no reason for his military operation to go undercover. Ahimelech became even more suspicious when David requested five loaves of bread, since five loaves would never feed a group of soldiers.[1] One may even discern a sense of desperateness in David's words, "whatever you can find" (v. 3). These details clearly convey that David was on the run and in great need of provisions for a lonely journey.

The priest Ahimelech, however, went along with David's story, although he noticed its mendacity. The narrator revealed the reason in verse 7: "Now one of Saul's servants was there that day, detained before the LORD; he was Doeg the Edomite, Saul's chief shepherd." Doeg was a foreign mercenary employed by Saul. It was not uncommon for ancient kings to entrust foreigners who had no local attachment with an important office. The narrator, in fact, emphasizes Doeg's loyalty by calling him "One of Saul's servants" (v. 7). The specific duties of his office as "Chief Shepherd" are not known, but a shepherd invokes the image of the king's intimate interaction with the common people based on the royal ideology. From this angle, the duty of "Chief Shepherd" may have related to gathering general intelligence for Saul. Thus Doeg may have been assigned as a spy to the sanctuary at Nob, where a lot of people tended to come and go. This is corroborated by the use of the Hebrew verb 'atsara, which is used elsewhere to refer to Saul's act of governing Israel (see 9:16: "rule over," NIV). The NIV translation, "detained," may be misleading since Doeg was not

---

1. Some scholars associate five loaves of bread with five sling stones, but the only connection between this episode and David's victory over Goliath is the Philistine town Gath. David was on his way to Gath, which is the town of Goliath, whom David defeated and killed in the battle of Elah. Rather, as Alter suggests, the number five may be an idiom for "a few" (Alter, *1 Samuel*, 131).

under custody. Rather, the sense is that Doeg was placed "before the Lord" in the sanctuary at Nob as one of Saul' watching eyes.

Ahimelech must have been aware of the presence of Saul's spy in the sanctuary, who would report anything suspicious to Saul. For this reason, Ahimelech trembled at the sight of David traveling without an attending entourage. If David was on the run from Saul, welcoming him at the sanctuary would put all the priests there in grave danger. Thus Ahimelech went along with David's lie about Saul's secret mission, even though the circumstantial evidence raised doubts about its veracity. By pretending to be a victim of David's lie, he would exonerate himself from the charge of treason, because he could claim that he thought he had been helping Saul's loyal servant, David.

The lack of ordinary bread launches the second round of dialogue between David and Ahimelech. Ahimelech proposes to give David consecrated bread, which was called "the bread of the Presence" (v. 6), if David's men were free from sexual impurities. The bread of the Presence refers to twelve loaves of bread laid out on a display table in a sanctuary. Priests could eat these loaves after they were replaced with fresh loaves.[2] But Ahimelech stretched the rule by offering to give the bread of the Presence to David and his men. In order to assure Ahimelech that his men were ritually clean, David said, "Women were kept from us three days ago when I started on a mission. The young men's bodies have been holy, although the mission was not holy. How much more so today!" (v. 5, my translation). Although his words are not totally clear, David was apparently making the point that, if the number of days of celibacy matters at all, David's men were now three times holier than they had been three days prior, since they had been kept from women for three days.[3] But what's jarringly unclear about David's answer is that he says, "although the mission is not holy" (v. 5). All military operations in Israel were holy, since God was ultimately the commander of Israel's army. So what kind of mission from the king would not be holy? In this statement, David seems to have accidentally revealed the nature of his fictional "mission," which had not been approved either by God or Saul. Afraid of Saul, David was defecting to Gath secretly, and he inadvertently defined that defection as "not holy."

After successfully acquiring food provisions for his "mission," David got down to the business of retrieving Goliath's sword, which he had brought there after killing Goliath (see 17:54). David needed it as a tribute to Achish, king

---

2. Alter, *1 Samuel*, 132.
3. Having sexual intercourse makes one impure for only one day (see Lev 15:18). If a man abstains from sex until the sunset, he becomes clean with the sunset.

of Gath. There could not have been a more appropriate gift than the sword of Goliath, the Gittite, whom David had killed himself. But he had to make the process of retrieving the sword look as natural as possible so as not to arouse suspicion. Knowing that Goliath's weapon was the only weapon in the sanctuary, David played innocent and asked for any weapon that happened to be in the sanctuary, adding that the urgency of the king's mission had not given him time to grab his own weapon. Ahimelech responded with a long answer, conveying that he not only noticed that David was on the run from Saul, but also that he was planning to flee to the Philistine town. First, he reminded David (and possibly Doeg, who was eavesdropping on the exchange) that he was the hero who had killed Goliath against all odds. His response was meant both to rebuke David – "what are you afraid of, hero?" – and also warn Doeg of the danger that he would get himself into by standing against the hero. Then Ahimelech the priest pointed to the presence of an ephod as he explained the location of the sword. By mentioning the ephod, Ahimelech was suggesting that David seek God's counsel before moving any further with his plans. An ephod was a priestly garment that priests used to seek God's counsel. In deciding to defect to the Philistines, David should have asked for God's counsel, but he did not, and he also lied to the high priest. Finally, Ahimelech told David what he wanted to hear: "If you want it take it; there is no sword here but that one" (v. 9). In contrast to Ahimelech's long speech, David's answer was very short, as if there were no need to think: "there is nothing like it; give it to me" (v. 9).

The dialogue between David and Ahimelech was carried out with the awareness that Doeg, Saul's chief shepherd, was eavesdropping on them.[4] Ahimelech was certainly aware of Doeg's presence at the sanctuary, and David must have known that Saul's spy was there, since he later confessed to the priest Abiathar, "That day, Doeg the Edomite was there, I knew he would be sure to tell him" (1 Sam 22:22). The narrator's characterization of Doeg as "the Edomite" may foreshadow his role in the massacre of priests at Nob, because the pagan would not have been restricted by any Jewish taboo.

21:10–15 DAVID AT GATH

After retrieving Goliath's sword, David left for Gath without delay and stood in Achish's court on "that day" (v. 10). Gath was one of the five city centers of

---

4. See Keith Bodner, *1 Samuel: A Narrative Commentary* (Sheffield: Sheffield Phoenix Press, 2008), 228.

the Philistines, located inland close to the border with Israel. It was a perfect place for a fugitive like David to find asylum because it was outside Saul's jurisdiction, but close enough to Israel to gather intelligence about Saul's army. The fact that David did not seek God's counsel in his decision-making partly explains his humiliating failure to gain entry in Achish's court.

Understandably, the servants of Achish were not willing to approve of David's surrender. In their estimation, David, a rock-star warrior in Saul's army, had no reason to surrender. The people of Israel chanted David's jingle when he came back from battlefields. Achish's servants worried that someone like David, who was highly respected and well-recompensed in his own country, would never try to defect to an enemy country except as a back-stabbing stratagem to defeat the enemy from within. The history of Chinese warfare confirms this as a legitimate worry, for impregnable fortress cities were sometimes conquered by enemy armies because they had accepted fake defectors. Thus defectors were usually subject to a strict examination before being accepted or beheaded. Though David was aware of the danger of being suspected as a fake defector and so brought Goliath's sword with him to alleviate such doubt, Achish's poor intelligence militated against David's effort to defect. Achish's servants knew nothing about Saul's attempts to kill David, nor the complex nature of Saul and David's relationship. They even called David the king of the land (v. 11)! Achish's poor intelligence about Israelite politics would have made it difficult for David to convince the court about his need to find shelter among the Philistines. When David sensed an air of suspicion in the words of Achish's attendants, he knew it was a matter of time before he would be decapitated by the Philistines, just as he had beheaded Goliath, their hero.

To save himself, David acted like a madman, making "marks [graffiti?] on the doors of the gate" and letting "saliva run down his beard" (v. 14). However, he did so only when the Philistines watched him, as suggested by the narrator's double mention of "in their presence" and "in their hands" (v. 13). Though the passage gives the impression that David's acts of insanity were short-lived, they actually may have continued for several days. In other words, Achish's rejection of David came after a probationary period. This is intimated by the fact that Achish rebuked his attendants twice for bringing the madman to him (vv. 14, 15).[5] As verse 11 makes clear, they objected to David, and if Achish had rejected David on the day of his arrival, his rebuke to his servants would

---

5. "Why bring him to me" (v. 14: *tabi'u 'oto 'elai*) may be taken as the court's decision to accommodate David in Gath temporally, instead of David's audience with the king.

have made no sense. His rebuke implies that David was allowed to live for a probationary period in Gath after a debate among Achish's servants. However, the author describes the event as if it all happened on the day of David's arrival. This dramatically conveys the abject humiliation that David had to inflict on himself to save his life out of the hands of the Philistines. This humiliation was a consequence of his decision to leave the land of his divine calling because he was afraid of Saul, a mere man. If killing Goliath from Gath was the glorious zenith in David's career, dripping saliva off his beard in front of the king of Gath constitutes its embarrassing nadir.

From the perspective of human politics, however, by pretending to be insane, David saved himself from mortal danger. The Chinese idiom *jia chi bu dian*, which means "it is better to be humiliated than to be killed out of pride," is hard to put into practice – especially for Asians, who regard honor more highly than a shameful survival. Chinese history, however, has witnessed several heroes who willingly humiliated themselves in order to escape a deadly situation. For instance, Liu Bang, the founder of the Han dynasty, was once invited to a banquet at Hong Gate hosted by Xiang Yu, his rival warlord, who planned to kill him after discerning his political ambitions during the banquet. To put Liu Bang to the test, Xiang Yu deliberately humiliated him by, among other things, giving Liu Bang the humblest seat and allowing a sword dancer to wield his weapon – against social protocol – dangerously close to him. But Lui Bang endured humiliation with a fake smile in order to survive. If he had let the color of his face change, he would have been killed and would not have been able to find the illustrious Han dynasty, which lasted four hundred years. In this regard, one may say that the narrator portrays David both as a sinner and a hero. David was a very complicated person – as we all are. He was not born as a king from the womb. Rather, God chose a man of humble origin and disciplined him through suffering to become a king after his own heart.

1 SAMUEL 22:1-23

DAVID BEGINS AGAIN

After failing to gain asylum in the land of the Philistines, David returned to Judah in deep despair, which marked another low point in David's circuitous journey to the throne. The downward spiral of David's fortune began with his decision to become Saul's son-in-law and hit bottom with his decision to defect to the Philistines and abandon the land of Israel. Both of these decisions were made without seeking God's counsel. Having gone broke both spiritually and physically, David had no strength, resources, or hope to continue pursuing his calling as the Lord's anointed. But grace asserts itself in the midst of our deepest despair. The Lord talked to David through the prophet Gad, and David began to seek the Lord's guidance through the ephod worn by priest Abiathar. This guidance by revelation characterized the second phase of David's rise to the throne.

The first part of chapter 22 describes the journey of David's band from Adullam to Mizpah in Moab and from Mizpah to the forest of Hereth in Judah. The second part takes place in Gibeah and describes Saul's horrible slaughter of priests and their family in Nob. In these episodes, we see two contrasting character traits in David and Saul. David is shown to be capable of having sympathy with the people, who are oppressed and marginalized, whereas Saul shows pure madness by killing innocent people to maintain his political power. More and more people flocked to sympathetic David while Saul's rule of terror pushed his loyal friends away from him. Although the author mentions it only in passing, David engaged with Gad and Abiathar to help him seek the Lord's will in his journey to the throne. In *Three Kingdoms,* Liu Bei acquired Pang Tong and Zhuge Liang as his advisers. Both Pang Tong and Zhuge Liang were brilliant military strategists in the late Eastern Han dynasty, about whom Sima Hui said, "Hidden Dragon [Zhuge Liang] and Young Phoenix [Pang Tong], if you can get either of them, you'll be able to pacify the empire."[1] After acquiring these two advisers, Liu Bei succeeded in establishing his own kingdom, the state of Shu Han.

---

1. See Luo Guanzhong, *Romance of the Three Kingdoms,* trans. C. H. Brewitt-Taylor (Create-Space Publishing, 2015), 247.

22:1–2 DAVID IN ADULLAM

David journeyed to Adullam in Judah after utterly humiliating himself in front of the Philistines.[2] Ironically, Adullam is located not far from the Elah Valley, the location of David's glorious victory over the Philistine giant Goliath. Instead of lodging in the city, David hid in one of the caves to seclude himself. No place would have been safe for "the most wanted" in Judah. When "his brothers and his father's household heard about it, they went down to David there" (v. 1). The entire family did not visit David merely to uplift his spirits, for they permanently moved in to live with and fight for David, the anointed king of Israel. For David to become king, it took his whole household, for it was more than a personal endeavor. Further, as some scholars argue, David's family may have had to support David because of the guilt-by-association system widely practiced in ancient times,[3] wherein the whole family or clan of someone who plotted treason was destroyed. Regardless, it must have been encouraging for David to have his family stand behind his cause. They had witnessed David's anointing and remained loyal and helpful.

Further, those who were in distress and debt or under persecution also flocked to David, and he became their shepherd leader. The Hebrew *mar-nepesh* (v. 2: "discontented," NIV) literally means "bitter of soul." This idiom often refers to those who are suffering unjust persecution or oppression (see 1 Sam 1:10; Isa 38:15; Job 7:11). Saul's reign of terror created discontented people who refused to become part of Saul's kingdom and became wandering misfits and outlaws. Around four hundred such people gathered around David, and he welcomed them as his own family. What a humble beginning for David's kingdom, which lasted more than four hundred years! David, who had sought the royal status in vain, became a shepherd for people in distress under Saul's oppressive rule.

During David's time in Adullam, the prophet Gad became his adviser and guided him out of the danger posed by Saul. Gad may have been among the four hundred who joined David in Adullam.[4] Chinese, Korean, and Japanese

---

2. Adullam used to be a Canaanite city, but Joshua conquered and annexed it to Judah. Interestingly, Adullam was the location for the story of the patriarch Judah and his daughter-in-law Tamar. In this place, one of Judah's descendants underwent a radical change in his orientation in his path to the throne.

3. The term "household" refers to a basic social unit in ancient Israel. The household of Jesse included his wife, children, servants, and foreign workers. Saul may not have fulfilled his promise to have Jesse's household exempt from taxes.

4. The text is ambiguous on this point, but the sudden appearance of the prophet Gad in v. 4, along with the fact that David obeyed him without hesitation, is best explained by assuming

children grew up hearing the story about Liu Bang, who rose from humble origins to the throne of the Han dynasty, which lasted four hundred years. Liu Bang's political career also began as a leader of three hundred social misfits, including runaway prisoners, beggars, and helpless peasants. Both David and Liu Bang understood that those who won the heart of the people would ultimately win the empire.

22:3–5 DAVID IN MIZPAH

We do not know how long David stayed in Adullam, but we are told that in short order David moved to Mizpah in Moab and entrusted his parents to the care of a certain Moabite king.[5] Then David stayed in "the stronghold" (v. 3). This episode depicts David as a filial son, just as the earlier episode when David commuted between Saul's court to his father's house (see 17:15). In Confucian culture, filial piety is praised as the most basic of all human virtues. Rebellious sons were excommunicated, whereas filial sons were often appointed to public office without going through the normal recruiting process. Confucius taught that whoever wanted to rule the world must first put his household in order, because king and father are one in substance. The fact that David was a filial son serves as a propitious sign that he would make a good king.

Further, David's time at the stronghold in Mizpah depicts him as a sincere seeker of the divine will. The literal meaning of "Mizpah" is an outlook at high altitude. As a result, many places of a similar geographical feature are called Mizpah. In Jewish tradition, the name also symbolizes the place of seeking God, namely a place of prayer.[6] We may argue that a similar nuance is attached to the "stronghold" (v. 4) that was usually built at high elevation in this context. The fact that David stayed in the stronghold in Mizpah for a while symbolizes a change in David's attitude, where he finally began to ask God before making any move. David's words to the king of Moab suggest this change: "Would you let my father and mother come and stay with you *until I learn* what God will do for me?" (v. 3, italics mine). David's next move was made on the basis of a prophetic command.

In sum, David fled to Adullam ("refuge"), where the people in oppression under Saul's regime joined him. Then he retreated to the stronghold in Moabite Mizpah, a place dedicated to prayer, in order to seek the will of the Lord. There

---

his presence among the four hundred men who pledged allegiance to David.

5. This request may be related to the fact that David's grandmother was a Moabite.

6. The people of Israel sought after God's forgiveness at Mizpah in Benjamin (ch. 7).

God spoke through the prophet Gad to David for the first time since Samuel had anointed him as king. Prior to this, David had made decisions based on his own initiative, but now he would follow the Lord's direction. The prophet Gad told David that he should not stay in the pagan land any longer, but he should go back to Judah, the land of his people, the land of his calling.

22:6–23 SAUL SLAUGHTERS THE PRIESTS OF NOB

Then Saul heard that David had resurfaced in the land of Judah with "his men" (v. 6). Although David's men were a ragtag band of misfits and outlaws trying to survive in the desert, Saul felt threatened by their presence. During Saul's court assembly under the tamarisk tree at Gibeah,[7] he claimed falsely that David had returned to lay ambush against him at Jonathan's urging (v. 8), and he complained about his attendants' failure to reveal the matter to him. Saul also accused his attendants of conspiring with the "son of Jesse" – a term used by Saul as a derogatory title for David.[8] By addressing his court officials as "men of Benjamin," Saul may have been referring to his inner group, who had been granted land and office in exchange of their loyalty to the reigning king. In ancient times, such land grants were a signature of a king's power. In this regard, Saul's remarks may be understood as accusing his attendants of treason for pledging their fealty to David: "Will the son of Jesse give all of you fields and vineyards? Will he make all of you commanders of thousands and commanders of hundreds?" (v. 7).

Then Doeg the Edomite stepped out of the ranks and reported what he had witnessed at Nob, as if to stress that he was not one of those Benjaminites. Referring to David as "son of Jesse" like Saul, Doeg brought three charges against the priest Ahimelech: inquiring of the Lord for David, giving provisions to David, and delivering Goliath's sword to David. The first of these charges was obviously a lie, but Doeg had to lie in order to indict Ahimelech for the other two charges. Doeg had to prove that Ahimelech had known that David was a fugitive when he helped him. For if David had been sent by Saul on a secret mission, then helping him would not have constituted an act of treason. But if the priest Ahimelech had inquired of the Lord, he would have realized

---

7. It appears that Saul does not have a sophisticated building for his residence, or for public affairs, for he officiated a meeting "under the tamarisk tree." Interestingly, the people of Jabesh-Gilead buried Saul's bones "under the tamarisk tree," possibly in memory of his best days.
8. Saul held a spear in his hand, which would have filled the room with terror. The founder of the Qin dynasty, Shihuangdi, was notorious for his rule through terror, which is illustrated by the fact that he used a military sword, instead of chopsticks, to eat at the table.

that David was on the run from Saul – which would serve as undeniable evidence for his collusion in David's crime. Thus Doeg invented the charge of unlawful divination and placed it first in his enumeration of Ahimelech's crimes. Moreover, Doeg did not call Ahimelech by the proper title of "priest," but by his patronymic, "son of Ahitub" – Eli's great grandson. This implies the Edomite's lack of respect for the Lord's priests and recalls an anonymous prophet's curse against Eli's descendants (see 2:31–33).

Then Saul summoned Ahimelech and all the priests at Nob to his court in Gibeah (v. 11). Saul began his accusation by addressing Ahimelech as "son of Ahitub," just as he had called David "son of Jesse" in order to denigrate him before the people. Ahimelech's polite reply, "my lord," did not abate Saul's anger, for he repeated Doeg's three accusations against Ahimelech and then added his own interpretation: "he has rebelled against me and lies in wait for me" (v. 13). Notably, Saul used imprecise language in naming the first two crimes, replacing Doeg's "provisions" (*tsedah*) with "food" (*lehem*) and replacing Doeg's "the sword of Goliath the Philistine" with "a sword," as if he were not really interested in these two charges. Saul's real interest was to establish that Ahimelech inquired of the Lord for David. If Ahimelech had divined for David, he could not plead innocent on the basis of his ignorance, nor could he argue that he had done so with a good conscience in order to help king Saul. Further, priestly inquiry of the Lord was reserved for a king, making Ahimelech's alleged service for David an act of treason in that Ahimelech was treating David as if he were king. Thus both Saul and Doeg went to great lengths to establish this lie as fact.

To this false charge, Ahimelech replies:

> Who of all your servants is as loyal as David, the king's son-in-law, captain of your bodyguard and highly respected in your household? *Was that day the first time I inquired of God for him? Of course not!* Let not the king accuse your servant or any of his father's family, for your servant knows nothing at all about this whole affair. (v. 14–15, italics mine)

Ahimelech's strategy in refuting Saul's accusation is twofold. First, regarding the charges of giving provisions and the sword of Goliath to David, he pleads innocence because of ignorance. Although he admits to giving food and a sword to David, he did so without knowing that David was Saul's enemy. He flaunts his ignorance by declaring David's favor within the royal household at the beginning of his defense. But in doing so, he emphatically praises

David for his loyalty and respectability.[9] Although this praise was meant to prove Ahimelech's ignorance about David's fall from grace within the royal household, Ahimelech may have intended it to awaken Saul to the truth about David. But judging from Saul's reaction, Ahimelech's message made Saul even angrier. Second, in refuting Saul's accusation, Ahimelech denies the transgression behind the charge of priestly inquiry for David. The meaning of the Hebrew original behind the NIV translation, "Was that day the first time I inquired of God for him," is ambivalent. However, the general context and theme both demand that Ahimelech did not inquire of the Lord for David, for the text criticizes David for his complete failure to ask of the Lord (see 21:9). Thus Alter paraphrases Ahimelech's rhetorical question as follows: "I never previously consulted the oracle for David, and why on earth would I do it now?"[10] Having said all this, one cannot deny that Ahimelech lied when he said to Saul, "your servant knows nothing at all about this whole affair" (v. 15). As we have already discussed, he went along with David's lie about the secret mission because of Doeg's presence in the sanctuary.

In the end Ahimelech could not convince Saul, who was determined to kill Ahimelech and his whole family, just as he was determined to kill David and anyone who joined his cause (v. 23). After pronouncing the verdict – that "Ahimelech knew David to be a fugitive when he helped him" – Saul calls his "guards" to kill the traitor and all his priestly brothers present in court (v. 17). The Hebrew *ratsim* (v. 17 "guards," NIV) refers to the king's "handy men," who carry out any order, particularly dirty jobs such as torturing, flogging, or killing criminals. But Saul's order to kill the priests of the Lord was so preposterous, unprecedented, and inhumane that even the "handy men" were afraid and hesitant to obey. Saul then turned to the Edomite who had no compunctions against killing the Lord's priests, and Doeg carried out the blasphemous order swiftly. On that day, eighty-five priests "who wore the linen ephod" (v. 18) were killed. Doeg, however, did not stop there. He went to Nob and, obviously following Saul's order,[11] massacred the whole village, leaving nothing alive

---

9. The phrase "in your household" could mean "in your kingdom," because a kingdom is often expressed in terms of "the house of a founder." For example, the kingdom of Judah is often called "the house of David," while the kingdom of Israel is called "the house of Omri." In this sense, Ahimelech is saying that David is respected not only by Saul's family members but also by all the people in his kingdom.

10. Alter, *1 Samuel*, 138.

11. It is not clear in the text whether Saul ordered the massacre of Nob, but it is unthinkable that Doeg, a servant of Saul, would carry it out without Saul's order or permission. What is even more shocking about the massacre is the possibility that it happened before Saul ordered

that drew breath. Ironically, Saul failed to carry out the divine order of *herem* (total destruction) against the Amalekites,[12] but then he applied *herem* to one of his own Israelite towns through Doeg the Edomite.

By killing eighty-five priests who wore the linen ephod, Saul effectively sealed his doom. A key motif in this chapter is that of knowing and not knowing. This chapter starts with a scene where David grows in his knowledge of the Lord through the prophet Gad. In contrast, we see Saul reproaching his attendants twice for not "opening his ears" (v. 8: "tell," NIV). Unlike David, there was no prophet to reveal hidden things for him, and so in desperation he resorted to a false prophet with a lying tongue – Doeg the Edomite. As it turned out, the false prophet blocked Saul's eyes and ears completely by killing all the true priests who could help him seek the Lord. From then on David would have an upper hand, because God's revelation was available only to him. The story of the priest survivor Abiathar reinforces this point. When he escaped to David, he carried an ephod with him, which was a legitimate means to induce the Lord's revelation (see 23:6). Thus David took into his service the only legitimate means for divining the Lord's will: the prophet and the ephod.

ABIATHAR AND HAN XIN

Saul's rule of terror forced Abiathar to defect to David and become his high priest. Although the text is not clear, David probably conversed with God through the priest. The addition of Abiathar to David's force helped David outsmart Saul's search parties and survive long enough to see his enemy fall on the battlefield. This recalls Han Xin's defection from Xiang Yu to Liu Bang. Xiang Yu was known to be a brave but stern warlord. He applied military laws so strictly that his men were afraid of him. One day, he buried two hundred thousand prisoners of war alive to prevent them from draining war provisions. Disappointed by this brutal act, Han Xin, a military strategist, defected to Xiang Yu's arch-enemy, Liu Bang, who was known to treat his men with sympathy and love. Recognizing Han Xin's genius, Liu Bang appointed him as head of the entire army. Later, with the help of Han Xin, Liu Bang defeated Xiang Yu's army and became the founder of the Han dynasty. In contrast, Xiang Yu's dream of being the emperor of a united China was frustrated.

---

the death of all the priests present at court. The Hebrew syntax in v. 19 makes it possible to translate the event as a pluperfect: "He had already put to the sword Nob, the town of the priests . . . "
12. *Herem* is a specific mode of battle which applied to a holy war. It literally means "total destruction" in the sense that the object of *herem* is devoted to God.

David makes it clear that he knew about Doeg's presence at the sanctuary, and he also knew that the Edomite would tell Saul about his meeting with Ahimelech. Although David cannot be blamed for the massacre at Nob, his failure to consult God formed a link in the chain of events that led to its destruction.[13] Further, David told a lie to Ahimelech about his secret mission. Although he may have told the lie to acquit Ahimelech for helping Saul's enemy, things did not pan out as David had hoped. Most likely, David told the lie to save himself, which may explain why David acknowledged his responsibility: "I am responsible for the death of your whole family" (v. 22). These details reveal that behind the tragedy at Nob, there were many interlocking levels of human sins. No one was without blame – neither Saul, Doeg, David, nor Ahimelech. Saul and Doeg lied so that they could kill David and Ahimelech. David lied to save himself – and possibly to save Ahimelech. Ahimelech lied to prove his innocence to Saul. Of course, the blame cannot be distributed equally, for Saul's massacre of Nob cannot be defended or justified by any circumstances.[14] Sadly, many scholars recall the anonymous prophet's prophecy of doom against Eli and his descendants (see 2:27–36)[15] and argue that the massacre at Nob is the fulfillment of that prophecy! Of course, this does not explain why Eli's innocent descendants should be killed over the sins of their ancestors. At the end of all this, we can say that men lie for various reasons, but God never lies. His words never come back empty. Although David, like us, was not perfect, God never failed to make good on his words.

---

13. David could not have anticipated that Saul would put the whole city of Nob to total destruction because of his interaction with Ahimelech. After all, Ahimelech claimed that he was only trying to be of service to Saul by helping his loyal servant and son-in-law. Killing so many innocent lives – including women, children, and animals – because Saul judged that Ahimelech had conspired against David was an insanely disproportionate punishment. Nevertheless, David admits his sin of omission in order to comfort Abiathar. In the Hebrew original, the pronoun *anoki* ("I") is used for emphasis. In this way, David expressed his sympathy with Abiathar over the great loss, whereas Saul never repented of the massacre and continued to pursue David's life.
14. In this episode, Saul is the embodiment of evil. His action was not only against humanity in general, but also against the Lord – who had chosen David as king of Israel.
15. See, for instance, Jon Macon's article, "The Fall of Eli's House" at http://northcolumbiacofc.org/Bullentins/2014%2007%2027%20Bulletin%20The%20Fall%20of%20Elis%20House.pdf, accessed on 4 April 2018.

1 SAMUEL 23:1–29

DAVID NOT WELCOMED IN THE DESERT

This chapter begins and ends with reports of a new Philistine invasion in the land of Israel. The Philistine attack on Keilah gave David the opportunity to act as if he were the king of Israel by saving the city from the hand of the Philistines. The report of the Philistine invasion at the end of the chapter, however, underscores King Saul's negligence of his essential duty due to his obsession with David. The Philistine invasion also saves David from Saul's murderous hand at the last moment. In a sense, this chapter continues the theme of elevating David and denigrating Saul, but David is not welcomed in the desert of Judah. David has to endure an inhospitable climate and people, while also running constantly from Saul's search teams. Through this period of suffering and persecution, David learns the nature of the people he should ultimately serve, develops the habit of inquiring of the Lord, and therein grows to become a man of obedience. At every moment of decision, David turns to God for guidance, and God answers David immediately. This accounts for the way David outmaneuvers Saul constantly despite David's lack of logistics.

23:1–6 DAVID SAVES KEILAH

While staying in the forest of Hereth (see 22:5), David received a report of the Philistine attack on Keilah, a walled city located in the lowland of Judah. Since the city was located in the arable land close to the Philistine border, the Philistines regularly launched raids and looted its threshing floors, which were located outside the city gate for grain and domestic animals. Why did this report get to David, a fugitive, and not to Saul, the reigning king of Israel? The essential duty of the king of Israel is to save his people from the hand of the Philistines. We do not know whether or not Saul received the same report, but we are told that only David responded.

David "inquired of the LORD, saying, 'Shall I go and attack these Philistines?'" (v. 2). This is the first time we hear of David turning to God for direction. David did not seek the Lord's counsel when he defected to Gath, but here he sought divine guidance first before making any decisions. This marked an important change in David's journey because the job David was supposed to fill was not like that of a pagan king. The king of Israel was a vice regent of the Lord. In other words, he did not rule his people according to his own will, but he served the Lord's people according to the Lord's law. So, it was crucial for David to develop the habit of asking God what to do and then obeying his will. This character trait differentiated him from Saul as well as any other king in the ancient Near East. We are not told how David inquired of the Lord, but because the priest Abiathar defected to David with the ephod in the forest of Hereth, we may infer that David sought God through Urim and Thummim in the priestly garment.[1] The author presents the scene as David's direct dialogue with the Lord in order to emphasize the intimate relationship that David enjoyed with the Lord during this difficult season of his career. We see how God revealed his will to David, but not to Saul.

Despite the Lord's command to "save Keilah," David's men demurred – perhaps because they were a small band of misfits that had never been trained to fight in battle. If "saving Keilah" was worthy of the king of Israel's attention,[2] David's men felt themselves unworthy for and incapable of the task. David did not ignore his men, nor did he accuse them of cowardice. Although fear is a sign of lack of faith – remember that David himself once succumbed to fear and fled to the Philistines – David lifted up his men's fear to the Lord. In response, the Lord gave David assurance that he would "give the Philistines in your hand" (v. 4). David convinced his men of the Lord's promise and then his army went and saved Keilah.

Notably, "David's men" later becomes a term for David's elite army unit (v. 3). For instance, David's men captured Jerusalem without the help of any other army units (2 Sam 5:6).[3] Their heroic fight against the Philistines is also recorded in 2 Samuel 21:15–22. The bravest thirty men are called "David's warriors," whose exploits are recorded in 2 Samuel 23:8–39. These men began as a ragtag band of cowards who hesitated in fear before the Lord's command to save Keilah, but David's leadership turned them into fearless warriors – and with their help, David was able to fulfil his calling as king of Israel. If David had forced his fearful men to go to battle, he would have lost not only the

---

1. The NIV translation of v. 6, which is based on the Masoretic text, is a bit misleading because that verse says that Abiathar defected to David in Keilah. But we know that Abiathar defected to David in Hereth (see 1 Sam 22:20 and 22:5). In this particular case the Septuagint provides a better reading of v. 6: "And it happened, when Abiathar son of Ahimelech fled to David, that he came down with David to Keilah having an ephod in his hand." If this reading were original, it would imply that Abiathar fled to David when the latter was in Hereth and later followed David to Keilah with an ephod in his hand. Then it stands to reason that David could inquire of the Lord regarding Keilah with the help of the high priest.
2. The Hebrew *hosia* ("save," NIV) predicates the Lord's act (see 17:47) and by extension his human king (see 9:16).
3. John Woodhouse, *2 Samuel: Your Kingdom Come* (Wheaton, IL: Crossway, 2015), 582 fn 8.

battle, but also his men. David was a good leader because he was able to put the people above his political goal, even though that goal was set by God. Liu Bei, whose leadership is still praised among many East Asians, believed that the empire was built upon the people – not upon the expanse of their territory – and made it his first priority to win the heart of the people, not their land.

23:7–13 DAVID CANNOT STAY AT KEILAH

When Saul learned of David's arrival at the city of Keilah, he prepared to lay siege to the city and then pressure the people of Keilah to deliver David to him. Saul rejoiced when he learned that David was in Keilah, for it was a city with gates and bars. Although it is hard to conquer a fortified city such as Keilah, it is relatively easy to stop the traffic in and out of the city. Saul only needed to keep watch of a few gates around the city wall. David was "a rat in the trap" as Koreans would say, or "a bird in the cage," as Sennacherib once said about Hezekiah. Saul figured that God had given him a chance to arrest David, for he boasted, "God has delivered him into my hands" (v. 7). It is not clear whether Saul actually thought this, or if he made such a boast as propaganda. But if this reflects his inner thoughts, we see a serious degree of self-deception on Saul's part. As Abraham J. Heschel once said, self-deception is "a refuge, an asylum for the cruel, the violent, for consummate criminals."[4]

Meanwhile, when David was told that "Saul was plotting against him" (v. 9), he ordered the priest Abiathar to bring the ephod. The author does not give us any details about Saul's plot, but David clarified what he heard in his prayer: "Lord, God of Israel, your servant has heard definitely that Saul plans to come to Keilah and destroy the town on account of me" (v. 10). We are not sure about the source of David's intelligence, but most likely the people of Keilah also heard what David had heard. We can imagine how much pressure this rumor put on the people within Keilah, especially since Saul had recently annihilated Nob. The people felt that the only way they could survive was to deliver David into Saul's hands – just as a woman of Abel beheaded Sheba, the son of Bikri, and threw his head out of the city wall to save her citizens (see 2 Sam 20). Since Saul's goal was to capture David dead or alive, we may infer that Saul himself deliberately aired the rumor to David and the people in Keilah. In *Three Kingdoms*, Cao Cao utilized a similar stratagem when he aimed to capture Liu Bei dead or alive. After being defeated at Xinye by Cao

---

4. Heschel, *A Passion for Truth*, 158.

Cao, Liu Bei retreated to Jingxia and tried to form a military alliance with Sun Quan of the Southland. Afraid of their alliance, Cao Cao wrote an imperial letter to the effect that unless Sun Quan broke the alliance with Liu Bei, he would come in person and totally destroy his country. Cao Cao made three thousand copies of the letter and let them drift down the Yangtze river in order to instill fear into Sun Quan's people.

David's inquiry of the Lord consisted of two parts. One was to confirm the accuracy of the news that he had heard about Saul's intention to come to Keilah (v. 11b). The other was to divine whether the people in the city would deliver David and his men to Saul (v. 11a). This question of the people of Keilah was more important to David than the former, so that he put that before the question of Saul's attack, even though the question about Saul's intention to attack is a more logical first question. Further, David repeated the question about the people of Keilah to the Lord again in verse 12. When the Lord answered that the people would give in to Saul's pressure, David and his men – which had now increased to six hundred men – decided to leave Keilah and flee into the desert of Judah (v. 13).

The Philistine attack against the city of Keilah gave David a moment to shine as the king of Israel should. But he could not stay in the city he had saved, because the people were going to betray him to Saul.[5] Being betrayed by those in whom you have invested love and effort is always a bitter experience, but in God's providence, this was a necessary experience that taught David the nature of the people he would serve. The Israelites were far from an ideal people, for they were a bunch of sinners who constantly turned their back on their God and their king. David's calling was to serve the rebellious sinners so that they could be transformed into an obedient people of the Lord. Keilah's betrayal gave a priceless lesson to David about human nature. Cao Cao, the king of Wei, did not want to be betrayed. So he was known for betraying others preemptively. He boasted by saying that he would rather betray the world than let the world betray him. Cao Cao represents a worldly king, a counterpoint to who David would become.

---

5. Because Saul did not move his troops to Keilah, some scholars argue that David had not been welcomed by the people of Keilah in the first place. The argument is that Saul's threat was invented by the biblical author to make David's departure from the city inevitable. Regardless, David and his outlaws – who would not only drain food in the city but also pose a threat to the people – would not have been welcomed in the city. See J. Baden, *The Historical David: A Real Life of an Invented Hero* (Toronto, ON: HarperCollins, 2013), 87–89.

23:14–18 JONATHAN REASSURES DAVID

> David stayed in the wilderness strongholds and in the hills of the
> Desert Ziph. Day after day Saul searched for him, but God did
> not give David into his hands. (v. 14)

David was a fugitive on the run with Saul in hot pursuit. David hid himself in
the desert of Judah,[6] which features small hills, rocky outcroppings (strongholds), with deep rifts between them. This topography makes travelling by
foot very difficult, especially since the temperatures would have been high
and water in short supply. The occasional oasis provided the only support
for habitation.[7] To survive in such a desert would be a challenge in itself,
but David had to deal with Saul's search parties as well. Verse 14 summarizes
David's life in the wilderness, which is that he always managed to evade Saul's
searches because of God's help. Divine help came in many forms, and one was
Jonathan's friendly visit.

Jonathan visited David at Horesh in the Desert of Ziph. The location of
Horesh is not known. Rather than being a place name, it may refer to a wooded mountain. In biblical times, certain hills in the desert were covered with
evergreen trees. One of these wooded hills may have been a perfect hideout
for runaway fugitives such as David and his men. In the text, Jonathan's visit
is narrated between two episodes of Saul's pursuit of David's life, underscoring
the fatigue and fear that must have gripped David in his desert years. The
phrase "He learned that Saul had come out . . . " (v. 15) may be alternatively
translated as "He feared because Saul had come out . . . . "[8] This alternative translation better explains the motivation for Jonathan's visit to David.
Jonathan understood David's dire situation and decided to visit him. David's
life in the desert was so hard that he desperately needed someone like Jonathan
to reassure him of his calling and to encourage him to persevere. We do not
know how Jonathan found David's hideout, but David must have received
Jonathan as a godsend, which is implied by the fact that Jonathan "helped
him find strength in God" (v. 17).

In the desert, Jonathan and David renewed their covenant for a third and
last time. During their first covenant, Jonathan gave his royal vestments to

---

6. I use the term "the desert of Judah" as a catch-all term for the arid area in Judah. Various
parts in the desert of Judah may be called differently, such as the desert of Ziph, the desert of
Maon, the desert of En-gedi, etc.
7. Baden, *The Historical David*, 83–84.
8. This alternative interpretation assumes a different vocalization of the word in question.

David, a symbolic act of abdicating his right to inherit the throne from Saul to David (18:3–4). Although we do not hear Jonathan's words in this scene, the text predicates their relationship as "love," which is another technical term for loyalty. David and Jonathan renewed their covenant a second time when David decided to leave Saul's court permanently to become a fugitive, expanding their covenant to their descendants (20:16, 42). Now at Horesh in the desert of Ziph, they renewed their covenant once again.

> Don't be afraid. My father Saul will not lay a hand on you. You will be king over Israel, and I will be second to you. Even my father Saul knows this. (v. 17)

In this conversation, Jonathan made it unmistakably clear that David would be king of Israel. Prior to this, he had conveyed David's future symbolically by disrobing (see 18:4) or through the euphemistic expression, "May the Lord be with you as he has been with my father" (20:13). Here, Jonathan added to the covenant the term that he would be the second-in-command in David's kingdom. Although Jonathan remained loyal to his father, he believed that David was God's chosen, and he dreamt of the future when he could serve as David's chief official. Moderns may blame Jonathan for playing double between two rivals, but Jonathan's filial piety made him truly an ideal public official in the eyes of ancient Asians. Jonathan never abandoned his father until David's assumption of the throne, which can be compared with David's attitude towards Saul as God's anointed, for David never tried to kill Saul. In a sense, David remained loyal to Saul during his lifetime. However, Jonathan did not survive to see the day when he would serve in David's kingdom, for he died prematurely in the Gilboa battle with his father Saul.

Jonathan's love for David was related to Samuel's prophecy about how God would give the kingdom "to one of your [Saul's] neighbor – to one better than you" (see 15:28). On seeing David defeating Goliath without a sword, Jonathan knew that David was the better neighbor. Saul knew the truth as well, as Jonathan made clear in verse 17: "Even my father Saul knows this." But whereas Jonathan accepted the Lord's will as expressed through the prophet Samuel, Saul resisted it and rebelled against God. Although Saul knew that God had given his kingdom to David, he did his best to prevent it. Saul's hatred of David may have been an extension of his hatred of God, who had rejected him as king!

23:19-29 DAVID IN THE DESERT OF ZIPH

This episode vividly shows one of the dangerous situations that David found himself in regularly as a fugitive running from Saul. Fearful of the reigning king, the people in the desert were willing to deliver David to Saul's contingent. After all, David and his men were a bunch of social outcasts who had to depend on the kindness of the people for food and shelter. In other words, they were a burden on those who lived in the desert towns. Further, David's fame as Goliath's killer faded away once he became a fugitive. He was no longer Saul's favorite general! David's decision to defect to Gath ruined any fame he had left, and it also made him appear as an idol-worshipper in the eyes of the Israelites, since defection to a foreign land meant conversion to a pagan religion. Thus the direct intervention of the Lord was necessary for David's survival in the desert of Judah.

Ziph is a Judean city located about seven kilometers southeast of Hebron. As with other desert cities, the city of Ziph may have been a fortified city with gates and bars.[9] City dwellers, in contrast to the Bedouin who moved around with animals, had vested interest in their relationship with the central government. Further, the news about Nob's destruction had most likely reached the ears of the Ziphites. They did not want their city to suffer from the same fate as Nob, and so they decided to do what Saul expected from his subjects: "opening his ears" about David (see 22:8: "telling," NIV). They went up to Saul in Gibeah and gave coordinates for David's hiding place: "in the strongholds at Horesh, on the hill of Hakilah, south of Jeshimon" (v. 20). When they expressed their willingness to deliver David to Saul, Saul was delighted by their concern (v. 21). Earlier, he had accused his attendants of being disinterested in him: "None of you is concerned about me?" (see 22:8). Apparently, Saul found loyal subjects in the Ziphites, and so he blessed them in the name of the Lord (v. 21).

But strangely, Saul did not act on the intelligence he received from these loyal Ziphites. Instead, he cautiously ordered them to go back and investigate the matter more thoroughly and to "Come back to me with definite information" (v. 23). What kept him from running into the desert to capture David? Certainly, the intelligence was detailed and credible, but David had recently acquired a reputation which Saul describes as being "very crafty" (v. 22: literally, "craftily crafty"). Earlier David had been known to be brave, eloquent, and

---

9. It is not clear whether the city of Ziph was fortified at this time, but it was during the reign of Solomon (2 Chr 11:8).

fine-looking" (see 16:18), but he had not been called "crafty." Most likely, his new reputation was related to the addition of the prophet Nathan and the priest Abiathar to David's forces. In a similar way, the addition of Zhuge Liang to Liu Bei's force affected the way enemy armies approached Liu Bei's army in battles. The reputation for being crafty always goes ahead of one's army and affects the enemy's strategy. Zhuge Liang's reputation for craftiness turned Sima Yi's army back from pursuing the fleeing Shu army in Qi Mountain.

> Sima Yi watched the skies . . . he was pleased and excited and said to those about him, "Zhuge Liang is dead!" At once he ordered pursuit with a strong force. But just as he passed his camp gates doubts filled his mind and he gave up his plan. "Zhuge Liang is a master of mysteries: he can get aid from the Deities of the Six Layers." It may be that this is but a ruse to get us to take the field. We may fall victims to his guile. So he halted.[10]

Similarly, David's reputation for being crafty delayed Saul from sending his search unit into the desert, and as a result he let David escape at the last moment. But David's dramatic rescue can also be attributed to the report about the Philistine invasion that was delivered to Saul. When the Philistines invaded the land, he had to pull his forces out of the rocky mountains. Without this timely report, Saul would not have called off his pursuit of David. The text describes this scene in a very dramatic fashion. Saul's pursuit operation reached its dramatic climax in the mountains in the Desert of Maon. "The rock" in verse 25 is the same place with "the mountain" in verse 26. The Desert of Maon undulates with substantial rock mountains, and David went down to one of those rock mountains.[11]

> Saul was going along one side of the mountain, and David and his men were on the other side, hurrying to get away from Saul. As Saul and his forces were closing in on David and his men to capture them, a messenger came to Saul, saying, "Come quickly! The Philistines are raiding the land." (vv. 26–27)

Jonathan's arrival in the desert had brought divine help to David in his distress by confirming his calling as the future king of Israel. The timely attack

---

10. Roberts, *Three Kingdoms*, ch. 104.

11. Sela Hammahlekoth, or "Rock of Separation," is the name of the rock mountain where Saul's army came close to capturing David, but they had to break off the pursuit because of the Philistine invasion. Although the text approximates the location in the Desert of Maon, its exact location has not been identified yet.

of the Philistines was another form of divine help for David and his men as they were being pursued by Saul and his forces. Saul had everything he needed to achieve victory in his battle against David: the seal of office, the army, provisions, a network of people willing to "open his ears" (22:8). David, on the contrary, lacked everything except for the Lord's help. The Lord was on David's side, and he sustained him through the most difficult season of his journey to the throne. The Lord's intention was not simply for David to survive, but also for David to be transformed. Saul was rejected because of his failure to obey the Lord, and obedience was the definitive quality that God wanted in a king of Israel, a vice regent who would serve in God's earthly kingdom. David was not obedient in the beginning, for he decided to become Saul's son-in-law on his own, and he did not inquire of the Lord when he defected to the Philistines. He made these decisions based on what seemed right in his own eyes. But David started to change during his stay at Adullam and the outskirts of Moab. During his trials in the desert, David developed the habit of asking God before he made any decisions. The Prophet Gad and the priest Abiathar served as two legitimate channels for divine revelation. As David grew in his understanding about what it meant to be the king of Israel, he drew closer to the throne.

1 SAMUEL 24:1–22; 26:1–25

DAVID SPARES SAUL'S LIFE TWICE[1]

David could not do anything to establish himself as king. He was an outlaw, a fugitive on the run who had lost his popularity. Even the people in Judea did not welcome him. His failed attempt to defect to the Philistines had cut him off from all hereditary ties with Israel and labeled him as an idol worshipper. Saul was still in power; doing everything he could to capture David. David had no logistics, no army, no local base from which he could operate.

David might have been able to establish himself as king by assassinating King Saul. Koreans under Japanese oppression regarded assassination as an important means of fighting for independence. Jung Geun An, who assassinated the Japanese governor to Korea, was hailed as a national hero in Korea, but he was convicted and executed as a terrorist in Japan. David was on the run with a few hundred untrained soldiers, and so assassinating Saul may have helped him get the kingdom. In fact, the chance to assassinate King Saul was given to David twice – first in chapter 24 and again in chapter 26. But both times, David restrained himself from killing Saul at the last moment. What made David stop? The answer to this question gives us a very important lesson for what our mission strategy should be in realizing the kingdom of God in the modern world.

24:1–7 DAVID CUTS OFF A CORNER OF SAUL'S ROBE

After Saul returned from pursuing the Philistines, he was told, "David is in the Desert of En-Gedi" (v. 1), which is an oasis on the west side of the Dead Sea in the Judean wilderness about fifteen kilometers west of the city of Ziph. As its meaning "spring of the goat" indicates, a lot of goats are said to have lived in the nearby rock mountains. This piece of intelligence prompted Saul to take his three thousand strong army into one of those rock mountains called "the Crags of the Wild Goats" in order to pursue David. Considering that "The three thousand able young men" amounts to the total number of Saul's standing army (see 13:2), Saul arguably spent all his available forces in trying

---

1. The present writer has decided to treat chapters 24 and 26 in one chapter, mainly because literary and theological meanings of the two similar but distinct events are best revealed in so doing. Readers will be equipped with a better perspective when reading the two texts in juxtaposition.

to capture and kill one fugitive on the run. What a waste of state resources! Some people even argue that Saul's kingdom disintegrated because Saul spent too many resources trying to deal with David.[2]

On his way to the rocky mountains where David had been reported to be hiding, Saul found a cave near the sheep pens on the slope and decided to enter it to relieve himself (literally, "to cover his feet"), without knowing that David and his men had secluded themselves far back in the cave. David's men urged David to kill him: "This is the day the LORD spoke of when he said to you, 'I will give your enemy into your hands for you to deal with as you wish'" (v. 4). Following their advice, David stealthily approached Saul to kill him, but he only cut off a corner of Saul's robe, without finishing him off. Many commentators assume that David had no intention of killing Saul, but it is more plausible to assume that David started out to kill Saul and then changed his mind at the last moment. The fact that David approached Saul at the urging of his men to kill the king (v. 4) intimates that David was tempted to assassinate Saul. What stopped David from doing so? When David commanded his men not to attack Saul, he said that he had not killed him because "The LORD forbid that I should do such a thing to my master, the LORD's anointed, or lay my hand on him; for he is the anointed of the LORD" (v. 6). In fact, the narrator says that David was "conscience-stricken" for having removed a corner of Saul's robe (v. 5).

Here we see two types of men in conflict: a man of principle versus a man of practical gain. David knew how to plan and execute in order to attain a goal, but in pursuing that goal, he set a boundary over which he never crossed. We can call this boundary his principles. David would do everything in his power to become king of Israel when the right time came, but he would not kill innocent people nor delight in unjust gain. This is what he meant by not killing the Lord's anointed. Assassination may have been the only feasible way for David to rise to the throne at that time, but he refused to violate his moral principles – even if doing so could give him the kingdom. David's men were more pragmatic and were willing to do anything to attain their goal. They had no moral boundary and even sold the name of God to achieve their goal by telling David that this was the day of which the Lord had spoken. But in their own words, killing Saul would be doing "what is good in their own eyes" (see v. 4: "to deal with as you wish," NIV).

---

2. See Rev Emmanuel Oghene, *Between Honorables and Hooligans* (UK: Xlibris, 2017).

Cao Cao, the founder of the Wei kingdom, was a man of practical gain like David's men. When he became a fugitive on the run after his failed assassination attempt on Dong Zhao, his uncle welcomed him into his castle at his own risk, and Cao Cao took shelter there. But suspicious Cao Cao killed his uncle preemptively, lest he betray him to the authorities for ransom. To justify himself, Cao Cao said, "I would rather betray the world than let the world betray me." He was willing to compromise everything for his goals. Many Christians easily fall into the trap of thinking that a godly goal can justify an ungodly means. For example, some Korean megachurch leaders have been criticized for "passing on" their absolute power to their sons under the pretext of minimizing confusion over a power transfer. But most Koreans compare this practice to the way that some Korean conglomerate CEOs bequeath their power to their sons. Obviously, there needs to be a moral boundary over which Christians never cross – regardless of how a particular course of action might seem to "help" the kingdom of God.

24:8–22 DIALOGUE BETWEEN DAVID AND SAUL

Then David went out of the cave and called out to Saul (v. 8). After a formality of obeisance, David delivered a long speech (vv. 8–15). David's rather repetitive speech may be summarized as follows: he pleaded innocent to the charge of intending to kill his way to the throne by presenting a piece of Saul's robe as physical proof of his loyalty. Calling Saul, "my lord the King" (v. 8), and "my father" (v. 11), David belabored the point that he intended no treason and that his "hand will not touch" Saul the Lord's anointed (v. 13). Noteworthy in David's speech is that he did not invoke a curse against Saul. The NIV translation, "may the LORD avenge the wrongs you [Saul] have done to me," is misleading in this respect (v. 12). The nuance of the Hebrew is: "may the LORD prove my innocence by delivering me from your hand" (v. 15). The focus of David's prayer is his deliverance out of harm's way, which will prove him innocent, rather than his vengeance on Saul. He truly trusts in the goodness and fairness of divine judgment. David was not concerned with whether God would make Saul fall in battle or let him live his full years (see 26:10). His concern was the Lord's rule over his life.

In response, Saul addressed David as "my son" for the first time, and "he wept aloud" (v. 16). It appears that he became repentant after hearing David's speech, but Saul's subsequent answer reveals that his intention to kill David would continue unabatedly in the future. First, he did not admit his sin. That

"You are more righteous than I" (v. 17) is less the confession of his sin than the praise of David's virtue. He could have said, "I have sinned. Come back my son David," as he does later in 26:21. Second, Saul did not promise that he would not seek David's life any longer. Although he invoked the Lord's reward on David's behalf after hearing about "the good" that David did to him (v. 18), he did not commit himself to returning "the good" to David. Read from this perspective, the proverb that Saul quoted sounds ominous: "When a man finds his enemy, does he let him get away unharmed?" (v. 19). Although Saul cited these words in the context of praising David's exceptional virtue, one may also discern Saul's veiled threat against David: "I will not let you get away unharmed!" Interestingly, just as David cited a proverb, "From evildoers come evil deeds" (v. 13) as a veiled accusation against Saul, so Saul cited a proverb as a veiled threat against David.

Although Saul's prophetic words in verse 20 ("I know that you will surely be king and the kingdom of Israel will be established in your hands") are usually taken as a later insertion, they are integrated into the narrative. They confirm Jonathan's words – "You [David] will be king over Israel . . . Even my father knows this" (see 23:17) – and also corroborate the pattern we have observed thus far, which is that Saul knowingly rebels against the Lord's will. Saul's subsequent request for David to swear that he would never kill his descendants nor wipe out his name (v. 21) is no sign of his surrender to David (v. 21). Rather, it could have been a sly stratagem to restore the throne to his family later. It was the well-known practice for a usurper to kill the family of the king he replaced and to confiscate all the property that would bear his name, all so as to prevent future retaliatory coups. Ancient Asians compared leaving any descendant of an enemy alive with planting a seed of disaster in their own backyard.[3] Thus David had to return to his strongholds of En-Gedi after this apparent rapprochement (v. 29), for he was smart enough to discern the negative nuance in Saul's words – and that Saul would not stop pursuing him in the desert of Judah (see ch. 26).

---

3. Following the oath that David made to Saul, David neither killed Saul's descendants nor confiscated his ancestral land. However, all of Saul's descendants except the disabled Mephiboshet were killed by the Gibeonites under David's auspice, and Saul's land was given over to Ziba's custody.

26:1–13 DAVID TAKES SAUL'S SPEAR AND WATER JUG

This episode repeats major motifs and themes from chapter 24, but it relates a different event that occurred in a different location. It also introduces two new rival characters into the story: Abishai and Abner. Further, this episode witnesses a significant change in Saul's attitude towards David.

Despite his tearful rapprochement with David in chapter 24, Saul set out to kill David when the loyal Ziphites went all the way up to Gibeah to inform the king of David's whereabouts in the desert of Ziph (v. 1; see also 23:19). Saul acted upon the intelligence without delay and went down to the hill of Hakilah in the Desert of Ziph. However, Saul failed to capture David again – not because the Ziphites gave him the wrong intelligence, but because David had learned from his own scouts that Saul's three thousand strong army had arrived and were encamped "beside the road on the hill of Hakilah facing Jeshmon" (vv. 2–3). David's use of scouts shows that he did not give up on gathering intelligence just because he could obtain divine revelation.

This episode turns out to be another chance for David to assassinate King Saul and thereby fulfill his ambition for the throne. The previous opportunity may have come too abruptly for David to prepare; since it was pure coincidence that Saul entered the cave where David was hiding to relieve himself. But this time, David crossed over to Saul's camp while Saul and his men were asleep, bringing along Abishai as his bodyguard and assassin. Clearly, his intention was to kill Saul, for he wouldn't have taken so great a risk just to steal Saul's spear and water jug. Because assassination was the only feasible means to turn the tables on Saul, Abishai volunteered to go with David.

Abishai was one of the three sons of David's sister, Zeruiah, who were not only known to be brave in battle but also to be violent and intractable. Even David found them to be difficult to control. Since Abishai had a vested interest in David's future kingdom, he was willing to do anything to make David king of Israel, and so it is no surprise that he volunteered for the killing mission.[4] This is clarified later by his words to David after they arrived at Saul's camp and found everyone sleeping: "Today God has delivered your enemy into your hands. Now let me pin him to the ground with one thrust of the spear; I won't strike him twice" (v. 8). These words mirror the message of David's men in the cave, but Abishai added his own color of violence at

---

4. We do not know much about Ahimelek the Hittite, who did not volunteer to go with David on the mission, except that he was one of the foreign mercenaries employed by David. Uriah, the husband of Bathsheba, was also a Hittite.

the end. Abishai may have taken David's successful entry into Saul's sleeping quarters as God's "go-ahead" sign for assassination.

But again, David aborted the mission at the last minute. He stopped Abishai: "Don't destroy him! Who can lay a hand on the LORD's anointed and be guiltless?" (v. 9). Although David crossed over to Saul's camp in order to kill him, his faith and conscience stopped him from doing something inhumane and ungodly under the pretext of doing the Lord's will. David may have had a moment like Chen Gong, a Hamlet-like character in *Three Kingdoms*. When he found out Cao Cao's true color – that he would do anything to gain the empire – Chen Gong decided to kill him while he was asleep. But looking over Cao Cao as he slept in his bed, Chen Gong had a moment of hesitation and said to himself: "I have left even my office to do righteous things. Now if I killed him, I would do unrighteousness. And the people [Heaven] would condemn me. I rather leave in silence."[5] David's words to Abishai resemble Chen Gong's.

> "Who can lay a hand on the LORD's anointed and be guiltless? As surely as the LORD lives," he said, "the LORD himself will strike him, or his time will come and he will die, or he will go into battle and perish. But the LORD forbids that I should lay a hand on the LORD's anointed. Now get the spear and water jug that are near his head, and let's go." (vv. 9–10)

After taking Saul's spear and water jug, David crossed back to his own camp. It was a miracle for them to escape without being noticed, because the king's tent during an expedition was heavily guarded. The narrator mentions divine help in their journey back: "They were all sleeping, because the LORD had put them into a deep sleep" (v. 12). Although it would have been just as difficult for David and Abishai to make it *into* Saul's tent without being noticed, the narrator does not mention the Lord's help at the front-end of the mission. The fact that the narrator mentions the Lord's help only after David's decision not to kill Saul intimates that the Lord approves of David's refusal to take an easy road to the throne. In these two episodes, David sets a good example of adhering to moral principles while working for the kingdom of God.

---

5. Roberts, *Three Kingdoms*, ch. 5.

26:14–25 DIALOGUE BETWEEN DAVID AND SAUL

Before engaging with Saul in conversation, David called out from a safe distance to Abner, Saul's chief general. David began by reminding Abner, "You're a man, aren't you? And who is like you in Israel?" (v. 15).[6] Then David rebuked Abner for failing to do his job as Saul's chief general: "Why didn't you guard your lord the king?" (v. 15). This speech marks an ominous foreshadowing of Abner's future, for he abandoned Saul on the battlefield on Mount Gilboa. When the Philistines pursued Saul and his sons to kill them, Abner was not there to protect his lords. Further, he betrayed Saul's successor, Ish-Boshet, and tried to capitulate to David. The treacherous Abner forms a foil for Abishai, who accompanied David in this dangerous expedition to Saul's camp. Unlike Abner, Abishai remained loyal to David until he established his kingdom. Although Abishai was violent and intractable, he made great contributions to David's kingdom. Lastly, David pronounced Abner's negligence of his duty as a crime deserving death, because it was ultimately a sin against the Lord's anointed (v. 16). Presenting Saul's spear and water jug as physical evidence for Abner's negligence, David's rebuke of Abner in Saul's hearing could have been intended to convince Saul of his misjudgment about David.

After rebuking Abner, David conversed with Saul, telling him that he spared his life a second time, even though he easily could have killed him. As in the previous speech, David pleaded innocent to the charge of regicide. He protested against Saul, "Why is my lord pursing his servant?" (v. 18). He then cursed those who attempted to drive a wedge between Saul and David by false words (v. 19). As all loyal Asian court officials would do, David attributed Saul's animosity to the misinformation whispered in Saul's ears by disloyal servants rather than to the king's petty jealousy. Further, David debunked the evil efforts of disloyal servants in Saul's court to cut off David from the land of his inheritance. They said to David, "Go serve other gods" (v. 19), which was equivalent to sentencing David to excommunication, or social murder. In all this, David did not criticize Saul, but rather humbled himself before Saul, comparing himself to a flea and a partridge (v. 20). David's speech underscores his political shrewdness. Though much shorter than his previous dialogue with Saul, it carried more weight, which is corroborated by Saul's response.

In Saul's previous encounter with David in En-Gedi, Saul did not admit his wrongdoing, but here he admitted it with sincerity: "I have sinned . . . Surely I have acted like a fool and have been terribly wrong" (v. 21). This was

---

6. The NIV translation, "you're a man, aren't you," makes no sense.

a great concession on Saul's part, because a king in the ancient Near East did not err and never apologized in his court. Further, he promised that he would no longer attempt to kill David (v. 21) – although he quickly reneged on this promise. Finally, addressing David as "my son" (v. 17, 21, 25), Saul blessed David: "You will do great things and surely triumph" (v. 25).

So how did David succeed in changing the king's heart? First, David persistently tried to do the right thing. Despite his servants' pressure to take a short cut to the throne, he did not compromise his moral principles for political gain. For David, killing the Lord's anointed was an absolute line he would not cross. Second, David's trust in the Lord enabled him to persevere in doing the right thing. He said to Saul, "The LORD rewards everyone for their righteousness and faithfulness" (v. 23). No matter what David's enemies said about him, he kept on doing the right thing in the Lord's eyes and asked the Lord for what he deserved instead of cursing his enemies or trying to harm them: "As surely as I valued your [Saul's] life today, so may the LORD value my life and deliver me from all trouble" (v. 24). Note that David did not judge Saul but valued his life. Thus David trusted in the Lord to prove his innocence by delivering him from his enemy. David teaches us that we should trust God's judgment and love our enemies.

1 SAMUEL 25:1–44

DAVID AND ABIGAIL

Chapter 25 illustrates how David took the initiative to establish his kingdom in Israel. Rather than being passive, as some scholars suggest, he did everything in his power to obtain the kingdom without crossing any ethical line.[1] After escaping from Saul's court, there was virtually nothing for him to do except hide in the desert, trying to survive. Even the people in the Judean desert turned against him. To top it off, Samuel, his mentor, died (v. 1). With so many circumstances against him, the episodes in 1 Samuel do not emphasize David's initiative in obtaining the kingdom – though this will shift after Saul's death, when David will make aggressive efforts to obtain the kingdom in the early chapters of 2 Samuel. However, the episode of David and Abigail in 1 Samuel provides one example of David actively pursuing the kingdom.

The highlight of this episode is David taking Abigail as his wife. This is not a romance story, for in ancient times, marriage was a business transaction. Most likely, David married Abigail, the wife of Nabal, to strengthen his tie with – or even his right to rule – the southern region of Judah, especially the area around Hebron. This is implied by the fact that Nabal was the de-facto ruler of southern Judah, as evidenced by his wealth. Later, when David came back to Judah from the Philistine lands, he presented his wife Abigail to the people of Hebron as a seal of kingship.[2] Doing God's will on earth entails both taking initiative as well as obeying the Lord's words. David's life shows us how obedience and initiative can work in harmony as we strive to live for the kingdom of God.

25:1 DEATH OF SAMUEL

Samuel did not live long enough to see David become the king of Israel. Rather, he died when the chance of David's success appeared to be most remote. The news of Samuel's death may have affected David negatively, for he most likely felt completely lost in his endeavor to survive Saul's persecution and fulfil his divine calling as king (see 27:1). The author describes Samuel's death and

---

1. See M. Halbertal and S. Holmes, *The Beginning of Politics: Power in the Biblical Book of Samuel* (Princeton, NJ: Princeton University Press, 2018), 17–66.
2. Joel Baden, *The Historical David: The Real Life of an Invented Hero* (New York, NY: HarperCollins, 2013), 97–98.

burial in a quick succession of four verbs, which belie the lustrous role Samuel played in shaping the early history of the Israelite monarchy.

We are not sure whether David attended Samuel's funeral, but after Samuel died, David moved to the Desert of Paran, which is usually understood to be located in the northeastern Sinai Peninsula. But since the subsequent story takes place in the Desert of Maon, which assumes that David and his men are operating in the city of Carmel (see v. 4), the Desert of Paran may better be read as "the Desert of Maon," following the Septuagint.

25:2–11 NABAL HUMILIATES DAVID

The story begins by introducing a certain man who lived in Maon and had business ("property," NIV) in the city of Carmel, about two kilometers north of Maon. His business was sheep shearing, and he was very rich, for "He had a thousand goats and three thousand sheep" (v. 2). To put this in perspective, during Solomon's reign, twelve district governors paid three thousand sheep per year for palace provisions (see 1 Kgs 4:23). In other words, this individual man owned more sheep and goats than the total sum of the annual tax collected in one tribal territory, which would have identified him as one who was as wealthy as a local ruler. In fact, the man was most likely the ruler of the area south of Hebron, which is corroborated by the fact he was a descendant of Caleb (v. 3),[3] who had acquired the right to the land of Hebron by conquest. Although the Calebites belonged to the tribe Judah, they had their own sphere of influence at that time.[4] The name of this rich ruler was Nabal, which means "A fool" (v. 3), and we are told that he was "surly and mean in his dealings" (v. 3). His wife Abigail, on the other hand, is introduced as "an intelligent and beautiful woman" (v. 3). These literary characterizations prove true as the story unfolds.

Living as an outlaw in the desert with six hundred mouths to feed left David with few options for earning bread for his troops. Either he had to take it by force from others, or he had to depend on others' generosity, or he had to run a protection racket like the contemporary Mafia. The last option appears to have been David's choice while he lived in the Desert of Maon after

---

3. The author devotes a full sentence to emphasize this fact, although he could have noted it with one word. See Baden, *The Historical David*, 97.
4. When David became the king of Israel and Judah, various clans in the land of Judah were united under one central administration. Prior to that, they formed a loose confederacy of independent clans.

Samuel's death. Naturally, Nabal – who had four thousand sheep and goats – was David's biggest customer. One should be careful not to judge David from a modern perspective, since such a business venture was not regarded as unjust or illegal – especially in a turbulent era when everybody was left to his own wits.

The plot is set in motion when David sent "ten young men" to ask for provisions from Nabal, who was shearing sheep at Carmel. Sheep shearing was traditionally an occasion for a banquet, during which wine and food were distributed to workers as well as neighbors. It was usually a party for the whole city, and the host tended to be more generous than usual, since he was gathering in the biggest "cash" for the whole year. When David heard the news of Nabal's sheep shearing, which was "a festive time" (v. 8), he decided to send ten boys to ask for food to feed his men. The number of the boys he sent represents the approximate amount of provisions he expected from Nabal.

According to what the boys said to Nabal, David humbled himself before Nabal by calling himself Nabal's son and by calling his boys Nabal's servants (v. 8). This was not only the language of outward decorum, but the language that informed the relationship between a sovereign and a vassal. By using this language, David recognized Nabal as ruler of the area. In a similar vein, David made sure that his request did not sound coercive: "Please give . . . whatever your hand ["you," NIV] can find for them" (v. 8). This can be likened to a Korean idiom, "His or her hand is big," which means, "He or she is very generous." Thus David was asking Nabal to give according to the size of his hand (generosity). But at the same time, David identified himself as an independent power. First, he directed his boys to "greet him in my name" (v. 5). Usually, a subject was summoned before a ruler; he did not approach him on his own. Moreover, a subject gave his name when asked; he did not greet a ruler in his own name. Further, David did not go in person to Nabal but dispatched an envoy, which points towards David's presumption as an independent power. Second, in asking for provisions, David did not beg for generosity but reasoned that he deserved it: "When your shepherds were with us [under our protection], we did not mistreat [harass] them, and the whole time they were at Carmel nothing of theirs was missing [we protected your flock from getting robbed]" (v. 7, brackets indicate an alternative translation). He also identified Nabal's servants as witnesses (v. 8). In Asian communities where honor is the ultimate virtue, it is generally considered a mandatory courtesy for a favor to be returned. If Nabal were a man of honor, he would return David's favor – whether David's service had been invited or not.

But David miscalculated, for though Nabal was rich and powerful, he was neither honorable nor diplomatic. As his name implies, he was a fool, for he not only rejected David's request for provisions but also humiliated David and his men. Nabal sullied David's name by regarding him as runaway slave and a man of no tribal heritage (vv. 10–11). If the former reflected Saul's assessment of David, the latter revealed how the people of Israel thought of him. David once complained of the people by saying, "They have driven me today from my share in the LORD's inheritance and have said, 'Go, serve other gods'" (see 26:19). What made Nabal's insult even more unbearable is the fact that he did not insult David in the heat of the moment but after taking time to deliberate on the matter. This is made clear by the author's brief note, "Then they waited" (v. 9). The Hebrew *wayanuhu* here may be translated literally as "they rested." In ancient China, when a king needed time to deliberate, he asked an envoy to rest in a guest house and to come back the next day or at another set time. The envoy waited for the king's answer while resting in a guest house. So we may infer from the note, "Then they rested/waited," that Nabal took time to deliberate about how to answer David's request. This made Nabal's insult deliberate and therefore even more preposterous.

Nabal is the embodiment of folly, for he deliberately insulted another human being – and even more disgraceful, a man in need. In an honor-shame culture, East Asians are willing to die rather than be humiliated. They would say, "Kill me, but do not humiliate me!" God may agree with Asians on this point, for God's many names reflect his acts in this world. Disgracing his name amounts to denying his salvific acts in the world. Blasphemers, therefore, are not to be forgiven. Nabal disgraced David's name, and therefore the punishment he deserved was total destruction.

25:12–17 DAVID DETERMINES TO KILL NABAL

As soon as David received the report of Nabal's insult, he strapped on his sword and ordered his men to do so as well. Then, after dividing his men into two groups – a four-hundred-strong attack unit and a two-hundred-strong logistics unit – David went up to the city of Carmel with his four hundred combatants. This division of force portrays David not as a leader of a ragtag gang but as a warlord of an organized army. We are not told here of David's *Chu Shi Biao*, or his reasons for the Carmel expedition, because the author deliberately delays revealing this until verses 21–22. The reason for the delay is explained below, but David is determined to take revenge for the shame by killing every male in Nabal's household.

CHU SHI BIAO

Chu Shi Biao originally referred to the letter that Zhuge Liang wrote to the emperor Liu Shan of the state of Shu Han in order to explain the reasons for his military expeditions to the northern part of China, where the state of Wei was located – the most powerful of the three kingdoms. In his *Chu Shi Biao*, Zhuge Liang argued for the necessity to preemptively vanquish the state of Wei before it would vanquish the state of Shu Han. This letter is famous not only for its literary excellence but also for its content reflecting Zhuge Liang's loyalty to his kings.

Meanwhile, Abigail also received a report from "one of the servants" (v. 14) and prepared to meet David.[5] The servant's report consisted of three parts. First, he summarized very briefly how Nabal had treated David's men, who had come during a festive time to ask for provisions. Second, the servant bore witness to the favor that David's men claimed to have given to Nabal. In so doing, he revealed that Nabal's insults were ill-advised and foolish. Third, he urged Abigail to do everything in her power to stop the imminent disaster in store for Nabal's household. The servant noted that his master "is such a wicked man that no one can talk to him" (v. 17). The NIV, "a wicked man," is an understatement of the Hebrew *ben-beliyaal*, whose literal meaning is "a man of Belial."[6] Since it would be very unlikely for a servant to insult his master in front of his master's wife, one may judge that this comment was purely literary, placed by the author in the servant's mouth to emphasize Nabal's foolishness. Be that as it may, the comment in question – whether the servant's or the author's – explains why the servant went to Abigail and not to Nabal, who was so wicked that no one could talk to him!

---

5. The NIV, "One of the servants told Abigail . . ." (v. 14), is better translated as, "One of the servants had told Abigail . . ."
6. The alternative meaning is "a man of worthlessness."

25:18–35 ABIGAIL CONFRONTS DAVID

The servant's report convinced Abigail that she needed to act quickly and shrewdly in order to avert a catastrophe. She loaded provisions, which David's boys had failed to acquire, on donkeys and left to meet David. The amount of food and drink enumerated in verse 18 shows "how big her hand was," as Koreans would say. Further, this crisis confirms the wisdom that was attributed to her by the narrator in verse 4. Her wisdom is discernible in two details describing her actions. First, she sent the donkeys loaded with gifts ahead of her. She may have reasoned, like Jacob, that she could pacify David's anger with gifts sent ahead (see Gen 32:20). The allusion to the Jacob story seems to suggest that Abigail was as shrewd as Jacob. Second, she kept the matter secret from her husband, for if she had told Nabal, he would not have let her go. This recalls the Shunammite woman who did not tell her husband about the son's death and left for the prophet alone (2 Kgs 4:23). This allusion seems to suggest that Abigail was as strategic as the Shunammite woman. Both allusions underscore Abigail's wisdom and foreshadow her success.

Abigail came down the slope of one mountain just as David and his men descended from another mountain. They were heading towards each other, but since she was passing through "a hidden area" (v. 20: "ravine," NIV) on her way down, neither party could see the other until the last moment. The note, "And she met them" (v. 20), carries a sense of abruptness and surprise. This abrupt confrontation between Abigail and David marks the highest point of tension in the narrative. Then the narrator inserts a flashback, as if to maintain the tension as long as possible. Verses 21 and 22, which comprise the content of David's *Chu Shio Biao*, interrupt the flow of the narrative and explain why David was heading to Carmel: "May God deal with David, be it ever so severely, if by morning I leave alive one male of all who belong to him" (v. 22). The revelation of David's murderous intention increases the narrative tension and also makes clear the tremendous challenge before Abigail, thereby making her success truly meritorious.

The suddenness of the encounter is further emphasized by Abigail's quick dismount from her donkey and her fall to the ground (v. 23). The narrator expresses Abigail's prostration to David in a succession of three verbs: "She bowed down . . . She fell . . . She fell" (vv. 23–24).[7] It may be read that she bowed down before David three times. Commoners approached the emperor

---

7. NIV translates the first "she fell" adverbially as part of the sentence that begins with "she bowed down."

in East Asia by prostrating themselves. Falling at the feet of one's ruler is the position of begging in the Old Testament (see Esth 8:3). Abigail further debased herself before David by calling herself "your servant."

Abigail's speech further illustrates her wisdom.[8] It consists of two parts. The first part (vv. 24–27) focused on appeasing David's anger. In the second part (vv. 28–31), Abigail spoke like a prophet, reassuring David of the Lord's protection and his success in establishing a lasting kingdom. By framing her speech in this way, she suggested that it would be in David's best interest not to kill Nabal. Her wisdom is evident in both her logic and her rhetorical strategy. The first thing she said to David was, "Pardon your servant, my lord" (v. 24). This is more than a courteous cliché for drawing attention to the speaker. The Hebrew original, *bi-ani adoni heavon,* may be rendered as, "In me, myself, O my lord, lies the guilt." In other words, she claimed that she was to blame. This may not have appeased David, but it must have piqued his interest. Abigail's most crucial challenge at this point was to get David to stop and listen. Her next words were also intended to hold David's attention: "Let me speak to you; hear what your servant has to say" (v. 24). The doubling underscores her desperation for David's attention.

Then she moved to the bones of the matter. First, she healed David's wounded pride by literally cursing her husband. She knew that this was ultimately a libel case, and so what needed to be treated was David's disgraced name. She cured David's hurt pride by disgracing her husband's name: "He is just like his name – his name means Fool, and folly goes with him" (v. 25). She even assumed that Nabal would soon die: "May your enemies and all who are intent on harming my lord be like Nabal" (v. 26). Then she broached the subject of provisions, speaking of them as not for David, but for his men. By so doing, she saved David's face, for he had asked for provisions.

In the first part of her speech, Abigail treated David's wounded pride by sullying Nabal's name; in the second part, she boosted David's pride by assuring him of his glorious future.[9] In this way, she sounded almost prophetic: "The LORD your God will certainly establish a lasting dynasty for my LORD" (v. 28). She went on to invoke the Lord's protection on David's life: "Even

---

8. In the Old Testament, wisdom generally refers to some knowledge that helps us to prosper in this world. It could refer to very practical skills: for instance, a wise sailor would know how to navigate the waters to a certain destination. As Abigail's speech conveys, a "wise woman" refers to a women who reveals wisdom in her speech.

9. The second part starts like the first, with Abigail's admission of guilt. The NIV, "Please forgive your servant's presumption," is as good as it gets in context, but it loses the nuance of guilt.

though someone is pursuing you to take your life, the life of my lord will be bound securely in the bundle of the living by the LORD your God" (v. 29). In her conclusion, she returned to the main theme of her speech, which was that David should not spill needless blood lest anyone accuse him of murder (v. 28), or lest it be a burden on his conscience (vv. 30–31). David was not only appeased by Abigail's words but also pleased with Abigail herself. After thanking God for sending Abigail into his path, he blessed Abigail and attributed to her the merit of stopping him from bloodshed, the very merit previously attributed to the Lord (see vv. 26, 34). Later, in answering Abigail's request to "remember your servant" (v. 31), David took her as his wife. But since marriage in ancient Israel was akin to a business transaction, more was involved in David's marriage proposal than romance.

25:36–44 NABAL DIES AND DAVID TAKES ABIGAIL AS WIFE

Abigail returned home to find her husband very drunk at the banquet, and so she did not tell him about what she had done for the household (v. 36). The next morning, when she told him, his heart failed him, and he became like a stone. Ten days later, he died. The abruptness of Nabal's death is underscored by the narrator's clever use of the word "heart." In verse 36, Nabal's "heart" was good (*lev*: "He was in high spirits," NIV), but then in verse 37, his "heart" "died" (*wayamot*: "failed," NIV). The failure of Nabal's heart cannot refer to the stopping of his heart, because he did not die until ten days later. In ancient Near Eastern cultures, the heart was related to the thinking faculty – or, in modern physiology, it was equivalent to the brain. Thus a "dead heart" might have referred to brain death, possibly as the result of a stroke from shock.

Be that as it may, the narrator attributes Nabal's death ultimately to divine punishment: "The LORD struck Nabal and he died" (v. 38). This raises a question about the sin that Nabal committed, which was deserving of premature death. Although David boasted of the Lord avenging Nabal for insulting him, the narrator provides a few hints that point to a different explanation. First, Abigail returned from her expedition and found her husband very drunk, which alludes to the golden calf event in Exodus 32, wherein Moses came back from his encounter with the Lord to find his people worshipping the golden calf in orgies. Second, the banquet celebrating sheep shearing was supposed to be for the whole community, but the narrator intimates that Nabal held the "royal" banquet for himself by placing Hebrew *lo* "for himself" before the word "banquet" (v. 37; the NIV omits it). Although Nabal pretended to care for his workers by rejecting David's request (see v. 11), he was not even generous to his own workers. The sin of idolatry and the sin of using other human beings for one's aggrandizement are one and the same in substance. The king of Israel, unlike pagan kings, should neither encourage idolatrous worship by laying claims to divinity, nor should he use his people as a means to glorify his own kingdom. To the contrary, the king of Israel should serve the Lord's people by obeying the will of the Lord. Many scholars regard Nabal as a caricature of Saul or other failed leaders of Israel.[10] Nabal's death symbolizes the divine verdict of the death sentence for idolatrous and oppressive leadership in Israel.

After Nabal's death, David proposed marriage to Abigail. This may have been his way of "remembering" Abigail, but she did not need to become David's wife to survive, because she would have inherited her husband's business and land. Moreover, Nabal's clan would have made sure that she found a husband within the clan in order to keep Nabal's property within the clan. Further, in ancient Israel, like Asian cultures, marriage was an economic and social transaction between families. Because Nabal had been the de-facto ruler in southern Judah, David was able to claim lordship of that region after he married Nabal's wife. In other words, the marriage was not for Abigail but for David. This raises a question about why Abigail accepted David's marriage proposal if it did not benefit her socio-economically. The answer to this question may be found in the language that Abigail used to accept David's proposal: "I am your servant and am ready to serve you and wash the feet of my lord's servants" (v. 41). She abased herself below David's servants, calling herself *shipha,* "a female slave" ("ready to serve," NIV). Most likely, she feared David so much that she could not turn down his marriage proposal. This may explain why Abigail disappears from the narrative once David became king of Hebron. David simply needed her no more.

David's marriage to Abigail portrays David as a strategic leader. Though he schemed and devised in order to achieve his goal, he could be distinguished from other leaders by his faith in the God of Israel. As a believer in a moral God, David did not violate his moral principles just to reach his goal much more quickly. This is illustrated by his taboo against killing the Lord's anointed. David appeared to be passive in pursuing kingship in much of 1 Samuel; however, the early chapters of 2 Samuel reveal how David did everything in his power to obtain the kingdom of Israel, trusting that this was God's will

---

10. See, for instance, Joseph Lozovyy, *Saul, Doeg, Nabal, and the "Son of Jesse": Readings in 1 Samuel 16–25* (London: T & T Clark, 2009), 67; Jon D. Levenson, "1 Samuel as Literature and as History," *JBL* 40 (1978): 11–28.

for him and for Israel. David's encounter with Abigail also reveals that true obedience to God's will involves discerning the will of God and then doing one's best to live that out.

1 SAMUEL 27:1–28:2

DAVID AMONG THE PHILISTINES

David's fortunes in the desert began to turn after two friendly encounters with Saul and his confrontation with Nabal, the foolish ruler. The encounters with Saul ended with Saul's prophetic blessing on and expression of goodwill towards David. The confrontation with Nabal led to David marrying Abigail in order to seal his lordship over the southern portion of Judah. In light of this turn of fortunes, it comes as a surprise that David decided to defect to the Philistines a second time. This question becomes more acute when we remember that defecting to Philistia would have been interpreted by the Israelites as abandoning the Lord. So why did David defect to the Philistines? Apparently, David feared Saul more than he feared God when he decided to defect to Philistia.

Yet his decision to defect to Philistia put him in a dilemma. On the one hand, he needed to earn the trust of Achish and his servants. To do so, he would have to render his service to the Philistines, the inveterate enemies of Israel. On the other hand, he had to avoid harming his own people in Judah. In dealing with this intractable problem, he was forced to compromise his moral integrity. First, he had to lie and then he murdered to prevent his lie from being exposed. Of course, this was not David's first time to lie or murder, nor would it be his last, but God could not keep him in such a situation for long.

One positive thing that came out of this dark period in David's life was the conditioning of his troops. Prior to this, they had been a ragtag gang of outlaws, but regular raids into desert towns transformed David's six hundred men into an organized group of elite combatants. These men rendered great service to David's kingdom, and many had their names go down in biblical history. We learn through this that God is indeed capable of making good out of our shortcomings for the advancement of his kingdom.

27:1–6 DAVID DEFECTS TO ACHISH AGAIN

In verse 1, the narrator reveals David's innermost thought when he decided to flee to the Philistine territory. David feared Saul:

> One of these days I will be destroyed by the hand of Saul. The best thing I can do is to escape to the land of the Philistines.

> Then Saul will give up searching for me anywhere in Israel, and
> I will slip out of his hand. (v. 1)

This comes as a surprise, because in David's two recent encounters with the reigning king, Saul not only prophesied David's victory but also extended a hand of reconciliation (see 26:21, 25). Further, David must have been aware that sojourning in a foreign country would entail serving foreign gods. If he did not want to give up his ambition for the throne, he must not sojourn in the Philistine land, as doing so would disqualify him from the throne in the eyes of the people. For this reason, Saul "no longer searched for him" when he heard that David had fled to Gath (v. 4). This was not simply because Philistia was outside of Saul's jurisdiction, for in those days, invasion could occur to retrieve a runaway criminal. But Saul did not invade Philistia because when David defected to the Philistines, he no longer posed any political threat. Thus David's decision to defect to Philistia cannot be explained solely by his fear of Saul. Two more factors contributed to David's defection.

The first factor was David's persecution by the people, which David himself complained of: "May they [the people] be cursed before the LORD! They have driven me today from my share in the LORD's inheritance and have said, 'Go, service other gods'" (see 26:19). Nabal's insults illustrate this persecution. We can further adduce the Ziphites, who were more than willing to turn David over to Saul. Further, David was betrayed by the people in Keila, whom he had saved from the Philistines. In sum, David was not welcomed and was persecuted by the people who sided with Saul.

The second factor that contributed to David's defection was Samuel's recent death. David may have thought of the prophet as a spiritual "womb" from which he had been born as king. With the physical evidence for his kingship gone, David might have felt he had no other choice but to defect to the Philistines. In a sense, David's decision to defect can be compared to his decision to become Saul's son-in-law. Both decisions put him in a difficult position from which he could not save himself. This episode underscores David's shortcomings. Nevertheless, David is revealed as the king whom God, not the people, chose out of his mysterious sovereignty.

Unlike David's first attempt at defection, this time he was not alone, for he took with him six hundred men along with their families. He also took with him his two wives, Ahinoam and Abigail, and settled in Gath under the care of King Achish, son of Maok.[1] This sizable group may explain why David's request for defection was accepted in Achish's court without any major objection. In ancient time, kings used to welcome foreign defectors, and once they proved loyal, kings hired them for important offices in court. As for David, he was likely judged to be harmless because he was no longer who he had been. He had shifted from being known as the famous Goliath-slayer, Saul's loyal general, and the people's favorite to a notorious leader of a group of outlaws, a fugitive from the Israelite authorities, an unwelcome burden on the people in the Judean desert. Achish would have discerned that David had every reason to defect, which explains how David and his people were able to settle in Gath, one of the five Philistine city centers.

ABIGAIL, DAVID'S "WIFE WHO ATE CHAFF AND GRAIN HUSK"

Although we do not know how and when David married Ahinoam, we do know that David married Abigail after Nabal died as a political maneuver to advance his interest in the area around Hebron. David took Abigail with him to the Philistine lands. This would have been no easy adjustment for her, as she fell from being a lady in her hometown to a defector's wife in a pagan land. In a sense, however, she lived through hard times with David and later helped him be king of Hebron. The Chinese call a wife who shares her husband's hard lot *zaokangzhiqi*, which literally means "a wife who ate chaff and grain husk." For David, Abigail was *zaokangzhiqi*, but sadly Abigail disappeared from David's life after he became king of Hebron. She was only one of his many wives and certainly not a favored one. Her son played no role in David's court. From an Asian perspective, one may say that it was a pity for David to favor another wife over his *zaokangzhiqi*!

But David did not stay at Gath for long. He asked Achish to grant him a city to rule as a vassal. The following words express David's *tatemae*, or "façade," concerning this matter: "Why should your servant live in the royal city with you?" (v. 5). He opined that he did not want to be a burden to the king any longer. It is true that supporting David and his people would have been a drain on the royal treasury. Certainly, Achish accepted David's request for this reason. But David's *honne*, or "true desire," was somewhere else: he

---

1. The full name of Achish is given in v. 1, possibly in order to increase historical verisimilitude. The narrator does not try to cover up David's time in Philistia.

wanted to escape from Achish's watching eyes. In the Old Testament, the expression of eating at the king's table often connotes life in house arrest or city arrest. For instance, Jehoiachin, the exiled king of Judah, is said to have eaten regularly at the Babylonian king's table after being released from prison (see 2 Kgs 25:27–30). Like Jehoiachin in Babylon, David was in city arrest at Gath. In David's case, the period of living in the royal city may have been a probation. After confirming the loyalty of David and his people, Achish granted David the city of Ziklag, intimating that David had successfully passed the probationary period. Yet Achish had nothing to lose in granting Ziklag to David. First, in an ancient feudal system, a vassal received a land or a city in exchange for his service to the king, mostly in the form of military service. A vassal would put his own army at the king's disposal upon request, and so Achish had more troops at his disposal by giving David vassalage. Second, Ziklag was in Philistine territory, but it was close enough to Judah to operate raiding campaigns against Judah, Achish's enemy. By giving the city to a foreign mercenary, Achish did not have to deal with the difficult problem of fighting against Israel himself. Further, this was an additional test of David's loyalty. But as the story unfolds, Achish was betrayed by David, for he did not invade Judah for the Philistine king. Further, Ziklag later became Israel's territory under David's kingship.

27:7–12 DAVID EARNS ACHISH'S TRUST

This section is demarcated by two notes about time. It begins with, "David lived in Philistine a year and four months" (v. 7) and ends with, "And such was his practice as long as he lived in Philistine territory" (v. 11). The period of one year and four months does not include David's stay in Gath,[2] making the time of David's sojourn in Philistine somewhat longer than sixteen months. During those months, David had to maintain, if not increase, Achish's trust while not doing what he was told to do: harm his own people. As Achish admitted, making David "so obnoxious" (v. 12) to his people was part of Achish's purpose for stationing David at that post.

---

2. The Philistine territory refers to the countryside of the Philistines. The Hebrew *sadeh,* "the field" ("territory," NIV), is often distinguished from the Hebrew *ir,* "the city."

To strike a balance between these two horns of dilemma, David lied and murdered. He raided Judah's enemy cities[3] rather than Judean towns,[4] and he lied to Achish, claiming that he had raided Judean towns. To cover up this lie, David murdered all the men and women in the cities he plundered. Let's put aside for a moment the historical question about how David could have kept the matter a secret for such a long time. The narrator is clear that David's strategy worked and that Achish trusted David so much that he appointed him as his bodyguard. The more relevant question is, as Christians, how can we justify what David did to the people in enemy cities, especially the innocent civilians?

Clearly, we should not endorse what David did during his residence in Philistia. His wrong decision to defect to Achish created for him the dilemma of earning the trust of Achish and not harming Judah. In order to solve this problem, he sinned by telling a lie and killing innocent people. He must have told himself that this was the cost he had to pay for defecting to the Philistines. David's sins are not to be condoned by any means, but they do underscore David's shortcomings and reveal him as a sinner just like any other human being. This was not the first time David lied to save himself from a difficult situation, nor would it be the last time. He lied to Ahimelek, the priest at Nob, in order to retrieve Goliath's sword as a gift for King Achish the first time David defected to Philistia. This was also not the first time David killed innocent people, nor would it be the last time. As David admitted, he was partially responsible for the slaughter of the priests of Nob and their families, because he knew that Doeg would tell Saul about his presence there, but he did nothing to prevent it. Later, he killed Uriah to cover up his rape of Uriah's wife.

David's status as a Philistine vassal caused him to fall into this vicious circle of sin, and the only way David could avoid this circle was to return to Judah, where Saul was still in power. Before long, God had to act once again to deliver David out of the land of the Philistines. David's decision to defect to Philistia may be compared to his decision to become Saul's son-in-law. Both decisions

---

3. The Geshurites are not to be confused with a country in northern Galilee, from which David later would get his wife. The Geshurites in question lived in the south closer to Philistine land. According to Josh 13:2, they are unconquered by Joshua along with the Philistines. The Girzites are otherwise unknown. The Septuagint omits it. The Amalekites are nomadic herders wondering around the Negev and in the Sinai Peninsula. These people were Israel's archenemy before the Philistines came along. For more details about the animosity between Israel and Amalek, see ch. 15.

4. Jerahmeel is part of Judah (see 1 Chr 2:9). The Kenites are the neighbors to the Jerahmeelites (see 30:29). For more details, see ch. 15.

were made without inquiring of the Lord. David decided to become Saul's son-in-law because it was right in his eyes. He decided to flee to the Philistines because he feared Saul more than God. Moreover, both decisions led David into serious troubles from which he could not save himself, and so he had to rely on divine intervention, whether directly or through divine agents. This episode is humiliating for both Christians and Jews who look up to David as the paragon of *messiah*. So they either do not talk about it (see Chroniclers), or they rationalize it by saying that defection was only David's stratagem to kill Judah's enemies, while keeping himself safe from Saul's pursuing army. But the better approach is to acknowledge David's shortcomings and praise the Lord for his wisdom and goodness to make out of a sinner a righteous king who sought the heart of the Lord and obeyed his will. The Lord is still doing the same work even now through the gospel of Jesus Christ.

28:1–2 DAVID BECOMES ACHISH'S BODYGUARD

In those days the Philistines and Saul were in constant warfare. Most of the time the Philistines sent raiding bands to Israelite towns near the border to plunder threshing floors (see 23:1). Once in a while military tension broke into an all-out war, with opposing armies facing each other across a battlefield – as in the Valley of Elah (see 17:1–3). Chapter 28 opens with a scene in which the Philistines prepare for an all-out war with Israel: "In those days, the Philistines gathered their forces to fight against Israel" (v. 1). Five Philistine rulers sent their armies to form combined forces against Israel. Achish was one of those who led his army to an assembly place (see 29:1–2).

Achish was depending on the addition of David's battalion to his army, as we see in verse 1, where Achish reminded David of his vassal duty. David and his men were required to participate in a war against Israel as part of Achish's army, an episode that would stretch David's relations with Achish to a breaking point. Although David was able to deceive Achish when he was away from his watching eyes, he could not deceive him while fighting as part of Achish's army. Either he would have to turn his back against Achish in the middle of the battle, or he would have to kill Israelites soldiers – if not King Saul himself. It is as if Achish knew David's dilemma when he said, "*you must understand* that you and your men will accompany me in the army" (v. 1, emphasis mine). Achish used an emphatic form of the Hebrew verb *yadah*, "to know," here. In response, David used another emphatic form of the same Hebrew verb, as if he caught Achish's innuendo, saying, "Then (*laken*) you *will see for yourself* what your servant can do" (v. 2, emphasis mine). David's answer was ambiguous, for it could change its meaning depending on one's perspective. Whatever David may have meant by it, Achish took it as a pledge of fealty and appointed him literally as the "keeper of his head" (v. 2: "body-guard," NIV). Interestingly, Achish used the same Hebrew adverb that David used: "Very well (*laken*), I will make you my bodyguard for life" (v. 2). "Very well" here and "Then" in David's preceding remark are different translations of this same Hebrew word, *laken*. It is as if both Achish and David spoke to each other with mysterious winks.[5] Whatever David and Achish were scheming in their hearts, in this episode David reached a critical point in his career as a Philistine vassal. Obviously, David could not remain in a vicious circle of sin forever, and so he could not continue in his role as a Philistine vassal.

---

5. One may assume that David had a plan when he said "yes" to Achish's order to march with him. In other words, just as David successfully deceived Achish about his raiding activity, he must have been planning to turn his back against Achish in the middle of battle in order to fight against the Philistines or possibly defect to Saul's army. But even if David hatched such a plan, there was no guarantee for success. There is also the possibility that Achish had a plan B for just such a case. For example, he may have ordered some of his soldiers to watch and kill David if he moved suspiciously.

1 SAMUEL 28:3–25

SAUL AND THE WITCH OF ENDOR

This episode concerns the last meeting between King Saul and the prophet Samuel. This meeting appears to have been arranged by a female medium, who conjured up the spirit of Samuel from the underground. Many Christians, who believe that the dead cannot interact with the living, feel uncomfortable about this story's apparent assumption that the dead Samuel came back to speak to living Saul, let alone the fact that he was invoked by a medium. This story is even more troubling for Asian Christians because their faith has often been promulgated in a polemic against ancestor worship or traditional practices of divination.[1] The moment one becomes a Christian, he or she stops offering an annual sacrifice to his or her ancestors and visiting a spiritual medium. But a closer examination of the text reveals that the narrator crafts into the story many elements that denounce pagan divination and authenticate biblical prophecy.[2]

Some elements in this episode recall Saul's first meeting with Samuel. Just as Saul visited the seer Samuel to divine the whereabouts of his father's donkey, which led to Saul's anointing as king, Saul visits an anonymous female medium at Endor in order to divine through the spirit of Samuel, which leads to his ultimate abdication from kingship: his death. In both meetings, Saul's servants lead the way to the seers. By describing Saul's last meeting with Samuel in terms that recall their first meeting, the narrator gives a sense of completeness to the story of Saul's tragic career as the king of Israel and also highlights the essential reason for his eventual rejection as king of Israel: his failure to "listen to" the words of the Lord as spoken through the prophet Samuel.

---

1. The practice of divination dates back to the eighteenth century BC in China. "No expedition was undertaken, no city or capital was built, no marriage was contracted, and indeed no decision was made without first consulting the spirits through divination by the use of tortoise shells." Win-Tisit Chan, "The Concept of Man in Chinese Thought," in *The Concept of Man: A Study in Comparative Philosophy*, ed. Radhakrishnan and Raju (New Delhi: Indus, 1995), 161.
2. For further details, see Koowon Kim, "Why Is the Woman of Endor Portrayed as a Heroine?" *Expository Times* 129 (2018): 399–407.

28:3–4 BACKGROUND

Three facts are presented as a backdrop for the subsequent story: Samuel's death (v. 3a), Saul's expulsion of mediums and spiritists from the country (v. 3b),[3] and the imminent war with the Philistines (v. 4). The first two facts happened before the current military confrontation with the Philistines. The information that Saul expelled mediums and spiritists is new to the reader, but we were told about Samuel's death and burial in 25:1. The redundant note about Samuel's death and burial is not only necessary to the plot of the subsequent story, but it also helps to frame Saul's motivation for expelling unlawful mediums of revelation. Apparently, Samuel's death awakened Saul's soul from spiritual stupor and urged him to clear the land of "the detestable practices" of the nation (see Deut 18:9–13), similar to Judah's reformers, Hezekiah and Josiah. But ironically Saul's reformation efforts put him in a dilemma, because God did not reciprocate Saul's pious gesture, but rather shut him out completely.

Meanwhile, the Philistines and the Israelites gathered their forces at Shunem and at Gilboa respectively. Shunem and Gilboa are both found in the Jezreel Valley – one to the north of the valley (modern Solem) and the other to the south. Unlike the last major war in the Valley of Elah (see 1 Sam 17), this time the Philistines chose the northern route through Aphek to invade Israel instead of their more favored route through Gath in the south. It had been a long time since the Philistines had taken this northern route to invade Israel, when they had achieved a great victory, killing Eli and his two sons and taking the ark of the Lord as a war trophy. The memory of this victory serves as an ominous sign for Saul's fate in the imminent war with the Philistines. Besides, Saul's army was not in good shape in terms of logistics. Saul had wasted too much energy and military provisions pursuing David in the wilderness. Ever since David's defection to Achish, Saul's already weakened army had lost much of his ground, especially in the Judean desert, against the Philistines. Achish's installation of David as a vassal in the desert city of Ziklag may have been part of his general program to control the Judean desert. This may explain why the Philistines took the northern route in this last war with Saul's army. Now Saul had to fight with the combined forces of five Philistine kings at the final line of defense in the Jezreel Valley. There was no turning back. If the Philistines

---

3. "Spiritists" always occurs in parallel with "mediums" in the OT. It appears that they are more or less synonymous in meaning. They refer to those who engage divination through the spirits of the dead. They conjure up the spirits out of the underground or their tomb to obtain secret knowledge from them.

broke through the Jezreel Valley, they could march straight to Saul's city of Gibeah without a major fight.[4]

28:5–7 SAUL'S PREDICAMENT

Saul was in great trouble: "He was afraid; terror filled his heart" (v. 5). The coupling of these two synonymous words ("afraid" and "terror") underscores the magnitude of Saul's psychological unbalance. Of course, the overwhelming power of the Philistine army filled Saul with terror. They were not only great in number but also armed with iron chariots. So, as any ancient king would do before a major war, Saul consulted his God, the Lord, by every means available to him. But the Lord did not answer him by dreams or Urim or prophets (v. 6). Dreams, Urim, and prophets were three legitimate means of obtaining divine revelation in Israel. Urim was one of the two magic stones – the other was called "Thummim" – that priests used for the purpose of soliciting the Lord's revelation. Since the priests usually served the king, the commoners inquired of the Lord through prophets when they were in trouble. The practice of obtaining revelation through dreams refers to a solicited dream. People who needed divine assistance spent the night in the sanctuary, hoping that a god would speak to them through dreams. This religious practice, called "Incubation," was very popular among ancient Greeks. The Old Testament includes only a few hints of dream divination. The most celebrated example is Jacob's dream at Bethel. Jacob, on his way to exile in Haran, arrived exhausted and full of angst at Bethel, a holy place. During the night there, he had a revelatory dream that gave him new strength and hope.[5] Saul inquired of the Lord using all three of these means of divination, but the Lord did not answer him. Dreams, Urim, and prophets were merely God's gracious measures for the Israelites. If they were living in right relationship with the Lord, the Lord would be gracious to speak through those means, but the Lord had no obligation to respond.

Out of desperation, Saul resorted to a detestable practice in the Lord's sight by ordering his attendants to make arrangements for a "psychic session"

---

4. Many scholars point out that this episode with the witch of Endor has been relocated from before ch. 31, which seems true in terms of time and place. At the beginning of this episode, we are told that the Philistine army was camped at Shunem in the Jezreel Valley. But we see in the following chapter that the Philistines still were in Aphek in the plain of Sharon and had not yet arrived at Shunem. As for time, according to Samuel's prophecy about Saul's death, the meeting of Saul and Samuel must have happened on the eve of the Gilboa battle, where Saul died.

5. For more details on the practice of incubation, see Koowon Kim, *Incubation as a Type-Scene in the 'Aqhatu, Kirta and Hannah Stories* (Leiden: Brill, 2011), 27–60.

with a female medium, an act he had previously criminalized. Even though Saul had expelled all mediums and spiritists, his attendants apparently had no problem finding one when they were ordered to do so. Further, they found one in a town called Endor not far from Saul's quarters. This intimates that there were many mediums and spirits illegally operating in Israel under the cover of night. The royal ban drove them into the shadows, not out of the country. Despite Saul's legislation against the pagan practice, the land was still in spiritual darkness. This teaches us that what counts in God's kingdom is the change of individual hearts, not laws. The land becomes pure only when people are renewed in their hearts through God's grace.

Noteworthy in this regard is that Saul asked specifically for a female. From a literary point of view, the image of the male authority figure of Saul consulting an anonymous female medium provides a foil for Hannah, an obscure figure of that time, who went to the temple and met with the male authority figure of Eli. This provides another link between Eli and Saul, both of whom were alienated from divine revelation in their own ways. In Korea, women have dominated in shamanistic professions. A priestess called *Mudang* goes into a trance in order to propitiate spirits of the dead, tell fortunes, or repulse evil. Belief in the power of *Mudang* is so deeply rooted among Koreans that even Christians visit *Mudang* when they are plagued by a series of unusual misfortunes or have a difficult decision to make. This sounds similar to what Saul was trying to do on the eve of his fateful battle with the Philistines. For sure, Saul was desperate that night, but it did not make his act less detestable in the eyes of the Lord. The author of Chronicles specifies Saul's consultation of a medium as an act of rebellion *par excellence* against the Lord's words which cost him his dynasty: "Saul died because . . . he did not keep the word of the LORD and even consulted a medium for guidance" (1 Chr 10:13).

28:8–14 SAUL ASKS THE MEDIUM TO BRING UP SAMUEL

The exact location of Endor is still debated, but a favored suggestion is Khirbet Safsafet, nearly seven kilometers north of Shunem, where the Philistine army pitched their war camp.[6] If this were the case, Saul had to go through the enemy ranks to get there, risking his own life. This would partly explain why Saul disguised himself and travelled there "at night" (v. 8). But more importantly, he did so because he was the king who had criminalized the practice of spiritual

---

6. See "En-Dor," *Anchor Bible Dictionary*.

mediums in Israel. It would have been both humiliating and very detrimental to his authority as leader if people discovered that he had practiced the very act he himself had criminalized. Further, he may have reasoned that if the female medium at Endor knew who he was, she would not render him her service.

The royal ban on the practice certainly made the female medium extra cautious in doing business. When asked to conjure up a spirit, she responded emphatically: "Surely you know what Saul has done. He has *cut off* the mediums and spirits from the land" (v. 9, italics mine). While reminding Saul of the recent ban on the divinatory practice, she changed the word "expelled (*hesir*)," which the narrator used to describe Saul's ban in verse 3, to a stronger and more emotional word, "cut off (*hikrit*)." This subtle change in her wording reveals how personally she took the recent ban. It amounts to her saying that she was putting her life in danger by conjuring up a spirit for Saul. Rather than suggesting that she was not doing business at that time, she was probably just testing the waters about her new customer. So Saul tried to calm her down by saying that he would not reveal the matter to the authorities. Ironically, he even swore by the name of the Lord. One rabbi famously lampooned Saul by comparing him to the woman who swore to her lover in bed by the name of her husband. Either Saul did not understand what it meant to be loyal to the Lord, or he was hypocritical in that his verbal profession did not match his deeds.

After assuring the female medium of her safety, Saul requested that she "bring up Samuel" (v. 11). In verse 12, the narrator omits the details about her conjuring up a spirit and gives us only the outcome. This omission is a literary device that minimizes the medium's control over Samuel. One may even argue that Samuel appeared on his own initiative, which is intimated by the fact that the medium was shocked to see a spirit coming from the underworld. The first thing she said in her consternation was, "Why have you deceived me? You are Saul!" (v. 12). It is not clear how the woman recognized Saul. There is no scholarly consensus on this question, either. But Saul could not see what the female medium saw, and so he set her at ease and then asked her what she saw (v. 13). The woman replied: "I see a ghostly figure[7] coming out of the earth" (v. 14). The expression "coming out of the earth" is a figure of speech and may not be used as evidence for any metaphysical claim about

---

7. Hebrew *elohim*. Scholars have spilled much ink in explaining its meaning here (see Tsumura, *The First Book of Samuel*, 624–625, for various interpretations). Since it cannot mean "God" in our passage, it is usually taken as a divine being, namely, an incorporeal spirit. But the problem is the plural form of its predicate, '*olim*, "coming out." Does this suggest that more than one spirit came up when she invoked Samuel from the underworld?

the state of a person after death. The ancient Israelites shared a belief with many other ancient peoples that the dead went down into the underworld. Such ancient ideas should not be normative for our concept of the world. Be that as it may, to make sure that the ghostly figure was really Samuel, Saul asked her again about his appearance. Then she characterized him as "an old man wearing a robe" (v. 14). Upon hearing this, Saul fell down to the ground to pay his respect to Samuel.

Interestingly, Saul recognized Samuel by his robe. The Hebrew *meil* ("robe") refers to an ornamental outer coat that only figures of authority used to wear. Samuel's robe symbolized him just as the staff symbolized Moses – or, to use a Chinese illustration, just as Red Hare symbolized Lü Bu.[8] In other words, Samuel's robe was the characteristic object by which people identified him. We remember how Hannah made "a little robe" for her son when he was under Eli's tutelage in Shiloh. Also, when Saul tore the hem from Samuel's robe, Samuel declared God's rejection of Saul as king: "The Lord has torn the kingdom of Israel from you today and has given it to one of your neighbors – to one better than you" (15:28). No wonder Saul immediately recognized Samuel by his robe. Ironically, Saul's formal recognition of Samuel was based on a symbol that recalled Samuel's proclamation that Saul was being rejected by God as king.

Many Christians feel uncomfortable with the idea that a pagan medium could control the spirit of one of the greatest prophets in biblical history. Apart from the question how Samuel could be manipulated by a medium, we wonder if it is ever possible for the dead to speak with the living. Historically, Asians have worshipped ancestors, and because an ancestor cult assumes that the dead continue to interact with the living, Asian pastors have emphasized that the dead can never come back to bless or curse the living. Thus Saul's encounter with the spirit of Samuel poses a conundrum to Asian Christians. However, one must understand that the Bible was written to a people who were living at a particular point in history, and so the Bible had to accommodate their worldview and culture. In the pre-scientific and ancient Near Eastern culture, invoking the dead was not uncommon, especially in the context of ancestor worship or of divination. Some of these cultural ideas made their way into the language and idiom, and so the idea that a medium could invoke the spirit of the dead may not have been as foreign to ancient readers as it is to us. But

8. Lü Bu was a legendary warrior in the period of *Three Kingdoms* and Red Hare was his horse, known to run 750 kilometers per day.

just because the Bible talks about divination does not mean that it should be "normative" for our thinking about the world. Rather than getting bogged down with the details in this episode, it is better to move onto the big picture that the author is drawing for us. As mentioned briefly above, the narrator conveys that Samuel was not controlled by the female medium, because he deliberately omits the process she went through in order to invoke Samuel's spirit, such as sacrifice, incantation, special gesture, and so on. The text reads as if Samuel appeared without being summoned, which may account for the medium's panic when she first sees Samuel. Further, the female medium did not have a role in the dialogue between Samuel and Saul. The narrator describes the conversation between the two males and then notes that the female medium entered the room (v. 21). These facts point to the possibility that she was not present during the séance. In sum, although the narrator accommodates the ancient idea that the dead may come back to speak with the living, the overall impression is that the witch was not in control of Samuel's spirit.

28:15–20 SAMUEL PROPHECIES AGAINST SAUL

Samuel sounded irritated, as if he had been awoken from deep sleep when he said, "Why have you disturbed me by bringing me up?" (v. 15). The Hebrew *ragash,* "to disturb," is a technical term often used in tomb inscriptions, especially as a warning to potential robbers.[9] It is as if Samuel was treating Saul as a tomb robber. Saul, in turn, explained to the irritated Samuel why he had to wake him up: "I am in great distress . . . The Philistines are fighting against me, and God has departed from me. He no longer answers me, either by prophets or by dreams" (v. 15).[10] The reader already knows most of Saul's defense because of the narrator's introduction in verses 3–4. But Saul's confession that God abandoned him is new. As Saul implies, God's silence was a direct outcome of God's rejection of Saul. Nevertheless, Saul called up the spirit of Samuel, the Lord's prophet. Samuel recognized this irony and said: "Why do you consult me, now that the LORD has departed from you and become your enemy?" (v. 16). The irony becomes more acute if Saul's purpose was not limited to acquiring knowledge of the future – namely, the fated outcome of

---

9. See Nerab Stela II, line 8.
10. Here "by Urim" is missing, maybe because Urim was not available to Saul any longer. He killed all the Elide priests at Nob. But see 28:5. Non-Elide priests may have helped Saul. The order of prophets and dreams are reversed maybe because Saul was speaking to the prophet Samuel.

tomorrow's battle with the Philistines – but expanded to seeking divine favor in the battle. Saul revealed his ultimate purpose in consulting Samuel: "I have called on you to tell me *what to do*" (v. 15, italic mine). Saul's purpose in consulting Samuel's spirit was to try to change his fate for the better, but Samuel's spirit could only inform Saul of his unchangeable fate.

In his speech, Samuel reminded Saul of the prophecy that he had already declared when the hem of his robe had been torn off by Saul (see 15:28). But here he identified "the neighbor": "The LORD has torn the kingdom out of your hands and given it to one of your neighbors – to David" (v. 17). Further, he mentioned Saul's failure to destroy the Amalekites as the reason for the Lord's rejection of Saul.

> Because you did not obey the LORD or carry out his fierce wrath against the Amalekites, the LORD has done this to you today. (v. 18)

Why did Samuel single out Saul's failure to carry out *herem* against the Amalekites as the definitive event that banned him from being the king of Israel? Why did the war against the Amalekites serve as a definitive test for Saul's obedience? We may be misled to think that God was unfair to Saul. Obeying the Lord is not the same as catering to God's unpredictable whims. The reason that obedience to God is exemplified in the act of killing every Amalekite has something to do with the symbolic meaning that is attached to the Amalekites in the Old Testament. It is well known that the Amalekites inflicted unspeakable pain on the Israelites when they wandered through the wilderness. They snuck up on Israel from behind and attacked the weariest and the weakest members who could not protect themselves, such as women, infants, the sick, the disabled. The Lord promised to Moses two things about the Amalekites: first, he would blot out the name of the Amalekites *from under heaven*. Second, he would be at war with them *eternally* (see Exod 17:14–16, emphasis mine). The eternal and ubiquitous animosity against the Amalekites surpassed the animosity against the Canaanites or the Philistines, which had a limitation in time and space. The Lord's eternal command to destroy the Amalekites teaches us that the crime against human nature is everywhere and never goes away, and so the fight against it must be eternal. For the king of Israel to obey the Lord, he must protect human dignity and treat his people as the object, not a means, for his own ambition.[11] Utterly destroying the

---

11. For more details about Amalek, see Yoram Hazony, *God and Politics in Esther* (New York, NY: Cambridge University Press, 2016), 62–69.

Amalekites symbolized the king's commitment to loving and serving God's people, especially those who had no protector except God. This contradicts and overturns the pagan ideology of kingship, where a king is a god, using his people as a means to his self-aggrandizement. Saul was rejected because he did not understand what it meant to be king of Israel and repeatedly refused to accept the role God had written anew for the monarchy of Israel.

Samuel concluded his speech with a new prophecy. Here Samuel finally tells Saul what he initially wanted to hear: the result of tomorrow's battle. But the news is disastrous, for Samuel predicted that Saul and his sons would be killed, and his army vanquished by the Philistines. Upon hearing the disastrous news, "Saul fell full length on the ground" (v. 20). Saul's prostration at the beginning of the séance was prompted by respect, but here it was caused by his mental and physical exhaustion. First, Samuel's words exacerbated Saul's fear instead of reducing it. Further, Saul had fasted for the past twenty-four hours because of his stress, just as Hannah could not eat anything due to her stress. No wonder Saul had no strength. His efforts to enlist Samuel's help had failed, and he found himself in greater distress at the end of his meeting with Samuel than he had been at the beginning.

28:21–25 THE MEDIUM RESTORES SAUL TO STRENGTH

This final segment of the episode underscores the heroism of the female medium. She had compassion on Saul and took the initiative to restore him to strength. Saul had been fasting because of his distress, but he still found no reason to break it after his meeting with Samuel, and so he ended up in greater distress and became like the dead. She came to the rescue at that moment. First, addressing herself humbly as "your servant," she boldly tried to persuade Saul to eat: "Look, your servant has *obeyed* you. I took my life in my hands and *obeyed* ("did,") what you told me to do. Now please *obey* ("listen to," NIV) your servant and let me give you some food so you may eat and have the strength to go on your way" (vv. 21–22). The repetition of the verb "to obey" is intentional on the part of the narrator to remind the reader of Saul's problem: Saul never learned to obey.[12] After his two servants joined the woman in urging him to eat, he sat up on the couch. She hurried to slaughter her own calf and baked *massot*, "bread without yeast," so that Saul might not wait too long. The quick succession of six verbs used to describe her meal preparation in verses 24–25

---

12. "To listen" was assumed after "He refused" in v. 23. For the expression of "refuse to listen" see Jer 10:11; 13:10; Neh 9:17.

show how much effort she put into restoring Saul to life, however temporary it might be. There is no sign that she did it for compensation. Although Saul regained his strength due to her selfless efforts, his heart was still heavy, and his future was still dark. This is expressed symbolically by the narrator's note that night had fallen by the time he walked out of her house.

Her care for Saul was noble and even heroic. The narrator portrayed her as a hostess that provided a secret meeting room for the two most important men in Israel at the time rather than focusing on her role as a spiritual medium. She was not present in the room where Saul conversed with Samuel, and Samuel's appearance seems to have surprised her. By minimizing her role as a spiritual medium, the narrator authenticates Samuel's message.

1 SAMUEL 29:1–11

ACHISH SENDS DAVID BACK TO ZIKLAG

Chapter 29 consists of narration and two cycles of dialogue. The narration bookends the chapter, providing a general outline of the episode, while the dialogue forms the main body, detailing how David was dismissed from his duty as Achish's bodyguard in his war against Israel. The narrator uses dialogue to slow down the narration and build up suspense, thereby emphasizing the theological significance of David's premature discharge from Achish's service. According to the narration, David made it to Aphek as part of Achish's army, but the dialogue makes it clear that he was then dismissed from his duty and returned to Ziklag, while the Philistine combined forces continued north to Jezreel to meet Saul's army.

David's dilemma was the inevitable outcome of his double life as a Philistine vassal, which had trapped him in a cycle of lying and killing innocent people. By compromising his moral principles, David earned Achish's trust, which led Achish to appoint him as "keeper of his head" (see 28:2: "bodyguard," NIV) in the battle against Israel. Of course, David could not refuse Achish's appointment, as it was required by his vassal agreement. His scheme had thrown him into a dilemma: either he had to kill his own people, including King Saul, God's anointed, or he had to rebel against his Philistine lord. If David killed his own people, he would have had to give up his ambition for the throne. But if David rebelled against his Philistine lord, he would lose Achish's protection from Saul, who was still in power. Only God could deliver David from this impasse. At that moment, the opposition from the Philistine rulers forced Achish to relieve David from his duty. This miracle released David from his old life of playing double in the Philistine land and opened a way for him to return to Judah. From this point on, David would never return to serve Achish.

29:1–2, 11 DAVID DISMISSED FROM HIS
DUTY AS ACHISH'S BODYGUARD

This scene at Aphek continues the episode that begins in 28:1–2, where Achish appointed David and his men as his bodyguards and left with them for Aphek to join other Philistine forces. In between, the narrator inserts Saul's nocturnal visit to Endor in 28:3–25 and then repeats what he said at the beginning of the episode: "The Philistines gathered all their forces at Aphek" (v. 1a; 28:1). Five Philistine city centers sent their armies to Aphek (modern-day Ras el-Ain) in the Sharon plain – a marshalling area – to march north together against Israel, whose army was camped near the spring in the city of Jezreel (v. 1b).[1] Verse 2 describes David and his men marching as part of Achish's army. The entirety of chapter 29 is devoted to showing through dialogue what happened to David as he tried to go with the other Philistine forces to battle.

29:3–5 DIALOGUE BETWEEN PHILISTINE COMMANDERS AND ACHISH

Although the narrator appears to differentiate the commanders (*sarim*) of the Philistines from the rulers (*seranim*) of the Philistines city centers, these two groups both had serious reservations about taking David's battalion into the battle (see vv. 3, 6). When they see David and his men marching along with Achish, they asked incredulously, "What about these Hebrews?" (v. 3). Their reference to David's men as "Hebrews" suggests contempt, because the term in those days had a derogatory connotation, parallel with "outlaws" or "fugitives."[2] Some scholars trace its origin to a group of social misfits and outlaws called *habiru* who were, according to the Amarna Letters, responsible for causing commotion in some Canaanite city states during the fourteenth and thirteenth centuries BC.[3]

Achish, however, came to David's defense. First, he introduced David as a former servant of Saul, king of Israel, who had repented and become his bodyguard (v. 3). We can sense a feeling of pride in Achish's words, "Is this not David?" (v. 3). Every king would have desired to have a loyal and brave fighter at his side – even if he had to steal one from his enemy king. Even Saul had the reputation of being an aggressive recruiter: "whenever Saul saw a mighty or brave man, he took him into his service" (14:52). Cao Cao, the founder of the Wei kingdom, was so infatuated with Guan Yu, the warrior of his rival Liu Bei, that he did not kill him when he captured him in battle, and he even presented Guan Yu with Red Hare, a legendary horse which had originally belonged to his own warrior, Lü Bu, to win him over. Cao Cao was

---

1. The city of Jezreel is identified as modern-day Zerin at the western foot of Mount Gilboa. The spring is found northeast of the city. *Anchor*, "Jezreel."
2. "Hebrew" is almost exclusively used by foreigners, either the Egyptians or the Philistines, to refer to the Israelites (see 4:9; 13:19; 14:11).
3. Provan, Philips, Longman, *A Biblical History of Israel*, 170–172.

very proud to have Guan Yu at his side when the latter decided to serve him. Achish may have felt similarly about David after he proved himself loyal to his new lord (see 27:12). It did not matter to Achish that David had been Saul's servant, and so he assured the other Philistine commanders that he had found nothing suspicious about David "for over a year" while he had been in Achish's service (v. 3).[4] The Hebrew *ze yamim 'o-ze shanim* ("for over a year") may be rendered literally as "days and years." Although its exact meaning is not certain, according to some scholars, "days and years" refers to a longer period than the NIV translation, "for over a year," seems to suggest.[5] From this, one may argue that Achish exaggerated David's time with him in order to convince suspicious colleagues of David's loyalty.

But rather than convincing the Philistine commanders, Achish's words caused them to become angry. They reasoned that Achish's blind trust in David would place all of them in danger in the battle against the Israelites, and so they ordered Achish to send David back to his outpost in Ziklag: "Send the man back (*shub*), that he may return (*shub*) to the place you assigned him" (v. 4a). Although the narrator does not use the word "order" to describe the Philistine commanders' demand, the force of their demand was certainly an order. Notice the imperative use of the repeated verb *shub*, which suggests that they twisted Achish's arm to send David back. Their worry was that David would turn against them during the fighting (v. 4b).[6] Further, they argued: "How better could he regain his master's favor than by taking the heads of our own men?" (v. 4). The phrase, "the heads of our own men," recalls Achish's appointment of David as the "keeper of his head" (see 28:2: "bodyguard," NIV). Thus the Philistine commanders lampooned Achish for trusting David and then further denigrated him by referring to him as *ze*, "this one" (v. 4: "he," NIV). As Koreans say, no one betrays only once. In the eyes of the Philistine commanders, David was a traitor who had betrayed one lord, and so it was only a matter of time before he would betray another. The Philistine commanders concluded their speech with the same phrase that Achish used at the beginning of his defense of David: "Is this not David?" (vv. 3, 5). But here David is not described as a loyal servant, but is remembered by the song of praise for killing tens of

4. The Hebrew *meuma* ("fault," NIV) is a versatile word, meaning "anything or something."
5. The NIV translation is based on the period specified by the narrator as David's residence in the Philistine land: "a year and four months" (27:6).
6. The Hebrew original for "turn against" is translated literally as "to become Satan to." Here Satan means "adversary" (see 1 Kgs 11:4).

thousands of the Philistines. In this way, the commanders criticized Achish for his blind confidence in David, against whom the Philistines had to keep alert.

The argument of the Philistine commanders is based on good logic and common sense, whereas Achish's confidence draws on his personal experience. Although truth may be revealed through personal experience more than general reasoning sometimes, that does not apply here, since David's loyalty to Achish was not genuine. The narrator implies this by letting the Philistine commanders have the final say in the dialogue.

29:6–10 DIALOGUE OF ACHISH AND DAVID

Although Achish did not share the concerns of the Philistine rulers that David would turn coat in the middle of fighting, he could not persuade them to share his faith in David. To please the other commanders, Achish ordered David to go back: "Now turn back and go in peace; do nothing to displease the Philistine rulers" (v. 7). This recalls David's first attempt to defect to Achish. Quoting the song about David's military prowess, Achish's attendants successfully persuaded Achish not to accept David into his service. But Achish's confidence in David's loyalty was not affected by his fellow rulers' doubt. This is revealed in the way he discharged David from duty. First, he praised David for being reliable (v. 6a). He also said he found no "evil" in David (v. 6b: "fault," NIV). Moreover, he swore this by the name of the God of Israel, a gesture of respect for David (v. 6). Second, Achish expressed his reluctance to discharge David in such a dishonoring way, making it clear that he would have preferred to have David serve him in battle. Third, Achish did not tell David why the Philistine rulers disapproved of him. Perhaps he did not want to hurt David's feelings or incite his wrath.

David must have understood what was happening, but he asked why the Philistine rulers disapproved of him and acted as if he were disappointed by their decision: "Why can't I go and fight against the enemies of my lord the king?" (v. 8). Inwardly David must have felt relieved that he would not have to battle against his people, but for Achish he put on a show. Through the Philistine commanders, God saved him at the last moment – just as God had saved him through the Philistine invasion at Sela Hammahlekoth in the Desert of Maon (see 23:27–29). The Lord did not abandon David in Philistia, but miraculously saved him. Rather than sending David back to his double life in Ziklag, the Lord prepared a better way for David out of the Philistine land.

After praising David by comparing him to an angel of God (v. 9), Achish repeated his wary decision: that David "must not go up with us into battle" (v. 9). For the sake of David's feelings, Achish dared not add: "or he will turn against us during the fighting" (v. 4). Instead, Achish suggested that David leave early in the morning – perhaps to save David from humiliation, as it was considered shameful to be discharged from duty in the middle of an operation. The repetition of the phrase "in the morning" (three times in vv. 10–11), which is used to describe David's return, takes on a different meaning when read in a broader context. David's return in the morning can be contrasted with Saul's nighttime return from Endor to the battlefield. If the former foreshadows David's positive future, the latter foreshadows Saul's death. This reading reflects the close relationship between these two events.

When David defected to Achish, he led a double life that could be maintained only by lying and killing innocent people. But this double life could not go on perpetually and would inevitably be revealed. Some people speculate that David wanted to go with the Philistines to battle against Israel so that he could turn coat and render victory for the Israelites. But even if David had been part of Israel's victory over the Philistines, he would have remained a fugitive. So God saved him from the mess he got himself into through the suspicion of the Philistine commanders. Though David was becoming a man after God's heart, he was not perfect. Likewise, God looks at the best in us and uses us for his good purpose, accepting us as we are and working with whatever we have to offer. Thus we need to remain humble even when we are used mightily by the Lord, and we should not be quick to judge our spiritual leaders. This does not suggest that we can somehow "balance" out our moral failures with our contributions to the kingdom of God! As the saying goes, we should be harder on ourselves than others.

1 SAMUEL 30:1–31

COMPASSIONATE DAVID

The Chinese idiom *sai wen shi ma,* "an old man's horse," is used to refer to the irony of fate. This idiom teaches that what appears to be an evil may turn out to be a blessing in disguise. For David, being released from duty in the middle of an operation certainly would have been a setback in the view of other Philistine soldiers. But this "old man's horse" exempted David from any suspicion or accusation of being involved in Saul's death. The lesson of "an old man's horse" may also be applied to the tragedy that befell David and his men in chapter 30. What appeared to be an utter disaster – the kidnapping of David's two wives and the families of his soldiers by the Amalekites – turned out to be the Lord's scheme to grow within David character traits that were essential for the future king of Israel: faith in the Lord and compassion for the people. Even the burning down of the city of Ziklag was a blessing in disguise, for the destruction of David's home city enabled him to return to the land of Judah. The total destruction of Ziklag left David homeless in Philistia, lest he become too comfortable with his life as a Philistine vassal or be tempted to keep playing double between Philistine and Israel.

Chapter 30 consists of two parts. The first part concerns David's pursuit and defeat of the Amalekites, who took advantage of David's absence to raid Ziklag and kidnap all the women, children, and elderly who remained there. In the midst of this despairing situation, David had faith that the Lord would deliver him and his people. Before pursuing the Amalekites, he asked for the counsel of the Lord. In the second part, we find David settling disputes among his soldiers about the distribution of the plunder. This led to the institution of a law that prescribed equal distribution of the plunder among all the people. Further David shared his booty with the elders of Judah, even though they had not welcomed him when he was a fugitive in Judah. These episodes confirm that David's kingdom will be built upon faith in the Lord and compassion for his people.

The narrator devotes a whole chapter to the episode of David's pursuit of the Amalekites, though it digresses from the larger story of the Philistine-Israel war at Mount Gilboa. Similarly, Saul's visit to the female medium at Endor in chapter 28 is a digression from the main storyline, and yet the narrator devotes twenty-one verses to Saul's meeting with the deceased Samuel and only one verse to the Philistine-Israel battle (see 31:1). These two digressions share a common interest in the characters' interaction with the Amalekites. In chapter 28, Samuel's spirit cites Saul's failure to carry out the Lord's wrath against the Amalekites as the reason for his rejection. This digression can be compared with the digressive episode in chapter 30 (in which David succeeds where Saul fails) as a way of contrasting Saul and David regarding their respective dealings with the Amalekites. As discussed previously, the Amalekites symbolized the eternal enemy of Israel, and the narrator's disproportionate treatment of these two digressive episodes teaches that the true king of Israel must diligently fight against and destroy the evil represented in the Amalekites. In chapter 30, the Amalekites attack those who were left in the city without defense and left their Egyptian mercenary in the desert without food or drink when he became ill. In this chapter, we see that David – rather than Saul – carried out the Lord's wrath against abominable evil.

EVERYTHING IN THE WORLD IS LIKE "AN OLD MAN'S HORSE"

This widely recognized idiom in China and Korea teaches that a loss may turn out to be a gain, and it finds its equivalent in the English idiom, "a blessing in disguise." Following is the story in which this idiom originates.

Once upon a time there lived an old man in Sebuk. One day one of his horses ran away to the enemy land. The townsfolk came and tried to comfort him for the loss but he said, "Well, this is not necessarily a bad thing." A few days later his runaway horse came back with a group of enemy horses. Then the folks came to congratulate him, but this time, the old man thought it might be a bad thing. The old man had a son who loved horse riding. One day, his son broke his leg while riding one of those enemy horses. When the folks came again to comfort him, the old man told them again that it might be a good thing. A few days later, when the war broke and all young men had to go to war, his son was exempted from military service because of his broken leg.

30:1–8 ZIKLAG SACKED AND ITS RESIDENTS TAKEN CAPTIVE

David and his men arrived at Ziklag after a three-day journey from Aphek. Although marching speed depended on the terrain covered, the baggage carried, and the weather, the Roman legion was known to have marched thirty kilometers per day. Since it is approximately one hundred kilometers from Aphek to Ziklag, we may infer from the marching pace of the Roman legion that David and his men forced their pace to cover the distance in three days. Part of the reason they hastened their walk was because Ziklag had been left defenseless since David had joined Achish's army. It was always dangerous to leave a city unprotected by mobilizing the entire army for a field expedition, as such cities tended to be easy prey. When David's entire force left the city, he was fully aware of the danger to which the people in the city were exposed, but he took the risk. As it turned out, however, David's worst nightmare became a reality. The Amalekites took advantage of the all-out war between Philistine and Israel and raided the Negev, the southern desert region of Philistine and Judah. Ziklag, which was located in the Negev, could not avoid the disaster. To be more precise, the Amalekites apparently gave special treatment to the home city of David, because from there David had regularly launched his attacks against the Amalekites. So as a means of retaliation, they not only attacked the city but also burned it (v. 1).

Attacking (Hebrew: *nakah*) a city usually connotes killing its inhabitants (see Judg 1:25), and so it is surprising to hear that the Amalekites did not kill the women and children but carried them off as captives (v. 2). Since David killed all the residents when he attacked the Amalekite cities (see 27:9), why did the Amalekites take the Israelites captive instead of killing them on the spot? This is a difficult question to answer definitively. One possibility is that the Amalekites feared David's retaliation, and so they dared not kill the women and children in his city. They may have reasoned that they could use hostages as leverage in negotiating with David.

Verse 3 repeats what is said in verses 1–2 from the perspective of David and his men: "When David and his men reached Ziklag, they found (*hinneh*) it destroyed by fire and their wives and *their* sons and *their* daughters taken captive" (italics original in the Hebrew text, but NIV omits). The Hebrew *hinneh*, literally "behold," is used here to represent the perspective of David and his men. Note also the accounting of those who were kidnapped in groups of family members: with the repetitive use of the personal pronoun "their," the narrator subtly reveals the deep pain that gripped David and his men when they returned to their destroyed city. To illustrate the intensity of their pain, the narrator devotes the whole of verse 4 to describing their emotions: "David and his men wept aloud until they had no strength left to weep." Although David lost two wives, Ahinoam and Abigail (v. 5), he could not act as a victim, because his men arose against him. Their grief turned into burning anger, which they vented at David, because they felt he was responsible for their pain and suffering. David's men conspired to stone David (v. 6), which distressed him, but he never shifted the blame to Achish, who had given the marching order, nor accused his men of rebellion or treason because he "found strength in the LORD his God" (v. 6). The narrator emphasizes David's intimate relationship with the Lord by calling him "his God" (v. 6). David believed that God would comfort and deliver his people, and so he ordered Abiathar, the priest, to bring him the ephod, and he inquired of the Lord:[1] "Shall I pursue this raiding party? Will I overtake them?" (v. 8). David did not simply ask for the Lord's permission, because he wanted God to assure him of his success in the rescue operation. His purpose in inquiring of the Lord was to seek divine help, and the Lord gave him the answer that he wanted to hear: "You will certainly . . . succeed in the rescue" (v. 6). David calmed down the bitter souls of his men with the Lord's promise of success in the rescue operation.

Before David resorted to the ephod, the narrator comments on David's faith in the Lord. David asked in faith for the Lord's salvation, which differentiated him from Saul. When Saul was in great distress, he inquired of the Lord by the same means, but the Lord did not answer him by dreams or Urim or prophets (see 28:5–6). According to an old Jewish tradition, *tsaddik,* "the righteous," have a power to which God is willing to yield,[2] but God does not allow himself to be manipulated by sinful men. David wanted to comfort his people, but he knew he was not capable, and so he turned to God in faith and prayed that the Lord would help him rescue their families from the Amalekites. God looked at David's heart and answered his prayer.

30:9–20 DAVID SAVES HIS PEOPLE FROM THE AMALEKITES

David and his six hundred men launched a search and rescue mission and arrived in the Besor Valley,[3] where two hundred of David's soldiers had set up a camp to manage logistics and support a combatant unit by delivering provisions and weapons. This is intimated by the use of a disjunctive syntax with the Hebrew perfect *'amadu* at the end of verse 9: "the Besor Valley, where the remnants *used to stay behind*" (italic mine).[4] David had divided his sol-

---

1. The narrator introduces Abiathar as the son of Ahimelech in order to remind the reader that he was the only survivor after Saul's massacre of the priests of Nob. Abiathar knew very well what it felt like to lose family and was more qualified than anybody else to help David to deal with angry and grieving people.
2. Abraham Joshua Heschel, *A Passion for Truth,* 268.
3. Its exact location is unknown. Either it refers to Wadi Besor, the greatest river in the northern Negev, or to its tributary.
4. NIV: "where some stayed behind." The Hebrew, *'amadu,* breaks the sequence of imperfect verbs and gives background information. It carries a pluperfect sense.

diers into two group, a logistics unit and a combatant unit, as in his punitive expedition against Nabal (see 25:13). Yet this time, David allowed those who were too exhausted to cross the valley to stay behind. The remaining four hundred followed David to cross the Besor Valley. This decision was based on compassion. His men had marched over one hundred kilometers at a quick pace in three days and had arrived to find their city burned to the ground and their families taken captive. Though they all agreed to go on the search and rescue mission, they were physically and mentally exhausted, and some of his weaker soldiers may have needed rest. So David compassionately decided to allow them to stay behind and entrusted them with weapons and provisions.

Meanwhile, those who crossed the Besor Valley soon found an Egyptian dying in the desert and brought him to David. Seeing that he had not eaten or drunk for three days, David cared for him until he regained his strength. The narrator describes in detail the compassionate care that David gave to the Egyptian: "They gave him water to drink and food to eat – part of a cake of pressed figs and two cakes of raisins" (vv. 11–12). David did not treat the Egyptian as a prisoner, nor did he restore him to life in order to get intelligence out of him. Instead David simply saved a human being from dying of hunger and thirst in the desert. The compassion David showed to this stranger brought David an unexpected bonus, for the stranger was a blessing in disguise.

When "his spirit came back to him" ("he was revived," NIV), the man identified himself as an Egyptian mercenary who had worked for the Amalekites. When he was still working for the Amalekites, he "raided the Negev of the Kerethites, some territory belonging to Judah, and the Negev of Caleb" (v. 14). We may assume that David's heart began to race when he mentioned "the Negev of the Kerethites," which was very close to the Philistine territory. And when the Egyptian confirmed that the Amalekites had burned Ziklag, David felt the invisible hand of the Lord at work in favor of his rescue operation. Further, David's kindness predisposed the Egyptian, who bore a grudge against his stern master, to cooperate. He agreed to help David and his men locate the Amalekites, as long as David would swear by God that he would neither put him to death nor hand him over to his master. This is understandable given his participation in burning Ziklag and kidnapping David's two wives and the families of his men. The intelligence provided by the Egyptian was crucial to David's success, since it saved a significant amount of time and energy in locating the criminals and also gave David a strategic advantage over the Amalekites by leading him to a place where he had a panoramic view of the Amalekites camped in the plain: "He led David down, and there they were (*hinneh*), scattered over the countryside" (v. 16). Note the use of Hebrew *hinneh* to represent David's perspective. Without the Egyptian, David would not have succeeded in his rescue expedition. In his infinite wisdom, the Lord coordinated David's act of compassion with his acquisition of a key informant.

David found the Amalekites "scattered over the countryside" (v. 16). The Hebrew *kol-ha'arets* literally means "all the earth." In other words, the Amalekites were so great in number that they could fill "all the earth," and yet they were "scattered," namely, not in battle formations. Further, they were not expecting an attack, as they were having a party to celebrate "the great amount of plunder they had taken from the land of the Philistines and from Judah" (v. 16). David knew immediately that the Lord had given them over to his hands, and so he ordered a surprise attack at the first light of day. The result was David's complete victory: "David fought them from dawn until the evening of the next day, and none of them got away except four hundred fighters who rode off on camels and fled" (v. 17).[5] Further, David miraculously "recovered everything that the Amalekites had taken" (v. 18) and "brought everything back" (v. 19) – thus no one was killed, no woman was raped, no animal was eaten. The narrator subtly intimates through the double use of the Hebrew verb *natsal*, "(David) recovered," in verse 18[6] that this miraculous salvation was given by the Lord, who used the same word (*natsal*) to assure David of success in his rescue expedition: "You will certainly . . . succeed (*natsal*) in the rescue" (v. 8). The repetitive use of inclusive terms – "all, everything, anything" (*kol*, used five times in vv. 18–20), "from dawn till evening" (v. 18), "young or old," "boy or girl" (v. 19) – may be hyperbolic, but this repetition underscores the faithful fulfillment of the Lord's promise.

This great victory turned the people's hearts around as well. Those who had conspired to kill David because of their extreme grief over the loss of their families now praised him: "This is David's plunder" (v. 20). Since the commander in chief usually had the right of disposal for all the plunder, there was no need for them to make this declaration, and so this statement signifies their change in attitude. But David did not entrust himself to the hands of the people, because he had learned through experience how quickly they could

---

5. The NIV has "from dusk until the evening of the next day," but the Hebrew *neshef* could mean either the beginning of the night or the end of it. I find the former more befitting the context. Also, the Hebrew *na'ar* refers to fighters in a military context. Regarding the Amalekites riding on camels, see Judg 6:5.

6. "David recovered everything the Amalekites had taken and his two wives David recovered" (my translation).

change. Those who had praised David for killing tens of thousands of the Philistines then betrayed him to Saul when he needed their help. Rather than seeking affirmation from the people, David found his strength in the Lord.

30:21–31 DAVID SHARES THE PLUNDER WITH ALL PEOPLE

Even though David's four hundred fighters declared David's right of disposal for the plunder, "all the evil men and troublemakers" (v. 22) must have felt entitled to some of the plunder, for they did not want to share any with those who had stayed behind in the Besor Valley. But this sense of entitlement derived from their ignorance, ungodly pride, and lack of compassion towards their compatriots. First, they were ignorant of the important role that a logistics unit plays in the battle. They also seemed to be ignorant of the fact that David had ordered these men to stay behind to watch the weapons and provisions.[7] Second, they did not ascribe the glory for the victory to the Lord, who had led them to the Egyptian informant and then delivered the Amalekites into their hands, while also keeping their kidnapped families from harm. These men acted as if they were responsible for the victory, which is made clear in their words: "We will not share with them the plunder *we recovered*" (v. 22, italics mine). The Hebrew *natsal,* "to recover," was part of the Lord's language in blessing David, but these evil men laid claim to their "recovery" independent of the Lord. Third, they lacked compassion for the weaker members of their community and so deserved to be called "all the evil men and troublemakers" (v. 22). The Hebrew *beney beliya'al,* "troublemaker," may be translated as "the sons of Belial (another name for Satan)," among other things. In their unwillingness to be compassionate towards those who were weak, they made themselves friends of Satan and friends of the Amalekites, Satan's agents.

David, on the other hand, proved himself to be compassionate to all of his people. Although he was entitled to have all the plunder for himself, he shared it with all the people – not only the four hundred fighters who followed him across the Besor Valley and the two hundred soldiers who stayed behind to manage logistics, but also with the elders of Judah, who had not welcomed him while he was a fugitive in Judah. In contrast to "all the evil men and troublemakers" (v. 22), David was fully aware that the Lord had delivered him a great victory against the Amalekites and had given him all the plunder (v. 23). When the two hundred men who had stayed behind came

---

7. The Hebrew original behind the NIV "and who were left behind at the Besor Valley" (v. 21) is literally translated as "and David made them remain at the Besor Valley."

out to meet the triumphant David, he asked about their well-being (v. 21). Normally, those who come out to meet a triumphant general greet him with high praise first,[8] but David recognized the role of the men who had watched the luggage and considered them as having equal participation in the rescue operation. David's response was honorable, whereas the troublemakers' assertion was selfish.[9] David's rebuke in the form of a question must be understood in this context: "Who will listen to what you say?" (v. 24). The situation can be compared with a soccer team who wins an Olympic gold medal, where all the players – whether they stood on the field or sat through the game – share the honor of the gold medal.

This controversy between David's men led to legislation prescribing an equal share for those who stayed with supplies and those who went to the battle: "David made this a statute and ordinance for Israel from that day to this" (v. 25). This has two important implications. First, by promulgating the law, David showed himself as a king. In the ancient Near East, only kings could make laws. Second, David's first legislation was about equality, which intimated that his kingdom would be built on the spirit of brotherhood. This would make Israel's kingdom different from their neighbors, where the king was a god, not *primus inter pares* (first among equals). Notice that David addressed his men as "my brothers" (v. 23) even when they acted against his will. David's kingdom would be different from all nations because God would rule his people through a human king. The people that David ruled would be both his brothers and the people of the Lord. As king of Israel, David should *love* his brothers and *serve* the people of the Lord. This principle should apply to all Christian leaders because the head of the Church is Christ, and we are all members of his body, and all members are equal. The calling of Christian leaders is not to dominate others, as worldly leaders would do, but to love and serve their brothers and sisters in Christ Jesus.

Chapter 30 concludes with a scene where David sent some of the plunder to the elders of Judah (vv. 26–30) even though they had not been willing to welcome David when he was a fugitive being pursued by Saul. Some of the elders even volunteered to be Saul's informants, and David fled to the

---

8. The Septuagint has the two hundred men greeting David and his followers, but it is better to keep the Hebrew text here.

9. Their sense of entitlement was individualistic. Their words, "because they did not go out with me," reveal this. Although the NIV corrects the Hebrew *immi*, "me," to *immanu*, "us," following the Septuagint, the Hebrew reading may be intended to highlight the crass individualism hidden in their claim to the group right.

Philistines in order to escape their hostility. But here David tried to befriend them with gifts, which he called "the plunder of the LORD's enemy" (v. 26). Through this gesture, David was identifying himself as the king of Israel who had fought the Lord's battle against the Lord's enemy. The cities mentioned in verses 27–30 cover the area between Hebron and Beersheba, the core area of Judah.[10] This is connected to the fact that later, David became the king of Judah first (see 2 Sam 2:3).

---

10. Some comments on the cities in vv. 27–30 are in order. First, "Bethel" in v. 27 is not the famous city north of Jerusalem but a village in Judah nine kilometers north of Beersheba. This may be the same as Bethul in Josh 19:4. Second, Aroer is not the city on the northern rim of the Arnon River but a city known as Ararah, which is located twenty kilometers southeast of Beersheba. Finally, all the cities – some of which are named only *hered* – are located in the area between Hebron and Beersheba.

1 SAMUEL 31:1–13

HEROES DIE ON THE BATTLEFIELD

In this chapter, we read about the defeat of the Israelite army and the deaths of Saul, its commander-in-chief, along with his three princes, just as the spirit of Samuel had predicted (see 28:19). Saul not only failed in his mission to deliver Israel out of the hand of the Philistines (see 9:16), but ironically his own fate was also sealed by the Philistines. The narrator's overall tone, however, does not accuse Saul, but rather portrays him as a hero who retained his royal dignity in his final moments and was "loved" by his people.

31:1–2 JONATHAN'S DEATH

The narrative focus shifts from David in Ziklag to Saul at Mount Gilboa. After being defeated by the Philistines, Saul and his men ran for their lives (vv. 1–2). Meanwhile, in the previous chapter, David and his men ran after and defeated the Amalekites. The narrator contrasts these two chapters to reveal that David, not Saul, was the king who would lead Israel into victory. However, the contrast between these two heroes goes deeper than their ability to lead, for it involves character. David was a man after God's heart and Saul was not. To put this in more practical terms, David proved himself obedient to the will of the Lord, whereas Saul rebelled against God's will to the extent that he resorted to an illegitimate medium for divination. In fact, the battle on Mount Gilboa represented a divine punishment for Saul's disobedience, thereby fulfilling the prophecy about Saul's doom by Samuel's spirit (see 28:19). This divine punishment revealed the seriousness of the sin of disobedience for an Israelite king, who was called to rule over God's people as a vice regent for the one God rather than a godlike king.

As verse 1 summarizes, the battle on Mount Gilboa ended with the Philistine victory: many Israelites died or fled for their lives. Verses 2–5 describe in detail the circumstances surrounding the deaths of Saul and his sons. The Philistines "were in hot pursuit of Saul and his sons" (v. 2). It may be argued that the Philistines were not aware that they were pursuing Saul and his sons. If they had known, they would not have left their bodies in the field and returned to "find" them the next day (see v. 8). More likely, they killed Saul and his sons unintentionally. This may suggest that Saul and his sons disguised themselves in the battle, since it was not uncommon for a king or a general to disguise himself in order to avoid being targeted during battle. One biblical example is Ahab, who disguised himself in the battle of Ramoth-Gilead (see 1 Kgs 22:29–40). In *Three Kingdoms*, Cao Cao threw down his characteristic red coat and even cut off his beard in order to give his pursuer, Ma Chao, the slip.[1]

The text says that Saul's sons fell first, though we do not know the manner of their deaths, whether by arrows or swords. The text simply lists their names: Jonathan, Abinadab, and Malki-Shua (v. 2). We do not know anything about Saul's sons Abinadab and Malki-Shua. We do know that Jonathan was the second-in-command in Saul's kingdom and a loyal friend to David. When Jonathan realized that David was the "neighbor" (15:28) to whom God would give Saul's kingdom, he yielded his robe, a symbol of his right of succession, to David (18:3). Later, when David was pursued by Saul, Jonathan made his way to David's hideout in Horesh and encouraged him. He even dreamt of the day when he would be the second-in-command in David's kingdom (see 23:17). But Jonathan died before he could see that day. Notice the concise and casual way that the narrator treats Jonathan's death in verse 2, which belies the depth of emotions that readers would have towards Jonathan's death.

31:3–7 SAUL'S DEATH

The text then moves quickly to narrate Saul's death in detail. The fighting between the pursuing Philistines and the fleeing Israelites went poorly, and Saul was shot by Philistine arrows and left writhing in great pain (v. 3b). The NIV's translation, "they wounded him critically" (v. 3b), misses the nuance of "pain" attached to the Hebrew *yahel*. Apparently, it was in pain that Saul asked his armor-bearer to kill him with a sword. When his armor-bearer demurred in fear,[2] Saul "took his own sword and fell on it" (v. 4). Why did the narrator provide this detail about Saul's death, since suicide is not condoned in the Bible? It may be to suggest that Saul both lived and died as a sinner. There is certainly a similarity between Saul's death and the death of Abimelech, Gideon's son, who killed his brothers to become the king. But on closer examination, we can conclude that even though a few cases in the Bible portray suicide in a

---

1. See Roberts, *Three Kingdoms*, ch. 58.
2. What did he fear? Since the object of the verb "fear" is missing in the text, one cannot say decisively that the armor-bearer did not kill Saul because of the same taboo that stopped David from killing Saul earlier. It can be argued that the armor-bearer feared violating the moral code of killing one's lord.

negative light, it is not necessarily always wrong. Historically, some instances of suicide have been accepted in East Asia. Suicide for a greater cause was considered heroic, but suicide was considered acceptable in order to avoid shame. When Yuan Shu was defeated by Liu Bei, he killed himself with his own sword because he deemed it more shameful to be taken alive into the enemy land than to be killed on the battlefield. From this perspective, Saul's suicide was acceptable, albeit not heroic, because he wanted to end his life not simply because of his physical pain, but also because of the shame that his capture would have incurred to his royal dignity. This is what he meant by the phrase, "these uncircumcised fellows will come . . . and abuse me" (v. 4). One may argue that Saul's final scene emphasizes his desperate efforts to maintain a degree of dignity as king.

This portrait of Saul is corroborated by the death of his armor-bearer. When the latter "saw that Saul was dead, he too fell on his sword and died with" Saul (v. 5). Following a lord to death was considered the highest expression of loyalty in ancient China, Korea, and Japan. Saul was fortunate and charismatic enough to have such a loyal man serving him. According to verse 6, Saul did not die alone, for many of his loyal servants – "his three sons," "his armor-bearer," and "all his men" – died on the same day. Dying on the same day as one's lord was also an expression of loyalty. The three oath brothers, Liu Bei, Guan Yu, and Zhang Fei, who were famous for their loyalty to one another, swore their loyalty in the following terms in the famous "peach garden" scene: "We . . . hereby vow to die the selfsame day."[3] Thus the text strikes a delicate balance in describing Saul's final moment: although Saul's death on the battlefield was a rightful punishment for his consistent and willful rebellion against the Lord, the manner of his death reminds us all that he was the king of Israel, deserving a proper tribute.

The defeat of the Israelite army at the Gilboa battle led to the loss of some territory among the Jezreel Valley and across the Jordan River: "They [the Israelites] abandoned their towns and fled. And the Philistines came and occupied them" (v. 7). The Philistines not only gained their foothold inland but also controlled an important trade route through the Jezreel Valley between the coastal area and the Transjordan.

---

3. Roberts, *Three Kingdoms*, 12. One may discern a negative connotation in v. 6, if one supposes that Saul dying with his three sons on the same day was predicted as divine punishment in ch. 28. But in v. 6, the armor bearer and "all his men" died on the same day with Saul, which opens the possibility of interpreting this verse in a positive sense.

31:8–10 SAUL'S BODY ON DISPLAY

The Philistines did not gather the corpses of Saul and his sons until the next day. The fact that they "found" their corpses when they came back to the battlefield to "strip the dead" intimates that they killed Saul and his sons accidentally in the mayhem of battle. But once they found their enemy king's body, they did what they were expected to do: they beheaded and stripped it and displayed it on the wall of the newly captured city.[4] They also "sent messengers throughout the land of the Philistines to proclaim the *good* news in the temples of their idols and among their people" (v. 9, italics added). They sent messengers to the temples because a military victory was always credited to a god in those days. The custom of capturing the idols of a defeated enemy and installing them in the temple of a victor's gods originated in this idea (see ch. 4). Interesting to note is the narrator's use of the Hebrew *basar* to refer to the Philistine messengers' mission (v. 9). Although the NIV translates *basar* as "to proclaim the news," the Hebrew *basar* almost always connotes good news. The death of king Saul was not only good news for the Philistines but also for the Israelites, because it prepared the way for David, the new king of Israel, to come to them. This reflects the Korean saying, "everything in the world is like an old man's horse," which means, in essence, that "a loss may turn out to be a gain" or "a blessing in disguise." The defeat of the Israelite army and the death of Saul in the battle of Gilboa was a big loss, but it would turn out to be a huge gain for Israel, just like "an old man's horse."

31:11–13 SAUL'S BODY BURIED

The people of Jabesh-Gilead retrieved the bodies of Saul and his sons from the wall of Beth Shan, burned them, and then buried their bones under a tamarisk tree in Jabesh. The people who went on this dangerous expedition without being asked were the people of Jabesh, whom Saul delivered from the threat of the Ammonites. Upon hearing of their trouble (see 11:4–5), Saul swiftly went to their rescue and defeated the Ammonites (see 11:9–11). The people of Jabesh may have sworn loyalty to Saul's family at that time,[5] and so when they "heard what the Philistines had done to Saul" (v. 11), they marched through the night to Beth Shan to save their king from further humiliation by giving

4. Beth Shan, which is located where the Jezreel Valley meets the Jordan River, traditionally belonged to Israel. The Philistines may have taken it from Israel after the battle at Mount Gilboa.
5. It is interesting to note that when David became king, he tried to bribe the people of Jabesh to follow him. David wanted to make loyal and brave people of his own men.

him a burial and funeral. This episode of repaying a favor properly ends the story of the first king of Israel, because it reminds us of Saul's best days as a king. Despite all his failures, Saul was the king of Israel who "fought against their [Israel's] enemies on every side . . . delivering Israel from the hands of those who had plundered them" (14:47–49).

Two things in this concluding episode deserve our attention. First, Saul's body was cremated; second, he was not buried in his hometown of Gibeah but under a tamarisk tree in Jabesh-Gilead. These two narrative details are related. The practice of cremation was originally adopted as an imperative of war to ensure that soldiers killed in foreign countries would have a homeland funeral that could be attended by their family.[6] In Saul's case, his cremation was necessitated by the geopolitical change that took place after the battle at Mount Gilboa (v. 7). In effect, the Philistines now ruled most of Saul's territory, and so it would have been impossible to bury Saul's body in Gibeah, Saul's hometown, as it was under Philistine control. Although the practice of burning a body was generally considered a divine punishment, the people of Jabesh may have burned Saul's body as an inevitable measure and then buried it provisionally "under a tamarisk tree" in Jabesh-Gilead in order to give Saul an approximated homeland burial. This is intimated by the fact that the place "under the tamarisk tree on the hill at Gibeah" is closely associated with Saul's career as king of Israel (see 22:6). David later reburied the remains in Saul's family grave (2 Sam 21:12–14).

Despite the author's efforts to portray Saul's last moments heroically, reflecting his royal status as king, the deaths of Saul and his sons on the same day fulfilled Samuel's prophecy of divine punishment. Saul's dynasty came to an end, with Saul failing to become a king after God's heart. Saul's failure mirrors the failure of the people of Israel, who asked for a king so they could be like all the other nations (see 8:5). They rejected God's reign in favor of the visible rule of a human king so that they could be like other nations. Although their request was idolatrous, God granted it by installing Saul as king, so that they might learn to seek God's rule after experiencing the consequences of their own sin. Yet Saul failed to deliver them from Philistine oppression, contrary to their expectations, and he also failed to enrich their lives economically or spiritually. But God was merciful and gave the people a second chance by preparing David, through whom he would establish his kingdom on earth. God still gives us a second chance. It's never too late to return to the Lord.

---

6. See "cremation," *Encyclopedia Britannica* (Chicago, IL: Encyclopedia Britannica, 2016).

SELECTED BIBLIOGRAPHY

Ackroyd, P. R. *The First Book of Samuel*. The Cambridge Bible Commentary: New English Bible. Cambridge: University Press, 1971.

Alter, Robert. *The David Story: A Translation with Commentary of 1 and 2 Samuel*. New York: W. W. Norton, 1999.

Baden, Joel. *The Historical David: A Real Life of an Invented Hero*. New York, NY: HarperCollins, 2013.

Bar-Efrat, Shimo. *Das Erste Buch Samuel: Ein Narratologisch-Philologischer Kommentar*. Beiträge Zur Wissenschaft Vom Alten und Neuen Testament. Stuttgart: Kohlhammer, 2007.

Birch, Bruce C. "The First and Second Books of Samuel: Introduction, Commentary, and Reflections." In *The New Interpreter's Bible*, vol. 2. Nashville: Abingdon, 1995–2002.

Bodner, Keith. *1 Samuel: A Narrative Commentary*. Hebrew Bible Monographs. Sheffield: Sheffield Phoenix Press, 2008.

Brotzman, Ellis R. *Old Testament Criticism: A Practical Introduction*. Grand Rapids, MI: Baker Books, 1994.

Brueggemann, Walter. *First and Second Samuel. In Interpretation*. Louisville, KY: John Knox Press, 1990.

Campbell, Antony F. *1 Samuel*. The Forms of the Old Testament Literature, vol. 7. Grand Rapids, MI: Eerdmans, 2003.

Cartledge, Tony W. *1 & 2 Samuel*. Smyth & Helwys Bible Commentary. Macon, GA: Smyth & Helwys Pub., 2001.

Chan, Wing-Tsit. "The Concept of Man in Chinese Thought." In *The Concept of Man: A Study in Comparative Philosophy*, ed. Radhakrishnan, 158–205. New Delhi: Indus, 1995.

Chapman, Steve B. *1 Samuel as Christian Scripture: A Theological Commentary*. Grand Rapids, MI: Eerdmans, 2016.

Chen, Ning. "The Problem of Theodicy in Ancient China." *Journal of Chinese Religion* 22 (1994): 51–74.

Dekker, John. "May the Lord Make the Woman Like Rachel: Comparing Michal and Rachel." *Tyndale Bulletin* 64 (2013): 17–32.

Dhorme, Paul P. *Les livres de Samuel*. Paris: V. Lecoffre, 1910.

Driver, S. R. *Notes on the Hebrew Text and the Topography of the Books of Samuel*. Oxford: Clarendon Press, 1960.

Finkelstein, Israel, and Neil A. Silberman. *The Bible Unearthed: Archaelogy's New Vision of Ancient Israel and the Origin of Its Sacred Texts*. New York, NY: Touchstone, 2001.

Firth, David G. *1 & 2 Samuel*. Downers Grove, IL: InterVarsity Press, 2009.

Fokkelman, J. P. *Vow and Desire (1 Sam. 1–12)*. In *Narrative Art and Poetry in the Books of Samuel: A Full Interpretation Based on Stylistic and Structural Analyses*, vol. 4. Studia Semitica Neerlandica. Assen, Netherlands: Van Gorcum, 1993.

Garsiel, Moshe. *The First Book of Samuel: A Literary Study of Comparative Structure, Analogies and Parallels*. Winona Lake, IN: Eisenbrauns, 1983.

Gordon, Robert P. *I & II Samuel: A Commentary*. Library of Biblical Interpretation. Grand Rapids, MI: Regency Reference Library, 1988, c1986.

Halbertal, Moshe, and Stephen Holmes. *The Beginning of Politics: Power in the Biblical Book of Samuel*. Princeton, NJ: Princeton University Press, 2018.

Hazony, Yoram. *God and Politics in Esther*. Cambridge: Cambridge University Press, 2016.

Hertzberg, Hans Wilhelm. *I & II Samuel: A Commentary*. The Old Testament Library. Philadelphia: Westminster Press, 1964.

Heschel, Abraham Joshua. *A Passion for Truth*. Woodstock, VT: Jewish Lights Publication, 2008.

Jobling, David. *1 Samuel*. Berit Olam. Collegeville, MN: Liturgical Press, 1998.

Keene, Donald, ed. *Anthology of Japanese Literature: From the Earliest Era to the Mid-nineteenth Century*. New York: Grove Press, 1955.

Kim, Koowon. *Incubation as a Type-Scene in ʾAqhatu, Kirta, and Hannah Stories*. Leiden: Brill, 2012.

——————. *1 Samuel: A Commentary for All Christians*. Seoul: Hongsungsa, 2016.

——————. "Is the Woman of Endor Portrayed as a Heroine?" *Expository Times* 129 (2018): 399–407.

King, Philip J., and Lawrence E. Stager. *Life in Biblical Israel*. Louisville, KY: Westminster/John Knox Press, 2001.

Klein, Ralph W. *1 Samuel*. Word Biblical Commentary. Dallas, TX: Word Books, 1983.

Leow, Theng Huat, ed. *What Young Asian Theologians Are Thinking*. Singapore: Trinity Theological College, 2014.

Levenson, Jon D. "1 Samuel as Literature and as History." *Journal of Biblical Literature* 40 (1978): 11–28.

Lozovyy, Joseph. *Saul, Doeg, Nabal, and the "Son of Jesse": Readings in 1 Samuel 16–25*. London: T & T Clark, 2009.

Luo, Guanzhong. *Romance of the Three Kingdoms*. Trans. C. H. Brewitt-Taylor. CreateSpace Independent Publishing Platform, 2015.

MacCarter, P. Kyle. *1 Samuel: A New Translation*. The Anchor Bible. Garden City, NY: Doubleday, 1980.

McKenzie, Steven L. *King David: A Biography*. Oxford: Oxford University Press, 2000.

Miscall, Peter D. *1 Samuel: A Literary Reading*. Indiana Studies in Biblical Literature. Bloomington: Indiana University Press, 1986.

Provan, Iain, V. Philips Long, and Tremper Longman III. *A Biblical History of Israel.* Louisville: Westminster/John Knox Press, 2003.

Roberts, Moss, trans. *Three Kingdoms: A Historical Novel Attributed to Luo Guanzhong.* Berkeley, CA: University of California Press, 1994.

Sáez, Lawrence, and Julia Callagher. "Authoritarianism and Development in the Third World." *Brown Journal of World Affairs* 15 (2009): 87–101.

Tsumura, David Toshio. *The First Book of Samuel.* The New International Commentary on the Old Testament. Grand Rapids, MI: Eerdmans, 2007.

Waley, Arthur. *The Analects of Confucius.* New York: Vintage Books, 1938.

Walton, John H., and J. Harvey Walton. *The Lost World of the Israelite Conquest: Covenant, Retribution, and the Fate of the Canaanites.* Downers Grove, IL: IVP Academic, 2017.

Woodhouse, John. *2 Samuel: Your Kingdom Come.* Wheaton, IL: Crossway, 2015.

Asia Theological Association

54 Scout Madriñan St. Quezon City 1103, Philippines
Email: ataasia@gmail.com Telefax: (632) 410 0312

OUR MISSION

The Asia Theological Association (ATA) is a body of theological institutions, committed to evangelical faith and scholarship, networking together to serve the Church in equipping the people of God for the mission of the Lord Jesus Christ.

OUR COMMITMENT

The ATA is committed to serving its members in the development of evangelical, biblical theology by strengthening interaction, enhancing scholarship, promoting academic excellence, fostering spiritual and ministerial formation and mobilizing resources to fulfill God's global mission within diverse Asian cultures.

OUR TASK

Affirming our mission and commitment, ATA seeks to:

- **Strengthen** interaction through inter-institutional fellowship and programs, regional and continental activities, faculty and student exchange programs.
- **Enhance** scholarship through consultations, workshops, seminars, publications, and research fellowships.
- **Promote** academic excellence through accreditation standards, faculty and curriculum development.
- **Foster** spiritual and ministerial formation by providing mentor models, encouraging the development of ministerial skills and a Christian ethos.
- **Mobilize** resources through library development, information technology and infra-structural development.

To learn more about ATA, visit www.ataasia.com or facebook.com/AsiaTheologicalAssociation

 Langham
PARTNERSHIP

Langham Literature, with its publishing work, is a ministry of Langham Partnership.

Langham Partnership is a global fellowship working in pursuit of the vision God entrusted to its founder John Stott –

> *to facilitate the growth of the church in maturity and Christ-likeness through raising the standards of biblical preaching and teaching.*

Our vision is to see churches in the majority world equipped for mission and growing to maturity in Christ through the ministry of pastors and leaders who believe, teach and live by the Word of God.

Our mission is to strengthen the ministry of the Word of God through:
• nurturing national movements for biblical preaching
• fostering the creation and distribution of evangelical literature
• enhancing evangelical theological education
especially in countries where churches are under-resourced.

Our ministry

Langham Preaching partners with national leaders to nurture indigenous biblical preaching movements for pastors and lay preachers all around the world. With the support of a team of trainers from many countries, a multi-level programme of seminars provides practical training, and is followed by a programme for training local facilitators. Local preachers' groups and national and regional networks ensure continuity and ongoing development, seeking to build vigorous movements committed to Bible exposition.

Langham Literature provides majority world preachers, scholars and seminary libraries with evangelical books and electronic resources through publishing and distribution, grants and discounts. The programme also fosters the creation of indigenous evangelical books in many languages, through writer's grants, strengthening local evangelical publishing houses, and investment in major regional literature projects, such as one volume Bible commentaries like the *Africa Bible Commentary* and the *South Asia Bible Commentary*.

Langham Scholars provides financial support for evangelical doctoral students from the majority world so that, when they return home, they may train pastors and other Christian leaders with sound, biblical and theological teaching. This programme equips those who equip others. Langham Scholars also works in partnership with majority world seminaries in strengthening evangelical theological education. A growing number of Langham Scholars study in high quality doctoral programmes in the majority world itself. As well as teaching the next generation of pastors, graduated Langham Scholars exercise significant influence through their writing and leadership.

To learn more about Langham Partnership and the work we do visit **langham.org**

Printed in the USA
CPSIA information can be obtained
at www.ICGtesting.com
LVHW062233060823
754499LV00010B/209